Experimental Theatre
Creating and Staging Texts

Judy E. Yordon
Ball State University

WAVELAND

PRESS, INC.

Long Grove, Illinois

For information about this book, contact:
Waveland Press, Inc.
4180 IL Route 83, Suite 101
Long Grove, IL 60047-9580
(847) 634-0081
info@waveland.com
www.waveland.com

Photo Credit

All photographs are courtesy of the Ball State University Photographic Services.

Acknowledgments

For permission to use copyright material, grateful acknowledgment is made to the copyright holders below and on page 328, which is hereby made part of this © page.

Chapter 1
1–2, reprinted with the permission of Atheneum Books for Young Readers, an imprint of Simon & Schuster from *The Wind in the Willows* by Kenneth Grahame. Copyright 1933, 1953 Charles Scribner's Sons, copyright renewed © 1961 & 1981; **19**, from "Impulse" by Conrad Aiken in *The Short Stories of Conrad Aiken*. Copyright 1950 by Conrad Aiken; **22**, from "The Third Prize" by A. E. Coppard in *The Collected Tales of A. E. Coppard*. Copyright 1929, 1948 by A. E. Coppard, published by Robert Hale. Reprinted by permission of David Higham Associates. *(continued on page 328)*

Copyright © 1997 by Waveland Press, Inc.

ISBN 0-88133-907-5

Printed in the United States of America

11   10   9   8   7   6

This book is dedicated to Donald E. Heady

Contents

3 Readers Theatre: Staging Your Script   73

4 Chamber Theatre: Creating the Script   99

Preface

Experimental Theatre: Creating and Staging Texts is devoted to the investigation of experimental group performance types. The inspiration for the text comes from years of creating my own scripts and from observing the productions of others in my field whose work I respect. Primary among these others are Leslie Irene Coger and Melvin R. White. Their ground-breaking text, *Readers Theatre Handbook,* featured the nuts and bolts of creating and staging readers theatre and chamber theatre scripts. This text owes much to this work while expanding the dimensions of group performance possibilities. In addition to readers theatre and chamber theatre, this text deals with the creation and staging of ethnographic scripts, everyday conversations, and personal narratives. This text features group performance and the creative possibilities inherent when we—as the Beatles once sang—get a little help from our friends. It seeks to stimulate personal development, increase awareness of all types of literary genres, develop new and different performance experiences, expand performance techniques, and establish new performance conventions.

Experimental Theatre: Creating and Staging Texts is intended for students in a beginning or advanced class in oral interpretation/performance studies or students taking a beginning or advanced course in directing. It would also be useful for literature students or students of ethnography, conversation analysis, or storytelling. This is a practical book that focuses on creating and staging a variety of script types. While staging plays is an ancient and esteemed art form, more and more we are experiencing the inherent drama in other literary and nonliterary materials. This book features how to create these nontraditional scripts and describes theatrical formats for their "public soundings."

On and Off Broadway, for example, such experimental productions as *Cats* (the long-running, award-winning adaptation of T. S. Elliot's book of poems entitled *Old Possum's Book of Practical Cats*), Charles Dickens' novels *Great Expectations* and *Nicholas Nickleby*, John Steinbeck's novel *The Grapes of Wrath*, Homer's "The Odyssey," Nathaniel Hawthorne's *The Scarlet Letter*, as well as powerful productions of Anthony Burgess' *A Clockwork Orange* and Faulkner's *As I lay Dying* at the famous Steppenwolf Company in Chicago, have succeeded in exciting crowds as well as producing box office revenues. In fact, many commercially successful productions are really readers theatre or chamber theatre productions—though rarely are they labeled as such.

In academia, experimental productions have been developed of everyday conversations and of the diversity of popular culture. At the 1992 Speech Communication Association Convention in Atlanta, a script was produced of *Casing a Promised Land: The Autobiography of an Organizational Detective as Cultural Ethnographer*, which depicted a fictional detective trying to investigate Huntsville, Alabama's organizational culture. Studies have been done and scripts produced of a Chesterfield, Indiana spiritual camp and of Alcoholics Anonymous meetings, among many others. Personal stories of growing up in a coal-mining community or in the Arizona desert have been effectively translated into theatrical productions. The proliferation of these experimental scripts and the varied styles created to present them demonstrate that they deserve more attention than they have received. This text attempts to describe and define the theory behind these methods and the techniques involved in creating and staging these scripts so readers will have the tools they need to begin to produce their own experimental productions.

These special performance types appeal primarily to an audience's imagination. Scriptmakers/directors of these nontraditional scripts feature the "words" as the most important aspect; their stage is primarily acoustic space. This is one of the major elements that differentiates these performance types from traditional performance types, which rely heavily on the spectacle elements of set, set pieces, makeup, costumes, props, and so on. As Marion L. Kleinau and Janet Larsen McHughes write, "Everything a director does . . . is designed to stimulate the audience's imaginative response rather than to provide a pictorial illusion of life onstage."[1] Although many commercially successful productions rely heavily on spectacle because audiences expect it, we still seek to appeal to the audience's imagination as much as possible.

The fields of oral interpretation and group performance (now know as "performance studies") are currently in a state of flux. Questions arise as to what we mean by "text" and what we mean by "performance." Both terms have expanded to include types of texts and types of performances not before appreciated as fields of study. A text may be written, oral, or artifact. Performances exist in day-to-day encounters between people, in family gatherings, in rituals, in sporting events. Whereas once we thought of performance as primarily a means of communicating a text—of serving a text—we now redefine performance as a way of knowing; that is, as a way of learning more about oneself, one's ideas, beliefs, and values. Although literature is no longer the primary or sole focus of oral interpretation/performance studies scholars, when literature is communicated, the performer has been given the right of ownership of his or her own interpretation. Literature may be interpreted in ways that serve what the performer wants to say. In a group production, the scriptmaker is asked to decide what a text means to him or her—and then to transform that into a new medium.

One of the advantages of these experimental performance types is the opportunity they provide for turning scriptmakers into "authors" with creative autonomy. We see these performance types as opportunities for students to communicate their thoughts, feelings, and ideas on various issues. Students use literature, real-life events, or family stories to share their point of view. They have ownership of their finished scripts. Their ideas and inventiveness are communicated.

This text is divided into eight chapters. Chapter one introduces some of the basic conventions of experimental group performance, differentiates presentational theatre from representational theatre, and briefly defines the styles to be covered in this text: readers theatre, chamber theatre, ethnography and conversational analysis, and personal narratives. Chapters two and three deal with the creation and staging of readers theatre scripts, respectively. Chapter four covers the creation of chamber theatre scripts, while chapter five concentrates on the principles of staging chamber theatre scripts. Chapter six deals with ethnography and conversation analysis, chapter seven focuses on the creation and staging of personal narratives, and chapter eight includes sample scripts.

There are many people without whose support and talent this book could not have been completed. Those people include the students in my spring 1995 Chamber Theatre class: Andy Catron, Josh Coomer, Michael Downey, Emily Faulkner, Nick Foster, Marie Jennings, Amy Kosanke, Simone Lawson, Amy Rafa, Carrie Schlatter, Cassandra Strandin, Bill Surber, Natasha Tunstall, and Petra Wiehe. Immense thanks to

Cassandra Strandin for handling the permissions for this text and for functioning as general, do-everything assistant, and to Emily Faulkner for research assistance. Thanks also to Holly Lynn Tolosko and Gayle Jennings Wood for assistance with chapters six and seven. I would also like to express my gratitude to Laurie Prossnitz, my patient and creative editor, and to Neil Rowe, publisher of Waveland Press, who gave me the opportunity to write this text.

Special recognition goes to Leslie Irene Coger for encouraging me to write a group performance text and for trusting me to carry on the fine tradition she and Melvin R. White established with *Readers Theatre Handbook*. I would not have had the courage to write this text were it not for the inspiration and instruction of three people: Charlotte S. Waisman, who first introduced me to the field of interpretation; Wallace A. Bacon, who stressed the importance of discovering "the other"; and Robert S. Breen, who introduced me to the narrative voice.

Notes

[1]Marion L. Kleinau and Janet Larsen McHughes, *Theatres for Literature* (Sherman Oaks, CA: Alfred Publishing, 1980), p. 179.

Introduction to Experimental Group Productions

Read the passage below, and try to imagine it performed on stage.

From *The Wind in the Willows* by Kenneth Grahame

The Rat was sitting on the river bank, singing a little song. He had just composed it himself, so he was very taken up with it, and would not pay proper attention to Mole or anything else. Since early morning he had been swimming in the river, in company with his friends the ducks. And when the ducks stood on their heads suddenly, as ducks will, he would dive down and tickle their necks, just under where their chins would be if ducks had chins, till they were forced to come to the surface again in a hurry, spluttering and angry and shaking their feathers at him, for it is impossible to say quite *all* you feel when your head is under water. At last they implored him to go away and attend to his own affairs and leave them to mind theirs. So the Rat went away, and sat on the river bank in the sun, and made up a song about them, which he called "Ducks' Ditty."

When you first read the passage above from Kenneth Grahame's *The Wind in the Willows*, were you able to imagine it on stage with a group of performers? You might have found this difficult since only one voice speaks—the undefined narrator of the tale. Let's look, though, at one possible adaptation of this paragraph for group performance.

Chamber Theatre Adaptation
From *The Wind in the Willows* by Kenneth Grahame

Narrator (*to audience*)**:** The Rat was sitting on the river bank, (*Rat sings* "Down By the River Side") singing a little song.

Rat (*stops singing to say this line to audience, then continues singing*)**:** He had just composed it himself, so he was very taken up with it,

Mole (*to Narrator and audience, angry and upset*)**:** and would not pay proper attention to Mole or anything else.

Narrator (*to audience*)**:** Since early morning he had been swimming in the river,

Chorus of Ducks (*to audience*)**:** in company with his friends the ducks. (*The ducks suggest standing on their heads.*)

Narrator (*to audience*)**:** And when the ducks stood on their heads suddenly

Chorus of Ducks (*to audience*)**:** as ducks will,

(*Rat suggests diving down toward ducks.*)

Narrator (*to audience*)**:** he would dive down and tickle their necks,

Chorus of Ducks (*through their angry giggles, to audience*)**:** just under where their chins would be if ducks had chins,

Narrator (*to audience*)**:** till they were forced to come to the surface again in a hurry,

Duck 1 (*to Rat*)**:** spluttering

Ducks 2 and 3 (*to Rat*)**:** and angry

Chorus of Ducks (*to Rat*)**:** and shaking their feathers at him,

Narrator (*to audience*)**:** for it is impossible to say quite *all* you feel when your head is under water. At last they implored him to

Chorus of Ducks (*to Rat*)**:** go away

Narrator: (*to audience*) and

Chorus of Ducks (*to Rat*)**:** attend to his own affairs

Narrator (*to audience*)**:** and

Chorus of Ducks (*to Rat*)**:** leave them to mind theirs.

Narrator (*to audience*): So the Rat went away, and sat on the river
   bank in the sun, and made up a song about them, which he called
Rat (*to himself*): "Ducks' Ditty."

This group adaptation features six performers: the Narrator, Rat, Mole, and a chorus of three ducks. This adaptation allows these various characters to appear directly instead of merely being talked about. The adaptation features some experimental theatre conventions that might be new to you: the dramatization of characters suggested within the narration, the ability of characters to speak of themselves in the third person and the past tense, and the necessity of adding suggested stage directions to clarify who is being addressed and provide the performers with a sense of who moves where and when. This narrative passage, then, is transformed into a group performance script which hopefully captures and holds an audience's imagination and attention. Since *The Wind in the Willows* is intended for children (as well as adults), dramatizing the characters brings them to life and provides an element of excitement. Certainly there is nothing wrong with a solo performance of this text, but a group performance can more dramatically stage the conflict and interaction that add to the humor and make the piece more "dramatic." As a recent *TIME* magazine article put it, ". . . the Greeks were on to something when, 2,500 years ago, they brought a second performer onstage; that changed the product from incantation to drama."[1]

The intention of this text is to introduce you to various styles of group performance. While most of you may be well aware of how plays are produced on stage, you may be less familiar with various styles of group performance that feature literary or nonliterary texts other than plays. There is much that is fascinating about the idea of working with material not originally intended for the stage. One of the most exciting aspects is that you become an "author." You are the creator of a never-before-produced "original" script that ideally communicates what *you* want it to say. You have "ownership" of the script you develop. This produces a tremendous sense of excitement and pride as well as a sense of personal responsibility.

The performance styles to be considered are readers theatre, chamber theatre, ethnography and conversation analysis, and personal narratives. This initial chapter introduces you to group performance types, and gets you started creating and staging your own scripts. Before discussing these performance types, let us consider theatre modes.

Theatre Modes

As you consider texts to stage in these experimental group perform- ance formats, an important consideration is the **mode**—lyric, dramatic, or epic—of the material you select to include in your script. Mode has to do with the nature of the speaker(s), the type of experience, and the elements of time and place. The particular mode of the selection or of the created script may help an adapter/director (usually the same person) determine the appropriate production type.

A **lyric-mode** text features one undefined speaker revealing a personal experience. Although one voice is usually featured in a lyric-mode text, adapters may include characters suggested or discussed in the passage (such as we did in the passage adapted from *The Wind in the Willows*) or they may take advantage of the various dimensions or characteristics of this undefined speaker by casting more than one performer to assay the roles of one human being. The disintegration of self; the past, present, anticipated future; the superego, ego, id; the self and the alter ego or conscience are possible ways to turn a single-voiced text into a multi- voiced text suitable for group performance. In a script on the meeting, courting, and marriage of Elizabeth Barrett and Robert Browning, for example, the lyric sonnet "How Do I Love Thee" became Elizabeth and Robert's marriage vows. Lyric-mode texts project a sense of timelessness and have a strong emotional base. Lyric-mode material is usually appro- priate for readers theatre productions.

A **dramatic-mode** text features defined characters in conflict situ- ations. These characters are usually found in a specific locale at a specific time. Most dramatic-mode texts are written in the present tense and project the sense of "happening now." Audience members feel as if they are witnessing an event that is happening before their eyes. Most plays (without narrators) are dramatic in mode, but dramatic-mode prose fiction and poetry also exist where defined characters speak at a specific time and place. Ethnographic scripts (scripts that illustrate, illuminate, and document the everyday events and behaviors of various cultural groups), are usually dramatic in that they attempt to re-create events with defined "characters" which took place in a specific time and location. Conversation transcripts (scripts that derive from recorded everyday conversations) are also dramatic in that one defined person is speaking to another defined person in a specific time and place. When these types of scripts are staged, the author/director attempts to recreate what was said and done as faithfully as possible.

In **epic-mode** texts, there exists a combination of both the lyric and the dramatic as stories are told. In the epic mode, there is usually the presence of an undefined storyteller and characters who appear to speak for themselves. In other words, there is both narration and dialogue. Most epic-mode material is written from a past-tense perspective. An audience viewing an epic-mode script senses that it is receiving a vicarious experience: that what is before them is history—has already occurred— and is being relived or retold from a singular perspective. Many personal narratives (scripts that embody everyday life stories) are often epic in mode, with a narrator telling a personal story that involves others who also speak. Again, though many novels and short stories are epic in mode, there are also plays (*Our Town, Into the Woods*) and poems (*The Iliad, The Odyssey*) that are epic in mode. Epic-mode material is most often staged in chamber theatre. Personal narratives, which are often epic in mode, may also be staged in a chamber theatre fashion, or new performance styles and conventions may be developed. In epic-mode scripts, the nature of the storyteller and the particular characteristics of his or her story are the central considerations. Let us now summarize this discussion by describing the characteristics of lyric-, dramatic-, and epic-mode scripts.

A lyric-mode script features one "character" revealing personal experiences in a timeless present. Although there is only one primary character, other characters suggested or discussed in the passage may be included, but there is the sense that they are not literally present but are products of the major character's dreams, thoughts, remembrances, or fantasies. A dramatic-mode script features defined characters in the present involved in some type of conflict situation—much like conventional plays. Epic-mode scripts feature a narrator in the virtual present (the time in which the narrator tells us the story) relating events that occurred in the virtual past (the time in which the events of the story took place).

Theatrical Complement

Group performance is not new, of course. It is certainly not unique or unusual to go to the theatre and see a group of performers put on a play by Neil Simon, for example. Companies all over the world have staged plays since the Greeks first discovered the magic of live theatre. What is unique and special about this text is the concentration on material not originally intended for the stage—on material that must be made theatrical. In other words, one must not forget the "theatrical" aspects of these styles of presentation. One must find a **theatrical complement** for each production—a way of staging them which, while featuring the text and the adapter's vision, still displays a sense of theatrical inventiveness. Adapters/directors of these original, experimental group productions must ask themselves, "How do I take material not intended for performance and make it work on the stage?" This is both the challenge and the creative excitement of experimental group performance.

Historically, chamber theatre and especially readers theatre were fairly static. Very little, if any, movement was incorporated, scripts were often carried, and there was no attempt to create any visual reality. During those early days, there was a real desire to make sure that these forms were not confused with conventional productions of plays. With a play, **spectacle** elements—set, costumes, make-up, and so on—may often be the most memorable aspects of a production. As David Richards writes in his review of *Sunset Boulevard*, "Whether we like it or not, machinery and the voracious public appetite for spectacle are remaking the contemporary musical."[2] You may have attended a play or musical where the audience applauded as the curtain lifted revealing a sensationally detailed set. Some audience members marvel at the realistic costumes or the stupendous special effects (one immediately thinks of the falling chandelier and candle-lit boat ride in *The Phantom of the Opera* or that amazing helicopter landing on stage in *Miss Saigon*). And while the group productions which are covered in this text are primarily concerned with conveying the words—the language—and with featuring the ideas, images, and personal experiences, we still realize that we must pay attention to an audience's need for movement, action, and interaction—for spectacle. (One is reminded of a well-known cartoon in *New Yorker*. A man and his companion go to the theatre to attend a "traditional" readers theatre production. As they stand at the end of the aisle observing the stage lined up with stools and music stands, the man turns to his companion and whispers, "I don't like it already.") Nowadays, we attend a performance of *Cats*, for example, which is in essence a readers theatre compilation of poems by T. S. Eliot, and we marvel at the costumes, the set, the dance, the make-up. While we do not expect your initial productions to be this "spectacular," try to keep in mind the sense that theatre is usually something that people go to "see"—it is expected that there will be action, interaction, and some appeal to the visual. With ethnographic and conversational performances, we seek to [re]produce cultural "performances" that have already taken place. With these productions, we attempt to [re]produce the **text**—what was said and done—as well as the

context—time, setting, apparel, situation, audience response, and so on. Attention to the reproduction of context, then, contributes to the creation of spectacle.

Before we briefly describe each of the special kinds of theatrical forms that will be covered in this text, it is important to define two kinds of theatrical conventions: presentational and representational.

Presentational and Representational Theatre

Readers theatre and chamber theatre are two group forms of theatrical presentation that stage literature not ordinarily staged. Ethnographic studies, conversation transcriptions, and personal narratives are also potential material for group performance scripts. Readers theatre, chamber theatre productions, and the staging of personal narratives are, for the most part, **presentational** in that rarely is reality or a realistic impression of life attempted. Presentational theatre is **nonillusory**; it makes no attempt to fool the audience members into thinking they are looking at real life. Presentational theatre says, "This is theatre; these are performers. What you see may resemble life, but it is not life. It takes place only in this performance." The audience becomes involved but does not forget it is watching a production. This involvement is not dependent on spectacle elements; the audience sees and hears a production that is primarily text-centered.

One type of focus performers use in many presentational productions is called **offstage focus**—performers address each other in an imagined space directly in and above the heads of the audience. Some performers may even address the audience members directly. **Onstage focus**—where performers look at and address each other and audience members see profiles—may also be employed. The spectacle elements of conventional theatre—lights, props, set pieces, costumes, makeup, etc.—may be used, but are usually minimized so that the scene remains offstage in the audience's imagination.

The prevailing spectacle convention of presentational theatre is **synecdoche**—or the use of a part to suggest the whole. A tree limb, for example, might suggest a huge oak tree. The addition of a tiara and boa may suggest someone dressed formally. Taking a step closer to another performer could suggest flirtation.

Representational theatre offers an "illusion" of real life—a conformity to actuality—and the production provides relevant spectacle details for the audience. The illusion of life is so real that the spectators are expected

In this scene from a production of *84, Charing Cross Road*, both performers utilized effective offstage focus.

Onstage focus was used in this scene from Neil Simon's *Rumors*.

to forget they are in a theatre. Representational theatre is primarily associated with the "realistic" productions of playwrights such as Henrik Ibsen, Anton Chekhov, and August Strindberg. With productions of this type, there is an attempt by directors, designers, and actors to be as true-to-life as possible. Actors imagine that they are in a real place (not on a stage) at a particular time, wear the appropriate costume, have authentic props, and appropriate period furniture and set dressing. The actors act as if they really ARE the characters they portray and there is no open acknowledgement of the audience. As Bakshy states, "The representational form can be used for portraying life in its various aspects . . . but, whatever the aspect of life, its reproduction in the theatre is always based on creating the illusion that it represents a world entirely different from that in which the audience is while in the theatre."[3] Ethnographic and everyday conversation performances attempt in their reproduction of actual events to give us this illusion of reality.

Marshal McLuhan, a Canadian media expert, would call representational theatre **hot** because "it extends one single sense in 'high definition,'"[4] that sense being primarily the visual. As a result of this high definition, there is low audience participation (elements are fully realized; audiences need not creatively imagine them). Examples of "hot" media are drawings by Durer, movies, productions of Ibsen's plays, and many music videos. Presentational productions would be considered **cool** because they have low definition in the visual sense and consequently high audience participation (audiences must visualize elements that are only suggested). Examples of "cool" media are Chinese line drawings, the telephone, Shakespearean and Greek play productions, and mime performances.

The chart in figure 1-1 suggests many of the basic differences between presentational and representational theatre.[5]

We discuss presentational and representational theatre so that you may adopt those conventions that are necessary for the type of production you are creating and staging. If you establish from the outset that you are working in the presentational medium, you will want to concentrate on adopting presentational conventions. If you are working in the representational medium, concentrate on adopting representational conventions. Figure 1-1 details many of the choices available to you. You may, of course, use both presentational and representational conventions in a production, but be sure you aren't confusing your audience.

Figure 1-1 Representational and Presentational Conventions		
Convention	**Presentational**	**Representational**
Front curtain used		X
No front curtain—stage open to audience	X	
Flat floor		X
Raked stage	X	
Realistic set and set pieces		X
No walls	X	
Primarily offstage focus	X	
Onstage focus		X
Direct eye contact with audience	X	
No direct eye contact with audience		X
Actors enter through audience	X	
Actors may carry scripts	X	
Actors stay on stage throughout (no literal exits/entrances)	X	
Only defined characters appear		X
Presence of a narrator	X	
Use of asides	X	
Use of soliloquies	X	
Use of monologues	X	X
Use of song and dance	X	
Unison speaking	X	
One actor per role		X
One actor plays many roles	X	
Many actors play same role	X	
Characters refer to selves in third person/past tense	X	
Spectacle elements literalized		X
Spectacle elements suggested	X	
Visible lighting instruments	X	
Doors that open and close		X
Visible scene changes	X	
Scene changes in dark or behind curtain		X

A Sense of the Other

The experimental theatre types we discuss in this text emphasize performance as "knowing." We learn about "the other" as well as about ourselves through our participation in these productions. One of the values of creating and staging (or performing in) these types of scripts is the sense they give us of the other—a fictitious other in the case of most readers theatre and chamber theatre productions, and a real other in the case of ethnographic, conversational, and personal narrative performances. Re-creating the lives of these others increases your awareness of them and expands your knowledge of yourself. As Wallace Bacon writes, "This sharing of self with other, this matching of self with other is a profoundly human activity which in the richest sense of the word *educates*, . . . it is not, to begin with, a *study* of the experience but an engagement with it."[6] Participation in these experimental art forms increases your appreciation of the world in which you live through an engagement with and in it. As you engage in these kinds of theatrical experiences, monitor your reactions in order to document what you have learned.

Let's now briefly discuss the definition and characteristics of the types of group performance styles that will be included in this text: readers theatre, chamber theatre, ethnographic studies and conversation scripts, and personal narratives. More detailed discussions of each type are found in chapters two through seven.

What Is Readers Theatre?

Readers theatre is a flexible, creative medium for presenting all kinds of literary texts.[7] (There are variant spellings of this form of performance—most commonly *reader's theatre*—but *readers theatre* is the most accurate, as it is not a theatre for one reader but a theatre for all readers, thus "readers" is plural, not possessive, in this case.) The term "readers theatre" was probably used for the first time in 1945 in New York, when *Oedipus Rex* was produced by a professional group that called itself Readers Theatre, Inc. The group's stated purpose was "to give the people of New York an opportunity to witness performances of great dramatic works which were seldom if ever produced."

Readers theatre works best with texts that make their primary appeal to our auditory sense. Texts that feature evocative images, for example, can benefit from readers theatre staging, which features economy and suggestion (not literalizing elements) in order to promote audience participation. Readers theatre depends on synecdochical spectacle—using a part to suggest the whole, as earlier stated. Material that might be effectively staged in the readers theatre format include poems, letters, diaries, plays which cannot be staged in a traditional or conventional manner because cast or set requirements are too great, radio plays (which essentially call for an aural rendition which appeals to the audience's imagination), essays, historical events, lyric prose fiction texts, and songs.

In recent years, the popularity of readers theatre has grown tremendously (although rarely are "readers theatre" productions labeled as such. They are simply accepted as "theatre" productions and audiences may not be aware that they are witnessing material not originally intended for the stage.) Some shows, like *Cats*, run for years on Broadway. A. R. Gurney's *Love Letters* is a two-person play that is essentially a readers theatre compilation of letters exchanged between two fictitious characters. This production successfully played Off Broadway with a different duo of performers for each performance. A recent production of Homer's poem *The Odyssey* was first produced by the Royal Shakespeare Company in Stratford-on-Avon in 1992 and in London in 1993. It then moved to Washington, D.C., and played at the Arena Stage. The Open Book—a company in New York that only produces readers theatre scripts—holds an annual contest for new scripts; the best are produced by the company and published by Fireside Theatre.

Students enjoy acting in readers theatre productions because they have an opportunity to present rarely performed texts, they often originate the roles they play, and because readers theatre offers interesting challenges. Staging a production like *The Odyssey*, for example, calls for someone to portray a one-eyed monster, the Cyclops, to transform Odysseus' men into pigs, and to suggest a ship at sea. As Richard Corliss, the *TIME* magazine reviewer of *The Odyssey*, wrote, it puts "epic dreams on a bare stage, to evoke ancient empires with only words and a few props."[8] These types of challenges allow for and promote exciting and creative solutions. Audiences are afforded the opportunity to participate by using their imaginations, and thus they help the performers create elements that are suggested on stage. Since script creators usually double as directors, they enjoy the dual creative challenge of writing and staging "original" scripts which empower them to assume the role of "author." Audiences, too, benefit from being able to experience literature which does not normally get staged.

As stated before, the earliest readers theatre productions made almost no use of spectacle or physical movement and were staged very simply.

Readers attired in white shirts/blouses and dark pants/skirts usually sat on stools behind music stands or lecterns and read from manuscripts. There were no literal exits or entrances (the cast remained on stage throughout the performance, looking up or down or turning forward or back to suggest entrances and exits), readers often "read" more than one role, and there may have been unison or choral speaking. These productions appealed primarily to the audience's auditory sense, and the performers depended on the audience's ability to imagine.

We have experimented much since those early productions. Readers theatre practitioners now believe that there must be conflict, interaction, and some visual appeal for present-day theatre audiences, and they successfully employ staging, spectacle, and special effects to underscore the particular material being performed. Stools, music stands, and manuscripts are often discarded unless their use is necessary.

Today's readers theatre productions pose a dual responsibility on directors. They must make sure that the readers keep the text as the featured element of the production.[9] They must also strive to keep the *theatre* in readers theatre in mind—that "theatrical complement" we addressed earlier which pays attention to the needs most audience members have for visual stimulation, including physical movement and spectacle elements. Not that we want readers theatre to lose its special appeal to the audience's imagination, but we want also to involve the audience's other senses as well. The more involved audience members feel, the more they will appreciate and remember what they have experienced.

We will now discuss briefly three kinds of readers theatre scripts: single text, expanded program compiled script, and collage compiled script.

Single-Text Scripts

The first kind of readers theatre script is a **single-text script** which means that one text may be **orchestrated** (divided into voices as a musical score is divided into and played by different instruments) and presented for group performance. One could orchestrate a poem, an essay, a famous speech from history, a letter, or a diary entry. Some plays are suitable for readers theatre when they make their primary appeal to our sense of hearing. Many Shakespearean plays, for example, can be staged effectively in readers theatre because much in Shakespeare depends on the language and the audience's ability to imagine. Shakespeare's plays often call for elements that are difficult to literalize on stage (e.g., the storm, the blinding of Gloucester, and Gloucester's suicide leap off the Dover cliffs in *King Lear*). A readers theatre presentation keeps the focus on the words—on the language—and the audience imagines the rest, much the way they did in Shakespeare's day.

Single-text scripts offer manifold challenges for the director as well as for performers. A text that seemingly manifests only one voice can be creatively orchestrated for group performance based on any number of considerations. Although one voice is heard, other voices may be suggested or implied. For example, these other voices can be created to speak the lines which refer to them (as we did with the adaptation of *The Wind in the Willows* at the opening of this chapter). Orchestrations of single texts might feature the sound qualities, the images, or the rhythm depending on the text and the adapter's intention. (See chapter two for more information on single-text orchestrations.)

Here is a sample orchestration of a children's verse:

Peter (*to audience, sadly, munching on imaginary pumpkin*): Peter, Peter, pumpkin eater

Wife (*to Peter, indicating "we have no home"*): Had a wife and couldn't keep her.

Peter (*to wife, pretending to find and carry big pumpkin shell*): He put her in a pumpkin shell

Both (*entering the imaginary shell, to audience*): And there he kept her

Wife (*kisses Peter, then to audience*): very well.

Compiled Scripts

To compile means "to put together" or "to juxtapose" pieces of literature. There are essentially two kinds of readers theatre **compiled** scripts: the **expanded program** and the **collage**. With these types of productions, performers can investigate a theme, the works of an author, a literary style, or a historical period in more depth than a solo performer or a single-text readers theatre production can. With the expanded program, materials are gathered together by some common bond, but each selection maintains its original context and remains an identifiable unit. The "seams" show where one selection ends and the next begins. One could compile an expanded program on the theme of "love" or "Edgar Allan Poe," or "the sonnet," or "religion," or "war," etc.

Here is an example of an expanded program script from verses from Mother Goose. The theme is "Marriage and the Treatment of Women."

Man: Now what do you think of Little Jackie Jingle?
   Before he was married, he used to live single.
   But after he married, to alter his life,
   He left off living single and lived with his wife.

Chorus: Needles and pins, needles and pins,
   When a man marries his troubles begin.

Woman: As Tommy Snooks and Bessy Brooks
   Were walking out one Sunday,
   Says Tommy Snooks to Bessy Brooks,
   "Tomorrow will be Monday."

Chorus: Needles and pins, needles and pins,
   When a man marries his troubles begin.

Woman: Peter, Peter, pumpkin eater,

Man: Had a wife and couldn't keep her;
   He put her in a pumpkin shell

Woman: And there he kept her very well.

In collage[10] compiled scripts, each selection or part of a selection becomes part of a new context and ideally seams do *not* show. The collage compiled script is the newest and perhaps the most challenging type of readers theatre script—both for the performers and for the compiler-director. As earlier stated, in an expanded program, each literary selection is a recognizably separate part of the whole. Each selection is usually performed in its entirety, when possible, with introductory and transitional material provided to show how selections relate to each other and to the program's theme. In a collage compiled script, however, often only fragments of literary selections are used: a stanza from a poem, a few paragraphs from a short story or novel, a song lyric, a newspaper headline, a diary entry, a few lines of dialogue from a play, and so forth. The audience should not be concerned with individual selections by individual authors; they should be concerned with understanding the script's overall theme or message, to which each selection contributes. The selections or fragments of selections work together as though there were only one source, and the script reveals only one seamless message—that of the compiler. Here is an example of a collage compiled script using the same material used in the expanded program script. The theme here is "Marriage Regrets."

Man: As Tommy Snooks

Woman: and Bessy Brooks

Both: Were walking out one Sunday,

Man: Says Tommy Snooks

Woman: to Bessy Brooks,

Man (*hands her an engagement ring*): "Tomorrow will be Monday."

Chorus of Men: Needles and pins, needles and pins,
    When a man marries his troubles begin.

Woman (*calling*): Tommy Snooks, Tommy Snooks

Man (*with regret*): Before he was married, he used to live single.

Woman (*gleefully*): But after he married, to alter his life,
    He left off living single and lived with his wife.

Man (*remembering what he has heard*): When a man marries his troubles begin.

Woman (*calling, with more urgency*): Tommy Snooks, Tommy Snooks.

Man: Had a wife and couldn't keep her.

Chorus: Needles and pins, needles and pins,
    When a man marries his troubles begin.

Woman (*with contempt and anger*): He left off living single and lived with his wife.

Man: He put her in a pumpkin shell
    And there he kept her.

Chorus: Now what do you think of little Tommy Snooks?

As you can see from the above collage compiled script, certain changes must be made to make the material you are using fit this new script you are creating. For example, characters' names might change—here we changed "Peter, Peter," and "Jackie Jingle" to Tommy Snooks as we want to have one consistent character identified. Then we used only parts of lines, and repeated some lines to underscore the compiler's intention rather than the intention of any individual selection.

Casting in readers theatre is usually not as it is in conventional theatre. Since we are not attempting a realistic view of life, men may play women's roles and vice versa, and ethnic and age discriminations need not be made. Often an entire chorus of performers may suggest one character, and one performer may play a variety of roles. In one experimental production of *Macbeth*, for example, a man and a woman played Macbeth. The woman dominated in the first half of the show when Macbeth still has qualms about killing and is sensitive to his position as the king's friend, relative, and host. In the second half of the play, after Macbeth realizes that he has committed so many crimes it matters little how many more he commits, the male performer dominated.

EXPERIMENT

Select a poem that you particularly enjoy. Some possible choices are "Richard Cory" by Edwin Arlington Robinson, "Because I Could Not Stop for Death" by Emily Dickinson, "Death Be Not Proud" by John Donne, or "Do Not Go Gentle into that Good Night" by Dylan Thomas. Orchestrate your selected text for readers theatre by deciding who should say each line or part of a line and to whom each line or phrase should be delivered. Stage your orchestration in class. Then, using all four of the poems above, try creating an expanded program compiled script and a collage compiled script.

What Is Chamber Theatre?

The second type of group production form is called **chamber theatre**.[11] Chamber theatre was defined and developed in the early 1940s by Robert S. Breen of Northwestern University. Breen developed this form as a vehicle for the staging of prose fiction texts—short stories and novels. Breen called this format "chamber theatre" because of the chamber plays of August Strindberg, which demanded small, intimate productions. The staging of novels, though, is not new. In the first half of the nineteenth century, for example, most towns had stock companies which produced hastily dramatized dime novels.[12] The difference between these productions and chamber theatre is that the latter maintains many of the characteristics of prose fiction; it does not turn the material into a play. Often, when novels are translated into films or into theatrical productions the first thing tampered with is the narration, which is either excised or rewritten into dialogue. In a chamber theatre production the narration is often maintained as written, and the narrator's style of storytelling is the central and major consideration when adapting and staging.

Since Breen defined the form, it has become very popular. Chamber theatre productions (though like readers theatre not often designated "chamber theatre") have appeared all over the United States and Europe. A chamber theatre production of *The Grapes of Wrath*, adapted and directed by Frank Galati, a former student of Breen's, made a highly successful appearance on Broadway. Galati also adapted and directed William Faulkner's *As I Lay Dying* at the famous Steppenwolf Theatre in Chicago. Steppenwolf featured a wonderfully exciting and faithful production of Anthony Burgess' novel *A Clockwork Orange*, while Broadway has offered successful productions of *The Secret Garden, A Christmas Carol, Nicholas Nickleby, Les Miserables,* and *Beauty and the Beast.* The Chamber Repertory Theatre in Boston is a nationally acclaimed professional touring company. The National Repertory Theatre in Philadelphia tours with "6 Great Authors in 1 Exciting Show . . . on stage."

In a chamber theatre production, the nature and behavior of the narrator, his or her reasons for and manner of telling the story, are the central concerns. The narrator's **point of view**—his or her unique perspective and way of telling the story—is the controlling element of the adapting and staging process. Narrators who refer to themselves as "I" ("I walked down the street, and I saw an elephant") behave and interact in a different manner than narrators who show and tell their stories from the third-person perspective ("She walked down the street, and she saw an elephant"). Regardless, the remembered scenes (most prose fiction is written in the past tense) are presented from the narrator's point of view. We are not seeing events as they happen—we are seeing events replayed as the narrator remembers them.

Prose fiction written in the epic mode is best suited to chamber theatre, as the strong relationship between narrator and characters representative of epic-mode literature is what chamber theatre features. The strong relationship between the characters and the narrator in *The Wind in the Willows* makes this a rich novel for chamber theatre as the adapted scene at the start of this chapter suggests. The director of a chamber theatre production is guided by the narrator's attitude toward and relationship with each character when adapting and staging. To clarify the epic mode in performance, the narrator uses offstage focus (addressing the audience) when telling the story and the characters use onstage focus when replaying the past scenes. This combination of offstage and onstage focuses emphasizes the contrary pulls in epic-mode literature and often heightens the conflict within the story.

When turning a story into a chamber theatre script, you do not rewrite the story, change the verb tense, or the point of view. You read the material carefully several times and analyze the narrator's perspective. You then decide who is to deliver which lines and to whom. Normally, narrators take the narration, and characters take the dialogue—but within the narration there are often other voices suggested or heard. An **internal modal analysis** of the text will help you as you decide who is speaking to whom: **lyric lines**—characters speak to themselves or to the narrator or they may address God, a muse, an absent or deceased person; **dramatic lines**—dialogue lines where characters address each other; **epic lines**—speakers address the audience. (More is said about this type of modal analysis in chapter four.) Let us see how we can employ an internal modal analysis to this passage from "Impulse" by Conrad Aiken.

From "Impulse" by Conrad Aiken

Michael Lowes hummed as he shaved, amused by the face he saw—the pallid, asymmetrical face, with the right eye so much higher than the left, and its eyebrow so peculiarly arched, like a "v" turned upside down. Perhaps this day wouldn't be as bad as the last. In fact, he knew it wouldn't be, and that was why he hummed.

At first glance, only the narrator seems to be speaking in this passage. But if we examine the language closely, we sense a division primarily indicated by language usage which seems to suggest that the narrator is sharing with us some of Michael Lowes' lyric thoughts. One possible adaptation of this passage might look like this.

Chamber Theatre Adaptation
From "Impulse" by Conrad Aiken

Narrator (*assuming role of Michael's reflected mirror image, watches and listens to Michael, then says to audience*): Michael Lowes hummed as he shaved, amused by the face he saw—the pallid, asymmetrical face

Michael (*to himself*): with the right eye so much higher than the left.

Narrator (*looks at Michael, then to audience*): And its eyebrow so peculiarly arched,

Michael (*to self*): like a "v" turned upside down. (*to Narrator/mirror, hopefully*): Perhaps this day wouldn't be as bad as the last.

Narrator (*to audience, ironically*): In fact, he knew it wouldn't be, and that was why he hummed.

This passage suggests that Michael's thoughts in Michael's language are heard within the narrative lines, so the performer playing Michael can say these lines. Since the narrator usually has the advantage of knowing the end of the story before the story even begins, the last line the narrator speaks has an ironic edge because the narrator knows that this is going to be the worst day of Michael's life.

When staging a chamber theatre production, you have two factors to keep in mind: the attitude and behavior of the narrator in the present and the attitude and behavior of the narrator and his/her relationship with the characters in the past. As stated earlier, the narrator mediates between the audience and the scenes on stage and may use both onstage and offstage focus. The scenes in the past are staged with onstage focus and resemble conventional theatre more so than the staging in readers theatre. Characters in the past scenes relate to each other in a manner similar to the way characters react in conventional theatre except that the narrator is in the scene, is often addressed by the characters, often addresses them, and may participate in the action. Breen explains that the narrator should usually begin center stage and then move in accordance with his or her perspective and sympathies. The narrator's point of view determines where he or she stands, who he or she empathizes or sympathizes with, how involved or uninvolved he or she is with the events related, and so on. The narrator's purpose or intention in telling this story should be communicated. Rarely do narrators feel neutral about the events in the stories they tell. Decide, then, not only who the audience is, but also why the narrator needs to tell them this story.

Chamber theatre is a presentational form, but it also incorporates some representational elements. Performers may make realistic entrances and exits, and may use costuming, lighting, set, set pieces, and props, if the narration does not make these elements unnecessary. Often the description in a story or novel is so vivid that few spectacle elements are necessary. Narrators and characters may use offstage focus. Occasionally, narrator and characters may be **bifurcated** (bifurcation is the casting of two performers to play one role). This technique is often used to show the attitudinal, emotional, or psychological divisions within one person. The technique of **trifurcation** was used in a production of Charlotte Brontë's *Jane Eyre*, when three actresses were cast to play Jane. One of the actresses played Jane in the present—older and wiser. One actress played Jane in the past—young and inexperienced. One actress danced Jane in the past's inner feelings and emotions which Victorian convention forbid her to express. The trifurcation underscored the narrator's feelings and produced another layer of tension. Other conventions include allowing characters to speak of themselves in the third person and in the past tense. This device shows the closeness

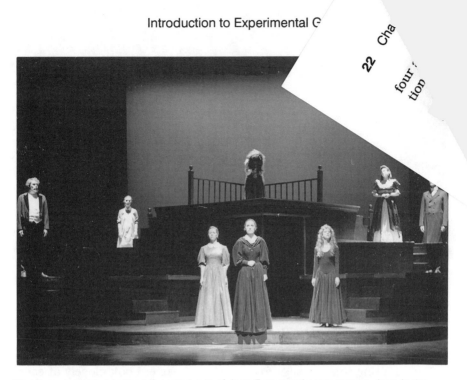

The three actresses in the trifurcated role of *Jane Eyre* stand center stage. Jane in the Present is down center; Jane in the Past is up right; and the actress who danced, portraying the inner turmoil of Jane, is up left.

between the character and the narrator, alienates or separates the character from the experience, and underscores the sense that the performer is presenting, not being, the character—as the scenes the narrator re-creates have really already occurred (for more information on acting in chamber theatre productions see chapter five). Last, spectacle elements are often mimed or suggested.

Whereas solo performers often have difficulty performing the narrative passages in a prose fiction text, group performance often solves this problem as the narrator's role must be the central consideration. The director should usually cast the strongest performer as the narrator, and the director must assist this person in developing the narrator's unique role (e.g., director, moralizer, puppeteer, camera-eye, reporter, double, conscience, alter ego, sympathizer, or judge, among others) and relationship with the other characters. In addition, the narrator, in conjunction with the director, must decide who the audience might be. The narrator must be able to find the best way to facilitate the general audience's transformation into the audience appropriate for this text. (See chapters

nd five for more detailed descriptions of chamber theatre conven-
s and techniques.)

Look at this narrative passage from A. E. Coppard's "The Third Prize." Can you hear more than just the narrator's voice here?

From "The Third Prize" by A. E. Coppard

Mr. Robins intimated that he could well understand such desires. Miss Margery retorted that then he was understanding much more than was good for him. Mr. Robins thought not, he hoped not. Miss Margery indicated that he could hope for much more than he was likely to get. Mr. Robins replied that, he would do that, and double it. And he asserted, with all respect, that had he but happily been in that train he too might have, etc. and so on. Whereupon Miss Margery snapped, would he? and Mr. Robins felt bound to say Sure!

Try adapting this passage for chamber theatre. Look closely at each line and decide who should speak it (the narrator or one of the characters), and to whom each line should be addressed. Stage your adaptation in class. Once you've made your own adaptation, check chapter four where four different adaptations of this story are included.

What Are Ethnography and Conversation Analysis?

Readers theatre and chamber theatre are two forms of group performance which rely on orchestrating, compiling, or adapting literary texts. The three remaining group performance styles discussed in this text—ethnographic and conversation analysis scripts and the personal narrative—create material out of everyday life experiences. As Richard Schechner attests, "If 'everyday life' is theatre, then people doing ordinary things are performers."[13] You may have already noticed that there is much in life that is theatrical. Performance is involved in our daily lives since we "play roles" all the time—deciding how to speak in a given circumstance based on "audience," wearing appropriate attire based on occasion, behaving in a certain way based on where we are and what is expected. Life is a kind of lived performance.

Practitioners in the field of oral interpretation once stressed the study of literature in performance as their emphasis. Now that oral interpretation programs in universities and colleges throughout the United States have been renamed "performance studies," the emphasis has expanded to include materials never before considered for presentation. Two of oral interpretation's most fundamental components have been reexamined: What is "text" and what is "performance"? Traditional definitions of text include literary texts: prose, drama, poetry—the three genres of literature. But the dimensions of what "text" means have grown. We now define text more broadly and include not just literary texts but oral texts. Personal narratives, stories of all kinds, are possible texts for performance. Aesthetic objects may be considered texts, as well. A quilt may be viewed as a text of a particular family, time period, or culture. Rituals may be viewed as social or cultural texts. Demonstrations, rallies, and sit-ins may be viewed as political texts. Studies of organizations or diverse cultural groups provide exciting material for group performance texts. Historical reenactments are potential performance material. Everyday conversations may be analyzed and performed as dialogic texts. Text, then, is a metaphor for all kinds of experiences.

Performance, too, has altered in meaning. The change from oral interpretation to performance studies reflects the field's new interest in the varied ramifications of what is now considered "performance." Performance is a reflection of humanness, of culture, of communication; performance is a way of knowing. In this section and in chapters six and seven, you will discover the theatricality in events and experiences that you may never have considered theatrical. More importantly, perhaps, you will also learn valuable information about yourself as well as about other people—how they think, operate, talk, interact—information that allows you to taste someone else's reality. Experience with these types of scripts stretches your creativity, makes you a more compassionate human being, and prepares you to perform a variety of different kinds of "characters."

Although ethnography (the study of cultural groups) and conversation analysis (the study of everyday discourse) are two distinct areas of study, we combine them because, in essence, conversation analysis is really one aspect of ethnographers' investigations. One question they ask is, "How do people use language and communicate with one another in particular groups." As fieldworker Michael Moerman concludes, "I now think it is a mistake to study conversation independently of the languages, cultures, and settings in which it occurs."[14]

Unlike readers theatre and chamber theatre, you will be creating ethnographic and conversation analysis scripts from nonliterary sources. Whereas with readers theatre and chamber theatre you began with a literary text and orchestrated or adapted it for performance, with ethnographic and conversation analysis scripts you begin with a detailed observation of an everyday life "performance," transcribe this into script form, then translate this script into a new performance experience. In readers theatre and chamber theatre, performers normally enact fictitious characters; however, in ethnographic and conversation analysis scripts, one attempts to suggest the presence of real people. In readers theatre and chamber theatre, you work from text to performance. With ethnography and conversation analysis, you work from recorded performance to script to [re]performance.

What follows is a very brief overview of these two related fields; a more detailed discussion is presented in chapter six.

Ethnography

Ethnography is the study of how people live and make sense of their lives. When dealing with ethnographic scripts, one selects a certain cultural group to study. In this text, an "ethnic" group is defined loosely as any group of people who share at least one characteristic in common. Possible "ethnic" groups you could visit include church members, nursing home residents, factory workers, farm families, lodge members, boy scouts, girl scouts, among others. An ethnographer's primary intention is to capture as accurately as possible the "aesthetic patterning of performances within specific cultural contexts."[15] Ethnographic scripts feature "the other." They often empower minority or marginalized voices not often represented in mainstream literature. We learn about these people in a close, personal way, and we share what we have learned with audiences.

Ethnographers are essentially interested in anthropological studies of people in other cultures which necessitates field research, but since extensive travel might not be possible for the traditional college or university student, there are many possible groups nearby from which to choose. Select a group you are really interested in learning more about. Do some prior research about the group and formulate a general idea of the focus of your project. You then need to find out the name of the person in charge so that you can gain access to that group. Call that person, describe your project, and gain permission to collect your data. We will discuss methods of data collection in more detail in chapter six, but the primary methods are participant/observer, observation, and interview. We recommend that you attempt to employ the participant/observer method, if this is possible. Regardless of the methodology you employ, you will probably need a video and audio recording of the proceedings. You must get permission to do so. Attend as many meetings/gatherings as possible. You will probably collect more data than you will need or be able to use. Work to free yourself of all preconceptions, and allow the cultural group to reveal itself to you as objectively as possible. You have an ethical responsibility to reveal this group as honestly as you can, so you might want to take notes as well as use the audio and/or video equipment. As stated above, ethnographic studies demand detailed observations of the performative structures within the group being studied and the ability to transcribe that research into script form so that others may share in the knowledge you have gleaned.

Once the material is collected, the job of scripting begins. Ask yourself these questions: How do I turn everyday-life material into a theatrical script? What do I use? How much should I include? How long is my script going to be? How do I edit? How do I organize what I am using? How do I make sure I am capturing both text and context? How do I make sure I am representing the group as ethically and objectively as possible with no hidden agenda or personal bias? In chapter six, we will provide you with the tools you need to record, transcribe, and stage ethnographic research.

Conversation Analysis

Other experimental scripts feature everyday conversations. These scripts transcribe real-life, naturally occurring conversations in an attempt to study the subtleties of spontaneous discourse and the reality of how we communicate with one another. Again decide on a project focus and employ either an audio or a videotape recorder. Once you have selected, gained permission from your subjects, and recorded their conversations, you will engage in hours of minute transcription so that the conversations can be accurately recorded, studied, and eventually performed on stage.

As stated earlier, a conversation analysis script is part of an ethnographic study. In conversation analysis you are minutely examining the language and communicative behaviors of certain people. As you study the conversation of these people, try to keep in mind the context, culture, and setting in which the conversation took place. The minute behaviors you record and script are then embodied by performers who memorize the transcript, and try to copy exactly the pitch, inflection, length of pause, body posture, gestures, etc. of the taped participants. One is successful if the performance matches the audiotaped or videotaped original. Although this is the ideal, we may need to balance this sense of fidelity to the demands theatre makes. We will say more on this in chapter six.

Performers engaged in conversational performances discover that they are able to suggest the "other" more closely than they were ever able to before. As one theatre student put it after participating in a script based on everyday conversation, "I never felt so close to another 'person' as I did in this performance—I really felt like I got out of myself and was breathing, speaking, moving like someone else. I was surprised at the difference between lines in a play and real-life lines."

Here is a brief example of what one conversation analysis script looks like. This conversation was recorded in 1992 between "K" and "L." See chapter six for an explanation of what each transcription symbol means.

L: ⌊He⌋ goes he go   I'm sure   that's what I mean I'm sure that's where
   he'll end up(.) and I don't know that   kinda   stuff↑scares   me

K: (.)Linne:a (laughs) that's   fine

L: =It does

K: I mean just look at Jeff

L: ⌊Because⌋I don

K: What does Jeff do nothing (.)

L: Yes but Jeff makes a lot of money an

K: He doesn't even he makes a lot of money doing nothing

L: (.) He does fun stuff though   he knows a lot about a lot of things

Ethnographic and conversation analysis scripts are very recent group performance forms and no conventions for production have been strictly formulated. The staging of ethnographic scripts depends heavily on the behaviors of those cultural groups being studied. Their interactions become your stage directions. The staging of conversation analysis scripts is determined primarily by the recorded behavior of the taped participants. This behavior is replicated when the conversation is [re]performed. This text will cover the creation of these types of scripts in terms of selecting, gathering, and scripting materials; any additional staging conventions can be incorporated from the staging principles already detailed for readers theatre and chamber theatre.

EXPERIMENT

Try creating an ethnographic or conversation analysis script. If you are interested in a certain group of people (e.g., an open meeting of Alcoholics Anonymous or Al Anon, members of a nursing home, candy stripers, boy scouts, girl scouts, etc.), find out the name of a person who is in charge. Call this person and see if you can attend several meetings. Tape the proceedings (if you have been given permission to do so), take copious notes, and see if you can structure what you saw and heard into a script that the members of your class can perform. Be sure to include physical behaviors and necessary background information.

If you want to try a conversation analysis script, you and a friend find two willing participants and videotape them for approximately fifteen minutes, or for a long enough period of time so that they hopefully forget that they are being recorded. (In some cases this may not occur at all, but this is the ideal.) Select approximately one or two minutes from your fifteen-minute tape to turn into a script. Replay the tape, starting and stopping so that you get each line recorded exactly as spoken. Use the transcription symbols outlined in chapter six, and include stage directions that describe body positions, gestures, inflections, pauses, laughs, hiccups, and so forth. You become one of the taped participants, memorizing the lines, pauses, and behavior; and your friend becomes the other. Perform the conversation for your class.

What Is a Personal Narrative?

We all have stories to tell; we all have favorite stories told to us by family members or friends. When we script and stage personal narratives, we preserve part of our oral tradition and give voice to our personal stories.[16] As Kristin M. Langellier writes, "Personal narratives emerge from oral culture and traditions rather than written and literary traditions."[17] Personal narratives are, in a sense, ethnographic studies of who we are and where we came from. Rather than being responsible for interpreting the text of another, you have personal authorship and ownership of your stories. When you script and present a personal narrative, you indicate a willingness to share parts of yourself with an audience.

When you create a script out of a personal narrative, you start by selecting a story from your own life—or a story you know well—that you are willing to share with an audience. You then find a way to structure it in much the same way as stories suitable for chamber theatre are structured. Work out a clear beginning, middle, and ending. Decide who will tell the story and how, how many "characters" will be involved, where the story will take place in the "then" and "now," how the story will be structured, and how transitions will be achieved. Consider also that if the story is too personal it will not have the universality that makes literature appeal to more than just a select few. Find a way to suggest that the story has broader implications which will make it possible for others to appreciate, relate to, and perhaps even learn from your experience. You learn from the experience as well. In addition to learning about the demands theatre makes in shaping your narrative, you will also learn from relating in objective terms the events that comprise your narrative.

One of the more unique aspects of adapting and staging a personal narrative is that you—as adapter/director—may indeed be casting and directing someone to play you in your production! (We recommend that you not be an actor in your own production. Directing provides you with the objectivity and distance you need to see your story from the outside. In addition, you really cannot adequately direct something you are in and consequently cannot see.) An equally daunting task is asking actors to portray the "real" people who inhabit your tale. You might consider whether it is judicious to show your cast videos of these real people; should they listen to audio tapes; should they meet them in person, if this is possible. You and your cast will feel an overwhelming responsibility to embody these real people as honestly and reliably as possible. See chapter seven for more detailed information on creating and staging the personal narrative.

EXPERIMENT

Select a short personal story and write it out. Adapt the story into script form complete with line divisions, direction of address, and any necessary stage directions. Stage the script in class using members of the class to take on the roles you have created. Lead a discussion afterwards so that the performers may relate how they felt about embodying the "characters" in your story.

Summary

This chapter has presented the basic philosophy of four different kinds of theatre forms: readers theatre, chamber theatre, ethnographic studies and conversation analysis, and personal narratives. Definitions were given for those terms necessary to understand the basic principles of creating and staging these group performance styles. The material that is staged in these texts falls into three theatrical modes: lyric, dramatic, and epic. A lyric-mode script features the experience of one person, deals with strong emotions, and usually presents a sense of timelessness. Dramatic-mode scripts depict delineated characters in a specific setting at a specific time. Dramatic-mode scripts, like play scripts, usually convey the sense of spontaneity, of events happening now for the first time. Epic-mode scripts usually feature a story told from the past tense. In epic scripts there usually exists both a narrator and characters.

Since much of the material included in these group performance formats deals with literature not originally intended for the stage, a theatrical complement needs to be found—a way to find the inherent "drama" in nondramatic material so it plays on the stage and appeals to audiences who are primarily visually oriented.

These theatre types are both presentational and representational. Presentational means that no illusion of reality is attempted—the audience realizes it is in a theatre. Representational theatre attempts to capture a feeling of verisimilitude—the audience is to believe that they are viewing life as it really is. Spectacle elements (sets, lights, costumes, makeup, etc.) are detailed and exact.

Readers theatre is a type of presentational group form that primarily stages texts not originally intended for the stage. The primary appeal in readers theatre scripts is to the ear—the aural dimension. Although, more and more, readers theatre productions, like *Cats*, are making strong appeals to all our senses, and incorporate more spectacle elements than traditional readers theatre productions back in the 1940s and 1950s.

Chamber theatre is a type of presentational theatre that stages prose fiction maintaining the narrator, the past tense, and the epic mode in which most prose fiction is written. Chamber theatre features a narrator telling a story from his or her unique point of view.

Ethnographic and conversation analysis scripts are more representational, and deal with everyday life experiences. Ethnographic scripts try to capture the cultural behavior of a particular group of people. Conversation analysis is an aspect of ethnography which deals with observing, understanding, and re-creating everyday discourse.

Personal narratives are part of the oral tradition. They are the autobiographical stories we collect and tell. Stories are heightened forms of discourse, and by staging them, we are able to preserve our familial ties and our cultural heritage. Personal narratives are, in a sense, ethnographic studies of who we are and where we came from. Turning stories into scripts empowers scriptwriters, and gives them a sense of existence and place as well as allowing others to benefit from their experiences.

Notes

[1] Richard Corliss, "Les Formidables," *TIME*, November 14, 1994, p. 86.

[2] David Richards, "Boulevard of Broken Dreams," *The New York Times*, Friday, November 18, 1994, C1, C30.

[3] A. Bakshy, "Representational or Presentational Theatre," in *Scene Design for Stage and Screen*, ed. O. K. Larson (East Lansing: Michigan State University Press, 1961), p. 263.

[4] Marshall McLuhan, *Understanding Media: The Extensions of Man* (New York: New American Library, 1964), p. 36.

[5] This chart owes much to a similar chart found in Stuart Vaughan's *Directing Plays* (New York: Longman), p. 62.

[6] Wallace A. Bacon, "The Case for Interpretation," in *Renewal and Revision: The Future of Interpretation*, ed. by Ted Colson (Denton, TX: NB Omega Publications, 1986), p. 22.

[7] See Judy E. Yordon, *Roles in Interpretation* (Dubuque, IA: Wm. C. Brown, 1993), pp. 408–417.

[8] Richard Corliss, "Club Adriatic," a review of "The Odyssey," *TIME*, October 31, 1994, p. 78.

[9] Joanna Maclay speaks of "featuring the text" in *Readers Theatre: Toward a Grammar of Practice* (New York: Random House, 1971).

[10] Marion L. Kleinau and Janet Larsen McHughes, *Theatres for Literature* (Sherman Oaks, CA: Alfred Publishing, 1980). See especially chapter 6.

[11] See Yordon, pp. 418–427.

[12] Foster Rhea Dulles, *A History of Recreation*, 2nd ed. (New York: Appleton, 1940), pp. 110–112.

[13] Richard Schechner, *Between Theatre & Anthropology* (Philadelphia: University of Pennsylvania Press, 1985), p. 248.

[14] Michael Moerman's "1987 Introduction" to "On 'Understanding' in the Analysis of Natural Conversation" in *Talking Culture: Ethnography and Conversation Analysis* (Philadelphia: University of Pennsylvania Press, 1988), p. 180.

[15] Elizabeth C. Fine, *The Folklore Text: From Performance to Print* (Bloomington: Indiana University Press, 1984), p. 2.

[16] See Yordon, pp. 394–395.

[17] Kristin M. Langellier, "Personal Narratives and Performance," in *Renewal and Revision: The Future of Interpretation*, ed. by Ted Colson (Denton, TX: NB Omega Publications, 1986), p. 140.

Chapter Two

Readers Theatre:
Creating the Script

As described in chapter one, readers theatre is a flexible, creative medium for presenting all kinds of literary and nonliterary texts. The beauty of readers theatre is this flexibility which makes it appropriate for young and old, amateur and professional. Readers theatre also draws on a wide range of styles, from the very presentational (stools, stands, little movement, scripts, no spectacle) to fully realized productions (like *Cats*) which incorporate realistic settings and much spectacle.

What readers theatre productions make possible is the theatrical "publication" of a myriad of various and varied materials that normally do not get staged. Readers theatre productions may include prose fiction, poetry, drama, letters, diaries, biographies, autobiographies, histories, journals, travelogues, essays, newspaper articles, song lyrics, oral narratives, jokes, interviews, and so on.

Although we will discuss basic principles, practices, and possibilities of creating readers theatre scripts, remember that there is no *one* way to present a text in readers theatre. We encourage you to modify or alter these suggestions to meet the needs of your particular production.

We will cover three kinds of readers theatre scripts: the single-text orchestration, and two kinds of compiled scripts: the expanded program and the collage. (For much of the material in this chapter and in chapter three on staging readers theatre productions, we owe a large debt of gratitude to the Coger and White text, *Readers Theatre Handbook, Third Edition*. This seminal text is the inspiration for many of the ideas in these two chapters.)

The Single-Text Orchestration

The **single-text orchestration** is a type of readers theatre script that involves only one text. As we have already suggested, the range of literature suitable for readers theatre is limitless. The following list of selections on which productions were based gives some idea of the variety that is possible: Neil Simon's play, *Last of the Red Hot Lovers*; *The Decameron* of Giovanni Boccaccio; W. Somerset Maugham's novel, *Of Human Bondage*; Hawthorne's story, "Dr. Heidigger's Experiment"; Millard Lampell and Earl Robinson's musical legend (once a radio script), *The Lonesome Train*; Edward Bond's one-act play, *Passion*; *84, Charing Cross Road*, Helene Hanff's collection of letters; Addison and Steele's essays, *The Spectator Pages*; and the comic strips and cartoons of Jules Feiffer.

Orchestrating means dividing a text into individual roles. You might know the word "orchestration" as it relates to musical orchestration. Much of what readers theatre scriptmakers do is related to music. When we orchestrate music, for example, we decide the instrumentation—which instrument will "say" which parts of the musical score. Each instrument has a unique quality which communicates a distinctive mood. The low-pitched oboe presents quite a different sound from the high-pitched piccolo and would be used to create different feelings. The violin sounds and feels different from the viola or from the bass. Listen to a recording of *Peter and the Wolf*, for example, and hear how the instruments underscore the qualities of each of the characters in the tale. When you orchestrate a text, then, you break it down into individual, distinct, or pervasive qualities—you make it possible for a group of performers to take part. Lines may remain as they appear in the original text, or they may be repeated, echoed, spoken in unison, given to a chorus, and so on.

Before you begin, be sure you have selected material with high literary values and strong dramatic potential, and then analyze the selection to devise your interpretation of it as well as your **production concept**—the main idea you wish to stress in your script. The best way to come to terms with your selection is to apply a **dramatistic analysis** by answering these questions: who is speaking, to whom, about what, where, when, how, and why. The answers to these seven essential questions will provide you with the basic information you need to devise a production concept—the message you desire your script to convey. If you were to perform a dramatistic analysis of the fairy tale "Little Red Riding Hood," for example, your analysis might reveal the following:

1. *Who is speaking.* A third-person, outside-the-story narrator is speaking. The narrator also allows characters to speak: Little Red, her mother, the wolf, the woodsman, and in some versions, granny.

2. *Who is addressed.* The narrator addresses a group of children; the characters address each other.

3. *About what.* The narrator's tale involves the story of a little girl's journey into the forest to bring a basket of goodies to her ailing grandmother. Although the little girl's mother has warned her not to leave the "right" path, the little girl meets a wolf who inquires where she is going and convinces her to deviate from that path to pick flowers. As the girl does so, the wolf gets to grandmother's house first, gobbles her up, and disguises himself as the grandmother to fool Little Red. Little Red gets to granny's, is confused by granny's appearance, and is herself eaten. A woodsman appears, kills the wolf, cuts open his stomach, and frees Little Red and her grandmother.

4. *Where.* There is no definite locale for the narrator as he or she tells the story, but the story itself took place at Little Red's house, in the forest, and at granny's house. The past locales are more important in this story than where the narrator is as he or she retells it.

5. *When.* The narrator is in a timeless present talking of the past.

6. *How.* The narrator tells the story with casual, simple language befitting the child audience.

7. *Why.* The narrator tells the story as a moral fable; to teach a lesson: "Obey your parents, and do not deviate from the 'right' path in life."

Once you have chosen and analyzed your selection and then devised a production concept you might also want to consider such external influences as the time limit of the performance, the available talent, the nature of the occasion and the audience, the physical characteristics of the theatre or other available performance space, and the overall mood to be established. Let us consider what material is available for the single-text orchestration.

Plays are often the easiest works to stage because they are written expressly for oral presentation. Plays that work best have compelling characters; provocative conflict; sustained action; vivid language; lively interchange of ideas; dialogue that reveals each character's motivation, personality, and depth; strong emotional climaxes; and make their primary appeal to the ear rather than to the eye. Good choices include radio dramas, for example, which appeal to the ear or "closet dramas" which were meant to be read rather than staged. Plays that cannot successfully be staged in conventional theatre because they require too many sets or too many performers, for example, may be successfully done in readers theatre. Since readers theatre emphasizes the audience's imaginative participation in the creation of the scenes, plays too demanding in the area of special effects and spectacle elements can be successfully done in readers theatre.

Plays that have been successfully staged in a readers theatre format include *Equus, Our Town, The Elephant Man, Amadeus, The Madwoman of Chaillot, The Matchmaker, The Devil's Disciple, Uncle Tom's Cabin, The Barretts of Wimpole Street, The Mikado* (a readers theatre version is available from Contemporary Drama Service, Inc.), *Skin of Our Teeth, Medea, Dream Play, Zoo Story, The American Dream*, and many of the plays of Bertolt Brecht and William Shakespeare. Many Shakespearean plays have been successfully done in readers theatre as so much of their spectacle is contained in the language of the text. In Shakespeare's day, the plays were staged very presentationally. The light source was the sun, and there were no literal sets or set pieces. Instead, close attention to the language of the text allowed audiences to visualize the setting. The first scene in *Hamlet*, for example, takes place on a guard platform on Elsinore Castle in Denmark. One guard, Francisco, is on watch and Barnardo comes to relieve him. The first two words of the play are Barnardo's "Who's there?" to Francisco. These simple two words accomplish two important effects. First, they indicate that something is "rotten in Denmark" because Barnardo should know who he is coming to replace and should not have to ask. He is fearful, however, because a ghost has been seen on the castle grounds, and Barnardo is not sure if Francisco or the ghost awaits him. The second effect created is to suggest to the audience that it is dark (midnight) because Barnardo cannot clearly see Francisco.

In addition to plays, readers theatre can effectively stage many other types of texts, including prose fiction texts, especially those written in the lyric or dramatic modes (see the discussion of modes in chapter one). Entire poems may be orchestrated, as well as songs, biographies, historical works, interview transcripts, and so on. In general, readers theatre works best with material that appeals to the performers' and audiences' imaginations. It has even been called "Theatre of the Mind."

Orchestrating

As stated before, when we orchestrate we turn a text into a script for a group of performers. To begin this process, we decide which aspect of the text we feel is the most pervasive, and we "release" this aspect in performance. We might release the character voices we hear in a text, the images, the sounds, or the rhythms, for example. Character voices include the actual or implied speakers in a text. Though releasing the voices in a text might be the most obvious choice, there may be parts of a text or entire texts where the voices are not as important or as significant as other aspects. In a lyric poem, for example, where an undefined persona speaks, what the persona says may be more important than the nature of the speaker. In this case, you may want to release the sounds (tone color), the images (sensory or literary), or the distinctive rhythm (meter or beat) in the text. Kleinau and McHughes call the voices, sounds, images, and rhythms in a text "power sources," and they describe the process of releasing those power sources as follows: "The process of releasing the voices in the text is a process of opening up the literary work. It requires breaking apart the lines of force in a work to tap the harmonic interplay of its power for your script."[1] Let us describe each of these forces which you could release in your orchestrations.

Releasing Character Voices

Probably the most obvious source for orchestration are the speakers in the text. Literature usually creates three kinds of speakers: characters, narrators, and personae. Speakers in prose fiction are called narrators and characters; speakers in plays are usually defined characters; speakers are called narrators in narrative poetry, characters in dramatic poetry, and personae (undefined speakers) in lyric poetry. In any literary or nonliterary text, it is important to ask who is speaking and to whom. In nonfiction works such as biographies, autobiographies, essays, letters, etc., the identification of the speaker depends on the given text. Oral narratives (performed stories of storytellers) usually have both narrators and characters.

Plays, for example, which usually involve only defined characters (although some plays also have narrators), are already "orchestrated." The playwright has decided who is going to say which line and to whom. Consequently, were you to stage a play in readers theatre, orchestrating is unnecessary. You may still need to cut or condense, but the task of dividing the play into character voices is complete.

The process of releasing the character voices in texts other than plays is more complicated. First, you must be able to identify and name the voices you hear—some may be defined and some may be undefined. In prose fiction texts, as we stated earlier, there are usually multiple voices. In a lyric-mode prose fiction text, the narrator dominates and there is very little character dialogue. Many works by D. H. Lawrence are lyric in mode. In dramatic-mode prose fiction texts, the narrator is secondary and there is an abundance of character dialogue. Many stories by Hemingway, who was once a newspaper reporter used to writing in a terse, objective manner, are dramatic in mode. Both lyric and dramatic-mode texts are best for readers theatre. Epic-mode prose fiction texts, where there is approximately an equal amount of narration and dialogue, are best suited for chamber theatre adaptations and will be discussed in detail in chapter four. Your job is to read the story over several times, and see if you can define the nature of the narrator and the kind of story he or she tells. Decide who will speak each line and to whom. If the narrator dominates, your production will want to show this. If the characters dominate, give them the emphasis, and relegate the narrator to a secondary position. Here is a passage from Hemingway's "Hills Like White Elephants" and then the same passage orchestrated into character voices.

From "Hills Like White Elephants" by Ernest Hemingway

The girl stood up and walked to the end of the station. Across, on the other side, were fields of grain and trees along the banks of the Ebro. Far away, beyond the river were mountains. The shadow of a cloud moved across the field of grain and she saw the river through the trees.

"And we could have all this," she said. "And we could have everything and every day we make it more impossible."

"What did you say?"

"I said we could have everything."

"We can have everything."

"No, we can't."

"We can go everywhere."

"No, we can't. It isn't ours any more."

"It's ours."

"No, it isn't. And once they take it away, you never get it back."

"But they haven't taken it away."

"We'll wait and see."

"Come on back in the shade," he said. "You mustn't feel that way."

"I don't feel any way," the girl said. "I just know things."

"I don't want you to do anything that you don't want to do—"

"Nor that isn't good for me," she said. "I know. Could we have another beer?"

"All right. But you've got to realize—"

"I realize," the girl said. "Can't we maybe stop talking?"

This passage very much resembles a play in that it is composed mostly of dialogue between a man and a woman. The narrator in this dramatic-mode story is undefined and plays the role of an observer, as the orchestration below illustrates.

Readers Theatre Orchestration
from "Hills Like White Elephants"
by Ernest Hemingway

(An American man and woman are sitting at a table outside a train station in Spain. On stage right are a round table with two chairs, a door frame is center stage representing the inside of a train station, and a bench is stage left. The couple has ordered drinks, and are now talking. As this scene opens, the woman rises, and walks to the end of the station, and sits on the bench staring straight out. The narrator stands to the far left, watching the couple, and sharing information with the audience. The woman in the scene uses offstage focus—she looks straight ahead and does not look at the man, unless otherwise indicated. The man primarily uses onstage focus—he looks at the woman.)

Narrator (*to the audience*): Across, on the other side, were fields of grain and trees along the banks of the Ebro. Far away, beyond the river, were mountains. The shadow of a cloud moved across the field of grain and she saw the river through the trees.

Woman: And we could have all this. And we could have everything and every day we make it more impossible.

Man: What did you say?

Woman: I said we could have everything.

Man: We can have everything.

Woman: No, we can't.

Man: We can have the whole world.

Woman: No, we can't.

Man: We can go everywhere.

Woman: No, we can't. It isn't ours any more.

Man: It's ours.

Woman (*she looks at him for the first time*): No, it isn't. And once they take it away, you never get it back.

Man: But they haven't taken it away.

Woman (*she uses offstage focus again*): We'll wait and see.

Man (*he goes to her at the bench*): Come on back in the shade. You mustn't feel that way.

Woman: I don't feel any way. I just know things.

Man (*sits next to her, touches her hand*): I don't want you to do anything that you don't want to do—

Woman (*looks at Man*): Nor that isn't good for me. (*She moves to the table, sits, finishes her drink.*) I know. Could we have another beer?

Man (*moves to table*): All right. (*The man snaps his fingers to get the attention of the Narrator to order drinks. Man sits, Narrator, acting as waiter, crosses to them.*) But you've got to realize—

Woman: I realize. (*Narrator stands upstage between Man and Woman waiting for them to order.*) Can't we maybe stop talking?

This orchestration illustrates some of the responsibilities the script-maker has when going from text to orchestration. The scriptmaker must decide where the scene takes place and what the setting will look like, where the furniture will be, and where the characters are as the scene opens. Notice that the story is reformatted in script form. There are many ways to reformat, but the way we have chosen is to include the name of the speaker, any stage directions in parentheses, a colon, and then the line the speaker is to say. Another job the scriptmaker has is to add stage directions so that the performers know where to look and where and when to move. You will notice that the first line the narrator says reveals a stage direction: "The girl stood up and walked to the end of the station." Since the girl can do that, the line becomes a stage direction and need not be said. **Tag lines** (the "he saids" and "she saids" writers use so that the silent reader will know who is speaking) may also be cut, because we know "she said" it. In readers theatre, as we will discover in chapter three, the primary type of focus is offstage—speakers deliver lines facing out toward the audience, and often directly to the audience—but a variety of types of focus may be employed. The scriptmaker should identify the type of focus the performers are to use and indicate where the focus changes. Notice, also, that the narrator may play the minor role of the waiter—necessitating only three characters in the scene.

Poetry may be orchestrated for readers theatre, although it is more often used in compiled scripts than by itself. Long poems such as Peter Bowman's "Beach Red," a story of war that describes the attitudes and feelings of soldiers, can furnish provocative and stimulating materials for a full-length program. When orchestrating poems based on releasing voices, begin by identifying and analyzing the nature of the speakers and their intentions. In many poems, there is only one primary speaker. Readers theatre, though, is a kind of *group* performance. How does one turn a poem with one speaker into a script appropriate for group performance? The answer is to look for complexity in the prevailing speaker. Does he or she manifest a good and evil side? an optimistic and pessimistic outlook? a feminine and masculine orientation? an anima and animus? a rational and an irrational side? and so on. Often one speaker manifests a variety of traits. These traits can be played by different performers. Since readers theatre is a presentational medium, not concerned with creating a realistic impression of life, readers theatre scripts can focus on manifesting the psychological complexity of human nature.

In lyric poetry, the speaker is usually an undefined persona—a speaker who is not defined in the poem and who may represent the mask or "persona" of the poet. The speakers in lyric poetry are usually intent on sharing an emotional experience. Lyric poems include "I Heard a Fly Buzz When I Died" and "After Great Pain" by Emily Dickinson, "The Road Not Taken" and "Fire and Ice" by Robert Frost, "In Just-" by e. e. cummings, "Daddy" by Sylvia Plath, and "Ode on a Grecian Urn" by John Keats.

Dramatic poetry features a defined character or characters engaged in conflict situations. Dramatic poems, then, resemble plays in verse. Defined characters dominate and they may speak to themselves ("Soliloquy of the Spanish Cloister" by Robert Browning), to the audience ("Wild Grapes" by Robert Frost), to a silent auditor ("My Last Duchess" by Robert Browning,) or to another character ("Is My Team Plowing" by Thomas Hardy). As we stated earlier, even though a dramatic poem may feature just one character speaking, look closely at the poem to see if other voices are suggested or implied. In the Browning poem "My Last Duchess," for example, there is only one speaker—the Duke of Ferrara—who is in his art gallery addressing a Count's emissary. The Duke is telling the emissary what he expects of his prospective new duchess (the Count's daughter) so that she doesn't end up like his last duchess—who is now deceased and represented by a painting the Duke has purposely revealed to the emissary. One possible way to orchestrate this poem is to divide the lines so that performers portray the characters mentioned by the Duke: the artist, Fra Pandolf; the last Duchess; the Count; the Count's emissary; the Count's daughter, in addition to the Duke.

Narrative poetry, as the name implies, features narrators narrating narratives! The narrators tell the audience about a series of events that happened in the past. If the narrator is defined it is a dramatic narrative. The narrator is undefined in the other types of narrative poems: ballads, metrical tales, and epics. Examples of narrative poetry include the dramatic narrative "The Prisoner of Chillon" by Lord Byron, the ballad "The Ballad of Rudolph Reed" by Gwendolyn Brooks, the metrical tale "Home Burial" by Robert Frost, and the epic *Iliad* by Homer. Narrative poetry normally features more than one voice, consequently orchestrating them is a bit easier. The narrator may take the narrative lines and the characters may take their dialogue lines. Orchestrating a narrative poem would borrow many of the techniques of chamber theatre which will be described in chapter four.

As you orchestrate your finished scripts, consider multiple casting. Since readers theatre is a presentational theatre format, more than one performer may play the same role, or one performer may play many roles. (The convention of bifurcation—casting two performers to play the same role—will be discussed in more detail in chapter four.) If two performers play the same role, you are manifesting some split or division in the character. If one performer plays many roles, you are showing the commonality among these roles. Here are two passages from a lyric story, "the letting down of the hair" by Anne Sexton, which features one central, undefined speaker. Afterwards, you will see these passages orchestrated and the speaker divided into four distinct voices.

From "the letting down of the hair"
by Anne Sexton

Attracting Thousands

I live in a stone room. Far from the luxury of draperies and transistors, far from the movie theaters and coffee houses, far from the men in their business suits, far from the children playing with their Lincoln Logs. I have only the daily newspapers and letters from Ruth. To tell the truth, I'm a recluse. I'm as hesitant as Emily Dickinson. Like a novice I'm all dressed in white. A recluse, yes. Yet each day I attract thousands.

The Stone Room

As I said, a stone room. Like the stones of Chile. Like the craggy rocks of Gloucester, that desperate seacoast. The steps of Rome and Michelangelo and his stone creatures. A stone room, a cupola five stories high. Like a lion in a zoo I adjust to my environment.

I came up here long ago. I didn't hide because I was ugly. I wasn't made of wolfsbane. I wasn't made of kidneys. I was made tall and of yellow hair. I'd had a normal life: men and lipstick, daiquiris and sunburns. My skin was the color of a teacup, fair but fragile. And hair, yellow-yellow hair. Brush. Brush.

A stone room as still and clean as a razor blade. All the time of the child in me this room was my secret. Oh, Mr. Man-in-the-Moon, where was your radar? Memory? Memory, here is your knife. A room to crawl into and hide. Better than the laundry chute. Better than the broom closet. A room unused except by birds.

Yes, as a child I would enter through a closet, standing tip-toe on a chair, up through the trap door into the forbidden—the dead maybe live up here, groaning every hour as they keep watch from the lookout window. Mother can't find me, little yellow ball. Father, you could find me if you would only look, but Father is too sleepy to look. Else he'd come flying, come flying. Brother, old sneak-mouth, can't find my hide-and-seek. You'll never see. A stone room five stories up, the shape of a merry-go-round, and eleven feet in circumference. A room like the inside of a church bell. A chalice, a cave, a perch queer bird that I am. A hidden place like the inside of a seed pod. Brush. Brush.

Here are the same two passages of the story orchestrated for readers theatre. (The entire script may be found in chapter eight.) The speaker has been divided into four parts based on different attitudes manifested. Voice 1 is the pessimistic/realistic self, who is suicidal and who realizes and struggles with the role women have been forced to assume in society. Voice 2 is the optimistic/idealistic self who tries to make the best of her "bondage." Voice 3 is the "Ruth" character—the symbol of unrealized hope. Voice 4 represents familial and societal influences. As the scene opens, the four women, dressed all in white, are seated on stools in a circle with their backs to each other.

Readers Theatre Orchestration
From "the letting down of the hair"
by Anne Sexton

All: I live in a stone room.

Voice 1 (*rises, moves stage right, and uses offstage focus*): Far from the luxury of draperies and transistors, far from the movie theaters and coffeehouses, far from the men in their business suits, far from the children playing with their Lincoln Logs.

Voice 2 (*rises, moves stage left, and uses offstage focus*): I have only the daily newspapers

Voice 3 (*rises, and stands next to Voice 1*): and letters from Ruth.

All (*Voice 4 rises, and stands next to Voice 2*): To tell the truth, I'm a recluse. (*All move toward the stools, then stop and turn to face audience.*) I'm as hesitant as Emily Dickinson. Like a novice I'm all dressed in white. (*The four sit on stools which have been arranged in a jagged line.*) A recluse, yes.

Voice 2 (*rises, happily*): Yet each day I attract thousands.

All but Voice 2: As I said, a stone room five stories high. (*Voice 2 sits on stool.*)

Voice 1: Like the stones of Chile. Like the craggy rocks of Gloucester, that desperate seacoast. Like a lion in a zoo.

Voice 2 (*to Voice 1*): I adjust to my environment.

Voice 1: I came up here long ago.

Voice 2: I didn't hide because I was ugly. I wasn't made of wolfsbane. I wasn't made of kidneys.

All (*all rise*): I was made tall and of yellow hair.

Voice 2 (*steps forward*): I'd had a normal life: men and lipstick, daiquiris and sunburns. My skin was the color of a teacup, fair but fragile. And hair, yellow-yellow hair.

All (*all sit and brush their imaginary long, yellow hair*): Brush. Brush.

Voice 1: A stone room as still and clean as a razor blade. All the time of the child in me this room was my secret. Oh, Mr. Man-in-the Moon, where was your radar? Memory? Memory, here is your knife. A room to crawl into and hide. Better than the laundry chute. Better than the broom closet. A room unused except by birds.

Voice 2 (*stands*): Yes, as a child I would enter through a closet, (*stands atop the stool*) standing tiptoe on a chair, up through the trapdoor into the forbidden— (*Voice 2 looks amazed at the wonders she creates, Voice 1 looks in horror, Voice 3 emulates Voice 2, and Voice 4 curls up in a ball.*)

Voice 1: the dead maybe live up here, groaning every hour as they keep watch from the lookout window.

Voice 4: Mother can't find me, little yellow ball. Father, you could find me if you would only look, but Father is too sleepy to look. Else he'd come flying, come flying. Brother, old sneak-mouth, can't find my hide-and-seek. You'll never see.

All (*rise and face out*): A stone room five stories up (*they put stools in a circle again*), the shape of a merry-go-round, and eleven feet in circumference.

Voice 1: A room like the inside of a church bell

Voice 2: A chalice

Voice 3: A cave

Voice 4: A perch

Voice 1: queer bird that I am.

Voice 3: A hidden place like the inside of a seed pod.

All (*seated with their backs to each other as in top of scene, and pretend to brush their long hair*): Brush. Brush.

Notice how simply this story was staged, depending on economy of movement and suggestion of character differences to capture and keep the audience's involvement. More will be said about staging in chapter three.

As we stated earlier, it is not just drama, prose fiction, and poetry that are appropriate for readers theatre. Letters, essays, and similar materials require special handling if they are to be used successfully. To convert an essay into appropriate material for readers theatre, it is often necessary to add characterization to the lines. More than one point of view needs to be represented to have some action or conflict or at least a degree of contrast. The Corey Ford essay "How to Guess Your Age," for example, although originally written as if it were spoken by one man, can be presented as though two men were standing in a bar exchanging comments on how the world is changing. "The Ten Worst Things About a Man," from Jean Kerr's *The Snake Has All the Lines*, can in a similar fashion be divided between the husband and the wife. Israel Horowitz provides sharp satire on modern theatre in his essay, "O, It All Rings So True to Life." Joan Wixen's interview-type essays on people adapt readily to group performance. When orchestrating Addison and Steele's *The Spectator Papers*, a secretary can be added so that conversation can occur between her and Sir Roger de Coverley. A letter could be orchestrated so that some of it is spoken from the perspective of the writer and some from the perspective of the recipient.

A description of the production of one nonfiction text might serve as an illustration of the creative possibilities of staging works one might never consider "theatrical" material. Not long ago, a book entitled *The Closing of the American Mind* by Allan Bloom was the talk of the academic world. Bloom bemoaned the awful state of the educational system, and proffered suggestions on various topics as to how to improve the condition. A production entitled "Bloomerang" was created out of this text in the form of a television talk show. After the "theme music" played, the two performers playing the talk show hosts entered with hand-held microphones, and said:

> Welcome. Author Allan Bloom describes the closing of the American mind as, "a meditation on the state of our souls, particularly those of the young and their education." On today's show, we have four college students who have studied Bloom's text, and will discuss his thoughts on four topics: books, music, sex, and what is meant by a "liberal education."

Each of the four performers had memorized one section of the Bloom text and presented their memorized sections as their opening remarks. The hosts then opened the discussion to the audience and to "home viewers" (taped questions from phone callers). Some audience members were given prepared questions to ask, but many of the questions were spontaneous, prompted by the audience's responses (often heated) to the memorized sections. The show was controversial, but it did reveal Bloom's ideas and "boomeranged" them back!

Releasing Tone Color—Sounds

We mentioned previously that texts appropriate for readers theatre have evocative language. What we mean by that is that the language is rich in sounds and images which help create impressions in the minds of the audience. One element that produces evocative images and is thus a power source that can be released in a text is tone color. **Tone color** is the repetition of like sounds throughout a work. These sounds become significant if they are repeated often enough to show a pattern. Though found most frequently in poetry, tone color is found also in other works which have a poetic quality. Alliteration, assonance, and onomatopoeia are among the most common devices imparting a poetic quality to language. **Alliteration** is the repetition of like consonant sounds, usually at the beginning of words in close proximity, throughout a work. **Assonance** is the repetition of identical vowel sounds in words in close proximity throughout a work. **Onomatopoeia** involves words that sound like their meanings—that imitate actual sounds. Alliteration, assonance, and onomatopoeia are readily identifiable in these brief illustrative passages:

> Alliteration:
>> The *r*umble of *r*everberation *r*ose to a *r*oar.
>> The *b*lazing *b*rightness of her *b*eauties *b*ecame . . .
> Assonance:
>> A *g*olden *g*low suffused the d*o*me.
>> The l*o*wing herd wind sl*o*wly *o*'er the lea.
> Onomatopoeia:
>> The hissing of the skates on the slick ice . . .
>> The moan of doves in immemorial elms . . .
>> And murmur of innumerable bees . . .

The sound patterning delights the ear and makes the meaning clear. Repetition of certain phrases or words, for example, can give cumulative power. Although a full-length script based on sound qualities alone would probably not be appropriate, parts of a script could feature the sound elements or sound could serve to underline or underscore various other elements of the script. Here is a short poem entitled "The Eagle" by Alfred,

Lord Tennyson. Notice how alliteration and the use of hard consonant sounds contribute to our impression of this proud bird and its sense of power and authority.

"The Eagle"
by Alfred, Lord Tennyson

He clasps the crag with crooked hands;
Close to the sun in lonely lands,
Ringed with the azure world, he stands.

The wrinkled sea beneath him crawls;
He watches from his mountain walls,
And like a thunderball he falls.

Here is a script of this poem which has been orchestrated to release the element of tone color.

Orchestration based on Tone Color
"The Eagle"
by Alfred, Lord Tennyson

This orchestration features two choruses, demarcated as C1 and C2. Any number of performers can make up each chorus. Chorus 1 represents "highness" and "stasis" while Chorus 2 represents "lowness" and "motion."

C1: He K-lasps the K-rag with K-rooked haaaaandzz

C1: K-lose to the suuuuun in looooonely laaaandzz,

C1: Riiiinged with the azzzure world, he STANDZ.

C2: (*said with an undulating rhythm*) The wrrrrinKled seeeeaaaa beneath him K-rawllllzzzzz;

C1: (*strong, still*) He watchez from his mountain wallllz,

C2: And——liiiiiiKe——a——T-H-U-N-D-E-R-B-A-L-L (*pause, say last two words with a decrescendo*) he fAAAAallllllllllZZZZZZZ.

Releasing Literary and Sensory Imagery

Enriched language also involves **literary and sensory imagery** that extend the possible meaning by evoking comparisons, making substitutions, bestowing lifelike qualities on inanimate objects, and involving the audience's sensory response, giving the writing stronger evocative power. Literary and sensory imagery exist in many texts, but are more obvious in the more crystallized, condensed poetry.

Literary imagery—or figurative language—helps to make a poem clearer, fresher, or more vital. There are eleven types of literary images:

1. *Allusion*. A reference to a person, place, or thing outside of the confines of the work. Example: "They went to Adam's Market and bought an apple."
2. *Apostrophe*. An address to an inanimate object, a muse, God, or an absent or deceased person. Example: "Death, be not proud."
3. *Hyperbole*. An exaggerated statement employing inflated language. Example: "If I've told you once, I've told you a thousand times."
4. *Litotes*. An understatement in which the affirmative is implied by denying its opposite. Example: "He's not bad looking."
5. *Metaphor*. A comparison in which something is associated with something else. Example: "She had pearly teeth."
6. *Metonymy*. One word or image is used to represent another with which it is closely associated. Example: "The guy was a real gumshoe (detective)."
7. *Oxymoron*. A contradiction that seemingly cannot be resolved. Example: "Parting is such sweet sorrow."
8. *Paradox*. A seemingly contradictory statement that turns out to be partly true. Example: "He was filled with loving hatred for her."
9. *Personification*. Bestowing human characteristics on inanimate objects, abstract qualities, or animals as with "hands" to describe the claws in "The Eagle" by Tennyson. Example: "The door groaned open; screamed shut."
10. *Simile*. A comparison employing *like, as,* or *as if.* Example: "Her teeth were like pearls."
11. *Synecdoche*. A device where a part is used to suggest the whole. Example: "She donated money so the wet eyes would cry no more." (Here "wet eyes" is synecdoche for crying children.)

Synecdoche—as a staging principle—is the heart of readers theatre productions, in general. Often, the presentational nature of readers theatre demands that a part be used to suggest the whole. More will be said in chapter three about how synecdoche becomes a dominant factor in the staging of a readers theatre production.

Sensory imagery appeals to our senses. To discover what sensory images are in a text, put yourself in the place of the speaker and ask yourself what the speaker is seeing, hearing, tasting, and so forth. There are primarily eight kinds of sensory images:

- *Visual*—appeal to sight
- *Auditory*—appeal to hearing
- *Olfactory*—appeal to smell
- *Gustatory*—appeal to taste
- *Tactile*—appeal to touch
- *Kinetic*—appeal to physical movement
- *Kinesthetic*—appeal to internal muscular involvement, the perception or feeling of movement
- *Thermal*—appeal to temperature, either hot or cold

Much of what performers do in readers theatre productions is related to kinesthesia. In *The Order of Poetry*, kinesthesia is defined as:

> . . . usually reserved for that kind of imagery which appeals, not to our senses of smell, hearing, etc., . . . but to our residual memory or imagination derived from the nerves and muscles which govern bodily movement and physical attitudes. Through kinesthesia we get "the feel" of an action, whether perceived directly or described in language; on the basis of having moved or arranged our own bodies in the past we can imaginatively identify ourselves with, or project ourselves into, the motions or postures of others. The use of "body-English" in games like pool or golf acts out our kinesthetic identifications . . . [2]

Kinesthesia is practiced when performers attempt to portray characters and behaviors that they have never experienced firsthand, but with which they can "imaginatively identify."

EXPERIMENT

Read the following passage from Ray Bradbury's *Dandelion Wine*, and see if you can empathize with—or feel with—the speaker in the text as he re-creates kinesthetic imagery. How could you direct a performer to release all the kinesthetic references in this passage?

From *Dandelion Wine*
by Ray Bradbury

But Mr. Sanderson—soon as I get those shoes on, you know what happens? Bang! I deliver your packages, pick up packages, bring you coffee, burn trash, run to the post office, library . . . you'll see twelve of me in and out every minute. Feel those shoes . . . see how fast they'd take me. Feel all that running inside? You stay in the nice cool store while I'm jumping all over town. But it's not me, really; it's the shoes. They go like mad down alleys, cutting corners . . . there they go! Whooooooooooosh!

Releasing Rhythm

Rhythm is the pulse or beat of a work. Again, the rhythm in poetry is more pronounced than the rhythm in other literary texts; but all literary texts—all lifeforms, really—have some kind of rhythm or repetitive patterning. Basing an entire script on rhythm or rhythmic variations might not be appropriate, but including a strongly rhythmic work in a larger frame can serve to underline the tension in your script. Analyzing the rhythm in the completed script can help you when adding movement in your production. As Kleinau and McHughes state, "Like rhythms of the human body, rhythms of the literary body are felt in terms of movement—the ebb and flow of strength—and are therefore of central interest . . ."[3]

EXPERIMENT

Read this poem, "Jazz Fantasia" by Carl Sandburg, which has a very distinctive rhythm. In addition, the sounds and images in the poem are very important, and contribute to the rhythm. How could this poem be orchestrated so that its rhythm and rhythmic variations are made manifest?

"Jazz Fantasia"
by Carl Sandburg

Drum on your drums, batter on your banjos,
sob on the long cool winding saxophones.
Go to it, O jazzmen.
Sling your knuckles on the bottoms of the happy
tinpans, let your trombones ooze, and go husha-
husha-hush with the slippery sand-paper.
Moan like an autumn wind high in the lonesome tree-
tops, moan soft like you wanted somebody terrible,
cry like a racing car slipping away from a motorcycle
cop, bang-bang! you jazzmen, bang altogether drums,
traps, banjos, horns, tin cans—make two people fight
on the top of a stairway and scratch each other's eyes
in a clinch tumbling down the stairs.
Can the rough stuff . . . now a Mississippi steamboat
pushes up the night river with a hoo-hoo-hoo-oo . . .
and the green lanterns calling to the high soft stars . . .
a red moon rides on the humps of the low river
hills . . . go to it, O jazzmen.

Evaluating Your Script Selection

Since you will always be the creator of a unique, new script—one that has never been done before—you have no paradigm to follow, but you also do not have to be restricted by convention or tradition. Do ask yourself if your finished script will secure the desired emotional and intellectual involvement of the audience. If you are concerned about the appropriateness of your selection for readers theatre, ask yourself the following questions:

1. Does the material excite you? Is it worth the time of those who perform in it and those who listen to it?

2. Will the material be illuminated more by group than by solo performance?

3. Does the script make a comment on life worth our time? Will it make us think, feel, see ourselves in a new perspective? Does it satirize our follies, express our frailties? Does it express ideas that are provocative and new? Does it express old ideas in a fresh manner?

4. Does it have the power to stir empathy; to draw us into its lifeworld; to leave "afterimages" in our minds?

5. Does it paint pictures and describe characters vividly? Catch the action in words?

6. Are the characters interesting? Unique? Does the story center on a conflict within or without characters?

7. If you are choosing a play, will this style of presentation give insights not revealed in a conventional theatre production?

8. Can it fit into the time allotted and present a complete action?

9. Can it be performed/staged effectively in the playing area available?

10. If the literature is not in the public domain, can you secure the rights to produce it? (See the information on copyright at the end of this chapter.)

EXPERIMENT

Find an interesting article from a newspaper. See if you can orchestrate this article and turn it into a readers theatre script by releasing its voices, its sounds, its images, or its rhythm.

The Expanded Program Compiled Script

The second type of readers theatre script is a compilation script called an expanded program. As we stated in chapter one, to compile is to put together or to juxtapose various texts on the same program. In this type of production, scriptmakers can investigate a theme, the works of an author, a literary style or period, or an historical period in more depth than in a single-text production. Programs may deal with a universal theme like love, hate, war, marriage, sex, death; investigate the life of a person, a type of poetic style, the works of one author; or they may commemorate an historical event such as the anniversary of the founding of a nation, a village, or a city. They may concern a special event or a special day, the ancestral origins of a citizen or citizens, or an ethnic culture, for example.

Selections are usually presented with an introduction and narrative transitions which are generally drawn from appropriate research on your theme, writer, style, or period. A clear example of an expanded program is the musical revue which is a compilation of songs by one composer. *Cole* is one such revue which features biographical material about Cole

Porter juxtaposed with songs. Another revue is *Jacques Brel Is Alive and Well and Living in Paris* which features a number of songs by the French composer Jacques Brel.

Here are examples of expanded programs and formats to give you an idea of the variety of possibilities.

Thematic Programs

1. *Save the Whales.* This was a production intent on changing the audience's mind regarding the senseless slaughter of whales. The creator used numerous media forms, and the production was staged with the audience onstage and the actors surrounding them.
2. *How Do I Love Thee.* This presented portraits of Elizabeth Barrett and Robert Browning using poetry, drama, and letters. The famous title sonnet was orchestrated to suggest the pair's marriage vows.
3. *Seasons Readings for and about Children.* This was an accumulation of prose, poetry, and drama on Hanukkah and Christmas intended for children.
4. *The Gladdest Things in the Toyroom.* This production analyzed the theme of marriage: why people get married and what happens when a marriage goes sour. The material was from R. D. Laing's book *Knots*, selections from May Swenson's book *Iconographs*, and selected concrete poems.
5. *Pretext.* A compilation of the "words before the text," including introductions, acknowledgments, forewords, and odds and ends. Cast of two.

Single Author Programs

1. *Twain by the Tale.* This is a professional script, compiled by Dennis Smee and available through a publisher (Bakers Plays), which features the works of Mark Twain.
2. *Lorca on Lorca.* This compilation included poetry and excerpts of plays by Frederico Garcia Lorca.
3. *Sylvia Plath: A Dramatic Portrait.* A compilation of poetry, prose, and letters by Sylvia Plath compiled by Barry Kyle.
4. *A Mixed-Media Approach to the Poetry of Gwendolyn Brooks.* As the title indicates, this program presented a number of

poems by Illinois poet laureate, Gwendolyn Brooks, and underscored each poem with slides, video, and music.

5. *The Mystery and Manners of Flannery O'Connor.* This is a collection of the works of this Southern writer showing her preoccupation with religion and her southern lifestyle.

Literary Style Programs

1. *Story Theatre.* This is a professional script written by Paul Sills which includes the improvised telling of favorite fables. It is available through Bakers.

2. *Love Sonnets.* This is a survey of the sonnet from Shakespeare to e. e. cummings.

Historical Period Programs

1. *Those Fabulous 40s: World War II from the Homefront.* This script can be found in chapter eight of this text. It is a collection of letters, songs, commercials, and personal narratives produced by a company called The Third Age Theatre—a group of performers over 55 years of age.

2. *Novel Voices.* This is an Off-Broadway show which features four performers (Arthur French, Paul Hecht, Lois Smith, Lillo Way) celebrating the 1940s—the war, the coming sexual revolution, and the American spirit as the century reached its halfway point, echoed vividly in the words of Carson McCullers, George Bernard Shaw, Norman Mailer, Truman Capote, and Mickey Spillane, among others.

The process of creating an expanded program script has eleven steps, usually, though not always, in the following order:

1. Select a theme, writer, literary style or period, or historical period you wish to investigate.

2. Decide on an assertion—a statement of your intention to which someone may respond "I agree" or "I disagree"—which will help you narrow the theme of your program and make selection choices easier. If you are preparing a thematic program, be sure to narrow your scope to fit whatever time limit you may have been given. If, for example, your theme is love, your assertion might be "love for animals is the only real love." If your program is on sonnets, you might decide to limit your choices to sonnets depicting nature or sonnets written by English Romantics.

3. Decide on the purpose of your program. Do you wish to inform, persuade, activate, entertain, shock, horrify, enrich, accommodate, confront, or achieve some other end?

4. Choose the material you wish to include. It is probably best to find more material than you will need and then eliminate selections based on what you want the program to say and on time limitations. (Check the reference section of your library for assistance in gathering materials. *Short Story Index, Play Index,* and *Granger's Index to Poetry* are excellent reference books for finding selections on a particular theme.)

After the material is gathered, look at it objectively and decide which would best communicate your assertion.

5. Analyze the material you have selected employing the dramatistic analysis described at the beginning of this chapter.

6. Decide the order of the selections. If you are not doing a script that depends on a chronological order, it might be best to start with the selection that conveys the strongest statement of your intended assertion to clarify this for the audience. Place the selection that makes the deepest impression and which has the most important or persuasive statement at the end. Depending on the nature of the script, you will want to provide variety by alternating short and long selections, comedic and dramatic selections, solo-voiced and multi-voiced selections, and the genres (if a variety of types of materials are included), and so on. Remember that the ordering of the selections will affect the way the audience perceives them. The juxtaposition of a selection that depicts a couple expecting their first child with another selection which depicts a couple who has just lost a child, for example, makes telling statements and provides insights that may not be in either selection. If a selection about divorce precedes a selection about marriage, the divorce is bound to suggest overtones in the marriage selection.

7. Decide which selections are to be performed by one performer and which are to be orchestrated for a number of performers.

8. Compose an introduction and transitions which might be performed by one performer or by different performers. Depending on the length of your program, you could introduce all your selections in the introduction, and then find a way to indicate to the audience without spoken transitions when one selection ends and the next selection begins. Transitions could be achieved with movement, lighting effects, music, and so on. If your script is long, then spoken transitions may be necessary.

9. Type the introductions, transitions (if used), and selections in script form, including who is to say each line and to whom. Include what the set will look like, and any appropriate stage directions. Give the script a title which will help the audience know what to expect.

10. Cast and rehearse your script.

11. Perform!

Here is an example of an expanded program which has been orchestrated for seven performers. Performers 1, 5–7 are male; performers 2–4 are female. The script is entitled *Witches Through the Ages*.

**Expanded Program Script
from *Macbeth* by William Shakespeare,
from *The Scarlet Letter* by Nathaniel Hawthorne,
and "For Witches" by Susan Sutheim**

Introduction

All: Witches Through the Ages

1: The depiction and characterization of witches has changed throughout time. The following three selections examine the evolution of the concept of "witch."

2: Witches were once depicted as frightening manifestations of evil, or, as Macbeth describes them, "secret, black, and midnight hags," with a tremendous power to foresee our destinies.

5: They were demons who lived in a dark world and represented the evil in nature meant to corrupt human will.

3: In this scene from Shakespeare's *Macbeth*, Macbeth asks the witches to conjure up his future,

4: which they do with a series of three apparitions. And now act IV, scene 1 of *Macbeth* by William Shakespeare.

1 (*Macbeth*):   How now, you secret, black, and midnight hags!
           What is't you do?

2, 3, 4 (*witches*): A deed without a name.

1: I conjure you, by that which you profess,

Howe'er you come to know it, answer me.

Though you untie the winds and let them fight

Against the churches; though the yesty waves

Confound and swallow navigation up;

Though bladed corn be lodged and trees blown down;

Though palaces and pyramids do slope

Their heads to their foundations; though the treasure

Even till destruction sicken—answer me

To what I ask you.

2: Speak.

3: Demand.

4: We'll answer.

2: Say, if thou'dst rather hear it from our mouths,

Or from our masters?

1: Call 'em, let me see'em.

(*Thunder. First Apparition: an Armed Head.*)

5 (*Apparition*): Macbeth! Macbeth! Macbeth! Beware Macduff,

Beware the Thane of Fife. Dismiss me. Enough. (*He disappears.*)

1: Whate'er thou art, for thy good caution thanks

Thou hast harped my fear aright. But one word more—

2: He will not be commanded. Here's another,

More potent than the first.

(*Thunder. Second Apparition: a Bloody Child.*)

6: Macbeth! Macbeth! Macbeth!

1: Had I three ears, I'd hear thee.

6: Be bloody, bold, and resolute, laugh to scorn

The power of man, for none of woman born

Shall harm Macbeth. (*He disappears.*)

1: Then live, Macduff. What need I fear of thee?

But yet I'll make assurance double sure,

And take a bond of fate. Thou shalt not live,

That I may tell pale-hearted fear it lies,
And sleep in spite of thunder.

(*Thunder. Third Apparition: a Child Crowned, with a tree in his hand.*)

1: What is this
That rises like the issue of a king,
And wears upon his brow the round
And top of sovereignty?

All: Listen, but speak not to't.

7:   Be lion-mettled, proud, and take no care
Who chafes, who frets, or where conspirers are.
Macbeth shall never vanquished be until
Great Birnam Wood to high Dunsinane Hill
Shall come against him. (*He disappears.*)

1:   That will never be.

Who can impress the forest, bid the tree

Unfix his earthbound root? Sweet bodements! Good!

Rebellion's head, rise never till the wood

Of Birnam rise, and our high-placed Macbeth

Shall live the lease of nature, pay his breath

To time and mortal custom. Yet my heart

Throbs to know one thing. Tell me, if your art

Can tell so much. Shall Banquo's issue ever

Reign in this kingdom?

2, 3, 4:   Seek to know no more.

6: In *Macbeth*, the witches are certainly not members of the community; they appear and disappear at will and exist in a netherworld.

7: In Nathaniel Hawthorne's *The Scarlet Letter*, Mistress Hibbins is a reputed witch who also happens to be the sister of the Governor of Boston. Because of this, she possesses a grudging respectability. She lives in town but visits the forest to serve her master. She is able, then, to function both in the light and dark worlds.

6: Like the witches in *Macbeth*, she is both feared and taken seriously, but whereas the witches in Shakespeare's play smile while Macbeth essentially causes his own downfall,

7: Mistress Hibbins actively seeks to steal the soul of Hester Prynne's mysterious daughter, Pearl.

6: This scene takes place in Governor Bellingham's house where he has summoned Hester to decide whether she should maintain custody of Pearl.

7: The scene includes a Narrator, Hester, Pearl, Reverend Wilson, Roger Chillingworth (Hester's estranged husband), Reverend Dimmesdale (Hester's lover), and Mistress Hibbins. *The Scarlet Letter* by Nathaniel Hawthorne.

3: Little Pearl's unwonted mood of sentiment lasted no longer; she laughed, and went capering down the hall, so airily (*she imitates Mr. Wilson with disdain on following line*), that old Mr. Wilson raised a question whether even her tiptoes touched the floor.

5: The little baggage hath witchcraft in her, I profess,

3: said he to Mr. Dimmesdale.

5: She needs no old woman's broomstick to fly withal!

6: A strange child!

3: remarked old Roger Chillingworth.

6: It is easy to see the mother's part in her. Would it be beyond a philosopher's research, think ye, gentlemen, to analyze that child's nature, and, from its make and mould, to give a shrewd guess at the father?

5: Nay; it would be sinful, in such a question, to follow the clew of profane philosophy,

3: said Mr. Wilson.

5: Better to fast and pray upon it; and still better, it may be, to leave the mystery as we find it, unless Providence reveal it of its own accord. Thereby, every good Christian man hath a title to show a father's kindness towards the poor, deserted babe.

3: The affair being so satisfactorily concluded, Hester Prynne, with Pearl, departed from the house. As they descended the steps, it is averred that the lattice of a chamber-window was thrown open, and forth into the sunny day was thrust the face of Mistress Hibbins, Governor Bellingham's bitter-tempered sister, and the same who, a few years later, was executed as a witch.

4: Hist, hist!

3: said she, while her ill-omened physiognomy seemed to cast a shadow over the cheerful newness of the house.

4: Wilt thou go with us to-night? There will be merry company in the forest; and I wellnigh promised the Black Man that comely Hester Prynne should make one.

2: Make my excuse to him, so please you!

3: answered Hester, with a triumphant smile,

2: I must tarry at home, and keep watch over my little Pearl. Had they taken her from me, I would willingly have gone with thee into the forest, and signed my name in the Black Man's book too, and that with mine own blood!

4: We shall have thee there anon!

3: said the witch-lady, frowning, as she drew back her head.

6: The last selection, "For Witches" by Susan Sutheim, takes us into the present, where "witches" are ironically women who try to function in the real world despite the handicaps and powerlessness of their everyday lives.

7: But beware—when their functioning is made too difficult, their tempers flare and a veiled curse is heard. "For Witches" by Susan Sutheim.

4 (*to imaginary man out center*):   today
i lost my temper

2: temper, when one talks of metal
means strong,
perfect.

3: temper, for humans,
means angry
irrational
bad.

4: today i found my temper.
i said,

2: you step on my head
for 27 years you step on my head
and though i have been trained
to excuse you for your inevitable
clumsiness
today i think
i prefer my head to your clumsiness.

All: today i began
to find myself.

tomorrow
perhaps
i will begin
to find
you.

The Collage Compiled Script

The collage compiled script is the newest and perhaps the most challenging type of readers theatre form—both for the performers and for the compiler/director.[4] As earlier stated, in an expanded program each literary selection is a recognizably separate part of the whole. Each selection may be performed in part or in its entirety, with introductory and transitional material provided to show how selections relate to each other and to the program's theme or major idea. In a collage compiled script, however, often only fragments of literary selections are used: a stanza from a poem, a few paragraphs from a short story or novel, a newspaper headline, a diary entry, a few lines of dialogue from a play, the opening of a personal narrative, and so forth. The compiler/director may still choose any type of literature as source material: prose fiction, essays, biographies, autobiographies, drama, poetry, letters, diaries, newspapers, song lyrics, journals, interview transcripts, and so on, but in this type of compilation script, each is recognized only as a part of the greater whole. The audience should not be concerned with individual selections by individual authors; they should be concerned with understanding the script's overall theme or message, to which each selection contributes. Ideally, the selections or fragments of selections work together as though there were only one source, and the script reveals only one seamless message—that of the compiler/director.

Creating a collage compiled script is similar in many ways to the process of preparing an expanded program script. Here is the most common order for creating a collage compiled script.

1. The first thing is to choose the theme or idea—like love, death, hate, war, presidents, loneliness, insanity, holidays, relationships—that will underline your script. Since it takes some time to compile a collage script, be sure to choose a theme you are particularly interested in and would like to spend more time investigating.

2. It is then necessary to narrow down your theme. Readers theatre productions are usually shorter than the two-hour conventional play—running perhaps from one hour to one hour and a half. Consequently, you cannot do justice to a theme such as "war" or "presidents" without restricting what you include. Narrowing your presidents theme might mean that you focus only on one person or compare and contrast two. (See the compiled script on the formation of the Constitution in chapter eight.)

3. Once you have selected a theme or idea and narrowed it down, decide on an assertion that will inform all your other decisions. As stated previously, an assertion is a statement of your specific purpose in sentence form. The sentence should be worded in such a way that someone hearing it could reply, "I agree" or "I disagree." In other words, your assertion should declare your position on the theme, e.g., "abortion is wrong," or "marijuana should be legalized." In the case of a script where you expect to persuade, activate, or confront, it is probably best to compose an assertion that everyone does not already agree with or believe. Compiling a script with the assertion that "murdering innocent people is wrong" would not take much convincing.

4. Choosing your assertion, then, is related to defining your specific purpose. Do you want to entertain, confront, accommodate, shock, persuade, etc?

5. You are then ready to begin gathering materials. Gather more than you think you will need. It is easier to eliminate selections or parts of selections than to search for and add more later.

6. Once you have collected enough material, edit, arrange, and rearrange the materials so that your attitude toward your theme is clear. Although you should strive to maintain your perceived intent of the source material as much as possible, you can put the source material into a larger context that may change or widen its dimensions. Were you to compile a script centering on an introspective youth, and you include "To be or not to be," you've added a new and frightening dimension to the speaker's thoughts.

7. As you gather materials, consider the eventual modal classification of your script. We spoke in chapter one of the characteristics of lyric-, dramatic-, and epic-mode texts. We now describe the characteristics of lyric-, dramatic-, and epic-mode scripts.

A modally lyric script may center on the investigation of one person; real or fictitious. The remaining cast members might represent various people that this person remembers or discusses. A lyric-mode script could also be an exploration of some idea or feeling, like love, hate, nature, and so on. The performers would not be defined characters, but instead personae intent on communicating an emotional experience. These scripts may seem abstract and ambiguous because they do not tell stories or have causal structures. The structure of lyric-mode scripts is often based on "**triggering**"—on a free association of ideas. One element of the script "triggers" another element, and so on.

A dramatic-mode script centers on individualized characters who are involved in some sort of conflict situation. Dramatic-mode scripts resemble conventional plays—except that the lines come from various sources. Dramatic-mode scripts usually take place in the present tense, and have defined locales and time periods.

A script which is epic in mode contains both a narrator and characters. Modally epic scripts are usually in the past tense, and focus on storytelling.

8. Probably the most difficult aspect of the collage script—and an aspect not required in single-text or expanded program scripts—is deciding on a structural format for linking all the pieces of literature together. Structure is what gives the content of your script form and definition. When considering structure, you can look toward three broad areas for assistance; **composition structure** (the way literature is put together), **speech structure** (the way a speech is organized), and **music structure** (the way music is composed). We will discuss these various structural formats in a following section.

9. Once the collage compiled script is structured, the compiler/director then orchestrates the script by deciding who will take each line. One way to do this is to divide the script into character voices, as we outlined earlier in this chapter. How many performers you cast will depend upon the number of different attitudes or individual characters that are represented in your finished script. If, for example, your theme is the draft, one character (or attitude) could be in favor of the draft, one could be against it, one could be apathetic, and one could be a flag-waving patriot. As you go through your script to orchestrate it, you label each line depending on its attitude toward the draft. In addition to attitudinal voices, there are other ways to orchestrate your script. You could decide to create atmospheric voices (wind, rain, ghosts, creaking noises, and so on), qualities (death, love, romance, fortitude), or nonhuman speakers (trains, computers, robots, animals), among others.

Composition Structures

Among the plots of short stories, novels, personal narratives, plays, and narrative poems, two types of structures are most common: **causal** structure and **contingent** structure.

Causal Structure

In causal structure, B happens because A happened, and C happens because B happened, and so on. In other words, all events in the story, play, or poem can be traced back to an incident that has already occurred. Most causal plots have the following order: exposition, development of conflict, crisis, resolution of conflict, climax, and denouement. The exposition establishes the time frame, introduces the characters, and sets the scene. Shortly after the exposition, a problem ensues. This problem produces conflict within the characters, between the characters, or between the characters and their environment. This conflict leads to the crisis which is the turning point—that moment when the direction the plot takes becomes more limited. After the crisis, the major character usually finds a way to resolve the conflict, which then leads to the climax or the highest point of action. After the climax, the denouement ties up loose ends and often projects the action into the future. With this type of structure, the audience is able to follow the cause-effect relationship and the logical flow of your argument. Use this type of structure for collage scripts which are basically narrative in nature.

Contingent Structure

The contingent structure can be used when you do not want to emphasize logical or causal connections between phenomena. This type of structuring often involves associative moments common to stream-of-consciousness literature, such as the works of Virginia Woolf and James Joyce. In the fiction of these writers, incidents happen and thoughts are triggered from no apparent cause or motivation. An idea in a character's mind triggers another seemingly unrelated idea which then triggers another, and so on. When you daydream, you often engage in free association—that is, you let your mind flow from one idea to another seemingly without any outside stimulus. James Thurber's short story "The Secret Life of Walter Mitty" is full of free association as Mitty allows noises or happenings in the real world in which he feels trapped to transport him to the fantasy world he prefers.

Often contingent structures lack even this triggering aspect. Something just happens next without cause or trigger. In one scene in Eugene Ionesco's absurdist play *The Bald Soprano*, for example, a couple sit and talk and discover they are married. In another scene, a fireman shows up for no apparent cause. Contingent plot structures, then, show the "accidental" nature of much of what happens in real life.

With the contingent structure, you may start with A, then go to C, then to F, then to Q, then back to A again. There is structure, but the structure is not the causal structure we are accustomed to. Ideas relate to each other, but not in a logical, narrative connection. Many lyric-mode scripts of an abstract nature have contingent structures. Use this type of structure when you want to investigate the seeming randomness of everyday life, an abstract idea, or show the complexity of the human mind.

Speech Structures

Speech composition formats provide additional structures for collage scripts. For a basically informative script, you may want to try this pattern: (1) introduction of basic assertion, (2) preview of main points, (3) body, (4) review of main points, and (5) conclusion.

Use a selection that presents the strongest statement of your assertion in the introduction. You might also consider using expository passages from different selections in the introduction. The preview of main points could be a simple list that you compose, or could be essential passages from selections in the script. Most of the literary selections go into the body of your script appropriately orchestrated, and the main points are repeated again in the review. You could save a selection that capsulizes the theme or which makes a deep impression to use for the conclusion.

For a script with a rhetorical or persuasive intent, try this structural pattern, called Monroe's Motivated Sequence: (1) attention, (2) need, (3) satisfaction, (4) visualization, and (5) action.[5]

The attention step introduces your theme and attempts to capture the audience's interest. Use something exciting, shocking, or thought-provoking in the attention step. The need step attempts to show the audience that there is a difficult problem to be solved. Include in this step the selections that present situations you wish to persuade the audience about. The satisfaction step proposes a solution(s) that will satisfy the need and alleviate the problem. The visualization step tries to show audience members how much better off they will be if they put your solution into effect, or how much worse off they will be if they do not. The action step gives specific information as to what this particular audience can do to effect change. [For an examination of the motivated sequence in song, look at "Trouble" from the musical *Music Man*. The speaker, Harold Hill, gathers the community together and warns them that there is trouble in River City (Attention). He tells them their children are wasting their time doing things like playing pool when they should be doing something more appropriate (Need). He proposes starting a boys' band (Satisfaction). He asks the community members to imagine "Seventy-Six trombones" leading "the big parade" (Visualization). He ends by asking for donations to buy uniforms and instruments for his boys' band (Action).]

Music Structures

The last kind of organizational structure is borrowed from musical formats and is often employed when choreographing dance. Music provides four kinds of structures useful for collage scripts: sonata, rondo, theme and variation, and antiphonal.

Sonata Structure

The **sonata** form is the basic life pattern: (A) we are born, (B) we live, and (A) we return to the unknown. With this format, you begin with the major idea (A) and then develop a related but different or contrasting idea (B). At the end of the script, you come back to the main idea (A), but it is usually different or at least changed (A' or A prime) because of what occurred in the developmental stage (B). Let's imagine that you are preparing a script on the theme of "marriage." In A, you would include materials that deal with a couple meeting, courting, and marrying. Search for materials that show young newlyweds who are full of idealistic dreams for their future. In B, include selections that deal with the realities and decisions married couples must deal with. Should they both work? Should they have children? Who is to take out the garbage? Who takes care of the money? What happens in A' will depend on your assertion. If your assertion is to persuade the audience that "marriage is a worthless institution with no hope for success," then your A' would include selections that show the break up and demise of the married couple. If your assertion is that "marriage works if you work at it," then you return to the married couple and show that they have come to an understanding and see the future more realistically. As we stated in chapter one, the materials you accumulate will have their own moods, character names, locales, time periods, etc. When you incorporate these texts into a larger whole (your script), you will have to alter them to fit the mood, names, locales, and time period of your script.

Rondo Structure

The **rondo** form follows the ABACADAEAF (and so forth) pattern. With this form, you begin with A, the main idea, then offer new or contrasting ideas on the A theme, and alternate these ideas throughout the script. If, for example, you compile a script on the Great Depression, your A or main statement could be: The Depression helped some people, but hurt others—*crash*. Your B,C,D, and so on, could be selections showing characters who were hurt and others who were strengthened or even benefited as a result of their experiences in the Depression. Your A' will be a repetition or restatement of the initial A, ending each time with the word *crash*—signifying the stock market crash of 1929. A variation of rondo is the **augmented** script. With augmented scripts, you begin with one recognizable text (A) that specifically relates to your theme, and you augment it—or make it larger—by adding material from other texts, B,C, D, etc. If your theme were "Suicide," for example, you could augment Hamlet's "To Be Or Not To Be" speech by adding other works inside of it. The A piece needs to be distinctive or recognizable to a majority of your audience because this helps to clarify your structure. The audience should know when you are in the A piece, and when you are adding new material. Possible texts to augment include Lincoln's Gettysburg Address; King's "I've Got A Dream" speech; "The Star Spangled Banner" or "America, the Beautiful"; the preface of the Constitution; and Carroll's "Jabberwocky."

Theme-and-Variation Structure

The **theme-and-variation** format presents the theme at the beginning of the script and then offers variants on this theme throughout the production. Your initial theme might involve the conventional marriage. You might then show variations on this theme by using selections that depict alternatives to conventional marriage: communal living, persons living together outside of marriage, extended family living, living single, and so forth. Another example of this structure might be to begin with a Brothers Grimm or Andersen fairy tale, and then compile updated versions of the tales by Thurber (fables), Sexton (found in the text *Transformations*), or James Finn Garner (found in the text *Politically Correct Bedtime Stories*).

Antiphonal Structure

Antiphonal patterns follow the ABABAB, etc. format. This format usually involves an argument involving two conflicting points of view. For example, your A literary selections could involve characters who have opted to go to college; your B selections could involve characters who have opted to go to work rather than to college. The A and B sections alternate, with each side presenting its point of view. When using the antiphonal pattern, deciding whether to finish with the A or B argument can be very significant.

With each of these structures, the individual sections (A, B, C, etc.) will not necessarily be composed of only one text. Consequently, internal compiling may be needed within each A and B unit as well as within the script as a whole.

EXPERIMENT

Gather the following list of selections: the short story "A Sense of Shelter" by John Updike, the song "Moonlight Drive" by Jim Morrison, the poems "Upon Julia's Clothes" by Robert Herrick and "She Was a Phantom of Delight" by William Wordsworth, and a scene between Rosalie and Jonathan in the play *Oh Dad, Poor Dad, Mama's Hung You in the Closet and I'm Feeling So Sad* by Arthur Kopit. Read the selections and see if you can decide what they have in common. What they have in common will be your overall theme. Then decide on an assertion on this theme. Compile the selections. Decide which selections or parts you will use, what structure you will use, who will say each line, and to whom.

Other Readers Theatre Considerations

Titling Your Script

It is usually a good idea to give your finished script a title. The title of a literary work helps the reader know what the writer thinks is important or significant. The title of your script could help clarify aspects of a particularly abstract script; communicate the main theme, locale, time period; and so on. A carefully considered title often acts as a key that helps the audience unlock the mystery of what your script means.

Employing a Chorus

In Greek tragedies, there was often a masked group of performers who sang and danced. This chorus usually chanted in unison, offering advice and commentary on the action. A chorus can be effectively employed in readers theatre productions for a similar purpose. Two choruses were employed in the orchestration of "The Eagle" which was reproduced earlier in this chapter. Because a chorus is a group, it has an aggregate power which individual members do not possess. This group can dictate how the audience as well as other characters in the production are to think or feel. In addition, a chorus can provide special effects. They can suggest weather conditions, they can highlight literary or sensory images, they can underscore sounds, they can heighten the rhythm. As Marion Kleinau writes:

> When images arise that cannot be embodied in single performers or in stage setting, a chorus might be the vehicle to carry them in production. Remember that the *anonymous character* of its members allows the chorus to assume a larger group identity, to become a force or an entity beyond the reach of the individual performing alone—a storm, the force of fate, an entire civilization.[6]

Employing a chorus can be tricky, though, in performance. We will say more about the use and staging of the chorus in chapter three.

Using Dance and Mixed Media

Dance and mixed media can be added to enhance elements of the script. Dance may be integrated in a performance by having one or more dancers extend the meaning as the literature is performed, or by having the performers speak and dance the material at the same time, if this is possible. Music can be used internally to heighten emotion or to provide a counterpoint, or it can be used to aid moving from one section of the script to another. Since locales usually are not literalized, film, video, or slides may be shown to spark the audience's identification of place.

Handling Transitions

Transitions are often a problem in compiled scripts. How do you smoothly get from one section of your script to another? **Cohesion**—creating a unified whole—is obtained through various means of linking the sections. One solution to the transition problem—especially in epic-mode scripts which focus on telling a story—is to create a narrator. A narrator acts like a mobile camera and facilitates fluidity between scenes without necessitating a "crosscut" from one moment to the next. If you do not include a narrator, then you must find another way to lead the audience from one mood, section, or idea to another, since a sudden switch may be jarring—unless that is what you intend. Transitions may repeat lines from the preceding material or may be original written comments that lead to the next selection. A striking statement of the overall theme can be repeated before each new bit of material. As Christie A. Logan puts it, "Clarity of presentational form is dependent on the audience's ability to adjust during the performance to shifts of time and place, of voice, of mode and style."[7] It is the compiler's responsibility to make those shifts clear. There also are staging techniques which can facilitate transitions which will be discussed in chapter three.

Securing Copyright

One last consideration involves copyright. One reason why compiled scripts are difficult to produce is that they can be very expensive. Were you to compile a script for eventual public performance and you intend to charge admission, you must write the publisher for permission to use every text or part of a text not in the public domain (over 80 years old). This is complicated by a "fair use" clause which allows you to use without compensation parts of selections—but how much of a selection you may use varies depending on the text. If cost is a consideration, there are two solutions to this problem: (1) do not charge admission for your performances or (2) use as much public domain, original, or unpublished material in your script as you can.

Reviewing the Basics

Once you have compiled your script, ask yourself the following questions:

1. Does the script have an identifiable structure that holds it together?
2. Does it have interaction among characters or between characters and the audience? Or among contrasting ideas, or ways of life, etc.?

3. Does the script have a sense of progression, of "going some-place?" Does it lead to a point of awareness, or some kind of insight?

4. Does it cohere? Does it have a unity despite the diversity of selections you may have included in your script? Is it unified by an author? An idea or theme? A period of history? An event? A class of people? A geographical section of the country? Through repetition of a word or phrase?

5. Does the script have an interest-catching opening?

6. Does it have a variety of materials in length, type, mood, genre?

7. Does it have interesting and effective transition materials?

8. Is the ending conclusive? memorable? Does it clinch the point of the script (if that is intended)?

Chapter three will take you from creating your script on the page to producing your script on the stage.

Summary

This chapter outlined how to create the three specific types of readers theatre scripts: the single-text script, the expanded program compiled script, and the collage compiled script.

The single-text script is one selection orchestrated into voices, sounds, images, or rhythms. Any kind of literary or nonliterary text may be orchestrated if the readers theatre format enhances the text.

The expanded program compiled script is a combination of individual selections on a theme, person, specific literary style or period, or a specific historical period. Each selection maintains its unique qualities, and transitions are given between selections to see how they relate to each other and to the overall theme or idea.

The collage compiled script conveys the seamless message the compiler/director wishes to convey. Again, a theme is selected and an assertion devised. Material is gathered and structured using composition formats, speech formats, or music formats. The material is then orchestrated and staged.

Miscellaneous considerations include giving your script a title, employing a chorus, incorporating dance and mixed media, handling transitions, and dealing with copyright.

Notes

[1] Marion L. Kleinau and Janet Larsen McHughes, *Theatres for Literature* (Sherman Oaks, CA.: Alfred Publishing 1980), p. 46.

[2] Edward A. Bloom, Charles H. Philbrick, and Elmer M. Blistein, *The Order of Poetry* (New York: Odyssey Press, 1961), p. 154.

[3] Kleinau and McHughes, p. 32.

[4] Much of this material is found in Judy E. Yordon, *Roles in Interpretation* (Dubuque, IA: Wm. C. Brown, 1993), pp. 414–17.

[5] Alan H. Monroe, *Principles and Types of Speech*, rev. ed. (New York: Scott, Foresman, 1939), pp. 208–23.

[6] Marion L. Kleinau, "Some Thoughts on the Readers Theatre Chorus," *Readers Theatre News*, Fall/Winter, 1981, p. 17.

[7] Christie A. Logan, "Form and Rhythm in Compilation Productions: Progressing the Audience's Field of Experience," a paper presented at the Speech Communication Association Convention, Boston, Massachusetts, November 1987.

Chapter Three

Readers Theatre:
Staging Your Script

Staging your finished script (though some scriptwriters never believe their script is "finished," as it is always in a process of rewrite and revision based on what happens in rehearsals) depends first on establishing a production concept. As stated in chapter two, a production concept is your vision of what the script and production will be. From this concept, the entire production evolves. The concept is the director's plan of action for illuminating the idea and structure of the script through set design, costuming, and the other technical devices, as well as decisions about focus. Varying concepts are primarily responsible for the different productions we get of the same Shakespearean play, for instance. Peter Brook's decision to stage *A Midsummer Night's Dream* in a circus setting informed every other decision. Begin, then, by deciding what you would like your audience to understand from your script and let that develop into a production concept. Edwin Wilson says, "The concept comes from a controlling idea, vision, point of view, or metaphor, which will result in a cohesive production and present the spectator with a unified artistic experience."[1] It determines the staging and the tone of the production, whether it is basically comedic or farcical, tragic or melodramatic, a mood piece or an intellectual stimulant.

Readers theatre styles of performance form a continuum ranging from the early days of performers on stools behind lecterns employing offstage focus to performers enacting all scenes onstage, with lines memorized, and spectacle added. At one end of the continuum, suggestive action is portrayed only through muscular tensions and facial expressions. At the other end, there is character interaction and physical movement. In chapter one, we discussed the need for the "theatre" in readers theatre to gain more emphasis. We stated that in today's world of multi-media, technological advances, MTV, and the like, audiences expect and demand character movement and interaction. Although there still may be some scripts which benefit from conventional readers theatre staging, most scripts will demand some kind of theatricality.

In this chapter we will discuss basic staging principles, including blocking, focus, and movement, and how to employ the spectacle elements of setting, lighting, costuming, props, and mixed-media devices. Before we discuss the staging principles, however, we first must cast our productions. We start then with some casting information.

Casting

Once you have readied your script for production, it is time to consider casting. When selecting your cast, the prime concern is not physical appearance (as it may be in some conventional theatre productions). Physical type-casting is often helpful to audience members in that it aids them in "seeing" the characters they hear; but of greater importance are sensitivity, a flexible voice and body, and an expressive face. The age, gender, or ethnicity of performers are not important considerations, therefore. Since readers theatre is presentational and nonrealistic, we do not attempt to find performers who may be perfect physical types for the roles. Our casting often works to emphasize psychological aspects of a character. Even when a character is bifurcated, the two performers playing the role need not physically resemble each other. If audience members are prepared for something different, if they can accept that two performers are playing the same role, then they should be prepared for these two performers to resemble the aspect of personality they play since the role has been divided with this in mind.

Think, too, about the number of cast members required. Whereas in conventional theatre there is normally a one-to-one correspondence between the number of characters called for and the number of performers cast, this is not always true in readers theatre. In readers theatre, many performers may play one role, and one performer may play many roles. If many performers play one role, this underscores the multiplicity of this character's personality. If one performer plays many roles, this emphasizes the similarity or common substance of these roles.

The best advice, therefore, is to cast performers who have a wide vocal and emotional range, can project variety in vocal quality, can project mental images, and are willing to take risks and try something new and different.

Blocking

Even in the most restricted readers theatre with little movement on stage, **blocking**—the movement of a performer in relation to the other performers and to the furniture or set pieces on the stage—is important. The audience must see the characters in relationship to each other, they must see "the man stalk out of the room," "the young couple sit on a bank of violets," "the woman leap from the window" even if all of this is suggested rather than literalized. We will focus on staging readers theatre in a proscenium-type setting—including a real stage, a classroom, or open space setting. A **proscenium stage** is typical of that kind of theatre one sees on Broadway where the action happens separate from the audience, which sits in front of and at some distance from the stage. Readers theatre productions also may be staged in other settings, but these types of productions tend to be more the exception than the rule. We will discuss some of these theatre designs later in this chapter.

A proscenium stage is divided into nine basic areas. Figure 3-1 identifies these playing areas:

Figure 3.1 Proscenium Stage

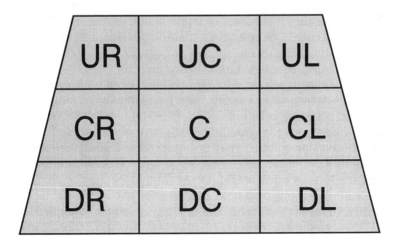

The geography of the playing stage includes downstage right, downstage center, and downstage left, right center, center, left center, up right, up center, and up left. Stage left and right are viewed as the performer on the stage views them. Upstage means away from the audience, as if one were walking uphill, and downstage means toward the audience, downhill. When you block your script—determine where performers will move and when—ask the performers to use the symbols in figure 3-1 to facilitate writing down their blocking. If a performer were told to cross downleft, for example, all he or she would have to write is XDL.

Strong stage positions include being downstage, elevated, moving from stage right to stage left, or being at the apex of a triangle with others focused on you. Weak positions include being upstage, being lower, and moving from stage left to stage right.

Body position on stage communicates. The full-front position is stronger than a quarter turn to right or left, and is much stronger than a half turn or a three-quarter turn. The full-front position is the one most associated with presentational theatre. The more a performer angles in, away from the audience, the weaker the position becomes. Playing profile is the norm of most representational theatre.

To "give" means to adjust your position to allow another performer to have focus. To "blend in" is to make minor body changes to obtain a better relationship to other performers. To "cover" is to be downstage of another performer thus blocking him or her from the audience's view. The downstage performer should take the responsibility for not blocking, but the upstage performer can help by "uncovering." To keep as open as possible to the audience, the performer should make gestures with the upstage hand. Performers should cross in front of other performers and furniture since they would not be moving if they were not the important person at that time. The triangle, with the apex upstage, is a useful device in composition. This opens the picture to the audience and allows all performers to be uncovered and thus seen.

Levels are effective devices for composition because they allow a variety of body positions. This variety may be achieved by employing lying, sitting, and standing positions. Variety in the height of stools or the use of ladders and platforms facilitates effective composition. Symmetrical balance in the stage picture may be achieved by having the same number of characters on either side of center stage. Asymmetrical balance may be obtained in several ways: by having more important characters separated from the group with more space around them or by having them on a different level from the others, usually on a higher level.

Emphasis is a very important component of the stage picture. The audience needs to know whom it should be watching. Having the eyes of the other characters focused on the important character is one way to indicate who should have the audience's attention. A hand or arm pointed toward the character adds emphasis. Placing important characters on a level different from the other characters will give them focus. Letting them have a full-front position features them. A movement attracts attention. An energetic stance will attract the eye, especially if others are not so alive in their way of standing or sitting. As a general rule, the person standing is more emphatic than the person sitting. As the attention shifts from one character to another, subtle changes must be made to adjust the composition so that the correct performer has the focus of the audience. In other words, someone must "give" stage so that the character who needs emphasis can "take" stage.

Directors may have done some preliminary blocking, but during the early, exploratory rehearsals, much of the early plan may be discarded as the creative performers, working together with the director, find new and unique ways of responding to the stimuli in the script. Before you can even pre-block, however, you must decide what set pieces or pieces of furniture you will use.

Focus

At both ends of the continuum, from conventional readers theatre to more representational readers theatre, focus is important. It is the director's responsibility to determine the type of interpretational relationship and contact the performers are to have with one another and with the audience during the performance. Imagination and experimentation are particularly valuable in this realm of readers theatre. The three possibilities from which the director chooses are onstage focus, offstage focus, and a combination of the two.

Onstage Focus

Onstage focus means that the performers relate to each other on the stage, looking at and reacting to each other as performers do in conventional theatre productions (see figure 3-2). It should be apparent, of course, that the larger the number of performers in a given scene, the more difficult it is to use onstage focus, because each performer has to be able to see and relate directly to all the others at various times. The

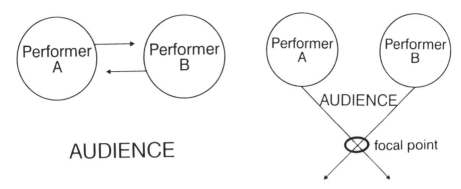

Figure 3-2 Onstage Focus   **Figure 3-3** Offstage Cross Focus

techniques employed for a production involving a large number of performers with onstage focus are quite similar to those used by the director of a conventional stage play.

Offstage Focus

Offstage focus refers to two techniques: in the first, called **open focus**, the performers look directly into the eyes of the audience; in the second, called **offstage cross focus,** the performers envision the scene and each other out in the audience, figuratively placing the scene of action in the midst of those witnessing the performance. Characters who are aware of an audience, or narrators who are sharing with the audience use open focus. Characters who are unaware of an audience and who are addressing each other may use offstage cross focus (see figures 3-3 and 3-4), which requires that they direct their words to the other characters as though they were out in the realm of the audience. Narrators usually look directly into the eyes of the audience, although they may occasionally look at the scene, then at the audience, and then back at the scene as if sharing with the audience.

In a scene with offstage focus, the performers' lines of vision cross or intersect in a hypothetical area about midway out in the center of the auditorium and slightly above the heads of the audience. This midway point is more effective than the back wall because it focuses the scene closer to all segments of the audience. Offstage focus puts the performers in a full-front position in relation to the audience, which allows their facial expressions to be seen easily.

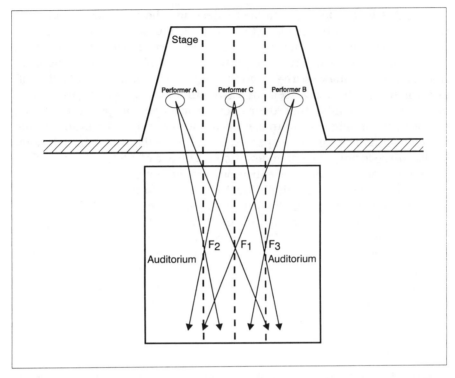

Figure 3-4 Offstage Focus; three performers. The focal point when A and B look at each other is F_1; for A and C, F_2; and for C and B, F_3. (This chart is an adaptation of a chart found in Coger and White's *Readers Theatre Handbook*, p. 102.)

In employing offstage focus, the director must emphasize to the cast the necessity for keeping in mind that they are not seeing a specific point or spot somewhere in the audience; they are seeing characters doing something in a definite locality—a scene. The four actresses in the orchestration of "the letting down of the hair" in chapter two, for example, must imagine seeing the small stone room in which they are housed, they must see the thousands they believe they attract to their secret place. In "Hills Like White Elephants," the woman must imagine seeing "fields of grain and trees along the banks of the Ebro." She must also imagine seeing the man who she only occasionally addresses with onstage focus. The performers can help themselves establish this imaginary scene or picture if they fill in the details; that is, in their mind's eye they should be seeing how the imagined characters are dressed, how they are standing or sitting, what they are doing, and how they are reacting.

With this type of focus, both the readers and the audience are creating the characters and the scene with their imaginations. In the use of both onstage and offstage focus for scenes, the narration is offstage, given directly to the audience. However, if the focus is offstage, it is imperative that the director make sure—from the audience's vantage point—that all performers involved in a scene at a given moment are placing that scene in the same locality, that their focus converges properly. If all the performers on stage are to make a wish on the moon, for example, the director should designate a specific place for all the performers to look so that there is only one imaginary moon. The use of offstage focus makes great demands on the concentration and creative imagination of the performers. They must actually "see" the action in this imaginary world at the place selected for their focuses to cross. To accomplish this, they could practice in front of a mirror. Another technique to try during early rehearsals is to place one of the performers out in the audience, while the performer sharing the scene remains on stage. They should run their lines in these positions making mental notes about how each other looks, sounds, reacts, so that when they are again standing side by side, they can rely on their memory to create an interaction.

Combinations

A third possibility is to combine onstage and offstage focus. Marion and Marvin Kleinau contend that the imaginary field in which the audience places the scene is a constantly shifting one that is determined by the nature of the literature being performed. In descriptive material the audience is more likely to see the scene close to themselves in their imaginations, but in dialogue, with the two performers physically present, the audience probably places the scene onstage with the performers. This, the Kleinaus say, is hypothetical, as is any theory of audience reaction, but they cite this example in support of their point of view:

> One example is from a Readers Theatre production of *Othello*, directed by Wallace A. Bacon of Northwestern University. Some of the scenes were deliberately set on stage and some were set off stage. In the fight between Cassio and Roderigo, Act V, Scene 1, the readers focused toward the audience. But when Iago wounded Cassio *from behind*, without explanation of the stage business in the lines of the text, Iago actually ran up behind Cassio to deliver the thrust. *What happened* was the point here—not what was heard or what the characters felt at the moment. The eye was the significant witness at the moment, thus the scene was presented to the eye. Later, in the murder of Desdemona, the

director felt that the significant action was the effect, on Othello, of his own action—not the deed itself, but what the deed did to the Moor. The actions were performed—the strangling, Desdemona's struggle—but the scene was focused toward the audience so that the major emphasis was placed upon Othello's face and thus on his personal suffering. Here an interesting tension was set up between *physical cues*, which tended to draw the scene on stage, and the readers' focus, which acted to draw the scene into the realm of the audience. This tension, it may be assumed, acted to reinforce Othello's own struggle within the audience member. . . .[2]

In general, when something is to be seen rather than heard (such as the stabbing of Roderigo by Iago), a director is wise to pull the focus onstage. Other reasons to pull the focus onstage are if the director wants to emphasize or contrast sections. If offstage focus has been used consistently and onstage focus is suddenly employed, this shift heightens the moment. If, for example, a couple—using offstage focus—argues about some issue but then resolves their differences, that resolution can be literalized with onstage focus as the couple literally sees eye-to-eye. In the final analysis, of course, you must make the decision on the type of focus or focuses to be employed at any given time. It takes time for some performers to get used to the convention of offstage focus. They wonder why they just can't look at the performer standing one foot away from them. You will have to be ready to explain the theory behind readers theatre's emphasis on audience members' ability to create a scene in their imaginations.

EXPERIMENT

Perform any orchestration or compilation in chapter two and practice using offstage focus. Make sure that the focal lines intersect somewhere in and directly above the audience members' heads. What effects are achieved with offstage focus? Try doing the scene with onstage focus. What different effects are achieved? See if you can discover when the focus should be onstage and when the focus should be offstage.

Action and Movement

Traditionally, little movement was used when presenting readers theatre productions. This lack of movement and of other stage devices was supposed to place the attention upon the language of the text itself. Therefore, literature of verbal richness and psychological insight worked best in readers theatre performances. As we stated earlier, however, this has changed. Not that we purport using movement just for the sake of adding action or to keep an audience used to special effects and constant motion awake and interested. Movement must be selective, and should suit the particular production and each particular character. The full-out movement of conventional theatre is not traditionally used. What is practiced instead are **suggestion** and **economy**—two essential terms involved in readers theatre staging. Suggestion means trying to avoid falling into the trap of making everything literal or representational perhaps by employing synecdochical movement—suggesting a part for the whole—or by using focus to create difficult to stage elements, e.g., giants, a person shrinking in size, a gigantic peach, a huge doll's house, bats flying in the sky, a man walking a tightrope, etc. Economy means finding the simplest way to stage elements so that the production features the language and the images rather than the special effects. If you were doing the balcony scene from *Romeo and Juliet*, for instance, you would economize by having both performers use offstage focus. The performer playing Juliet would look down when looking at Romeo in the garden, and Romeo would look up at her. Both performers switch to eye level offstage focus as Romeo climbs up to the balcony and now sees Juliet at the same level. The same scene could be staged with Juliet on a ladder and Romeo beneath her.

   Kinesic behavior is of tremendous importance in employing economy and suggestion. Kinesic behavior includes all bodily movement that has communicative value. The tilt of the head, leaning forward or backward, nods, facial expressions, ways of standing, walking or sitting, and tensions of the muscles are a few of the subtle movements that communicate attitudes and reactions.[3] This kinesic, nonverbal language completes the interaction between the speaker and the listeners in a scene. The way a reader sits is revealing. What is conveyed when one sits well back, completely balanced? When one sits on the edge? When one sits with the body leaning diagonally, legs crossed above the knee? This is related to **behavioral synecdoche**, where a small action may communicate much more to the audience.

   What types of movements, then, may be used? Of first consideration are those essential to the script. Getting characters on and off stage, or in and out of the scene, is a prime concern. The entrances and exits of the performers must necessarily be more symbolic, and in a physical sense, more restricted than in a conventional play. Of course, characters could come on stage as they would in conventional theatre, but this calls attention to their walking in, on stage, when the scene is to be in the minds of the audience members. This can be jarring if many performers enter at the same time and if there are many entrances and exits to be effected. One way to avoid having characters walk on and off stage is to have all of them sit or stand onstage at the back or sides and simply walk into the scene as needed. Peter Brook employed this technique in his experimental production of *A Midsummer Night's Dream*. He placed characters on a balcony above the stage until they were needed to make their entrances into the action. Another possibility is to have the entire cast enter in some symbolic or creative way, and then remain on stage, reacting in character to whatever happens throughout the production. If this is not desirable, you may employ the **freeze**—having performers hold a position without moving—to take them out of a scene momentarily. If a freeze is employed, be sure to freeze the performers in some sort of active position or attitude so that the audience knows they are frozen and not just passively uninvolved. This is useful if there are a series of short scenes being played in such a way that the action shifts back and forth rather quickly from one group to another.

Two other types of movement can provide wonderful effects: **speeded up action** and **slow motion**. When the director decides to speed up the action, the performers move in a kind of double time (this may be done in place, or by literally moving about the stage). This kind of behavior would indicate that the narrator or characters are hurrying over long sections of time, suggesting some type of chase or sections of a journey. This device was employed in a script where a boy is trying to escape from a man who is searching for him. The boy stood and ran as fast as he could in place, while the man, not able to move that quickly, stood next to him moving at a much slower pace. When time is slowed down, that moment becomes heightened and significant. In a script about a man murdering his mother by mistake, the action was slowed way down—as can be done in film, for example—to underscore the act and to show the reaction of the man doing the killing.

In general, movement in readers theatre illustrates psychological relationships among characters, illuminates symbolic action, and provides behavioral synecdoches for the stimulation of the audience's imagination. The more that offstage focus is employed, the more economy and suggestion are expected. When onstage focus is used, more movement and action are expected.

Setting and Set Pieces

Readers theatre is known as "Theatre of the Mind" because it concentrates on the audience's ability to create settings and set pieces (furniture) from language. This relates to a type of theatre that Jerzy Grotowski founded in Poland in 1959. Grotowski reacted against the "rich theatre" with its emphasis on spectacle, and created his "poor theatre" to take its place. Grotowski thought that the most important aspects of a theatrical production were the performers and the audience. For him theatre could happen anywhere. All that was necessary was a bare space, skilled performers, and an audience willing to suspend disbelief. While we do not propose going to this extreme, we do applaud Grotowski's emphasis on performer and audience to create imaginatively all that is required.

Symbolism and Simplicity

Since readers theatre does not attempt a literal representation of life, symbolic set pieces may be employed such as stools, blocks, ladders, crates, chairs, benches, and the like. These set pieces can be easily moved and reconfigured to suggest most any locale and the furniture in it. A piano bench may suggest a settee, a love seat, a davenport, a car, a bed, etc. A longer bench may suggest a train, a garden wall, or a dinosaur. A stool may become a chair, and a ladder may suggest a radio tower, a balcony for Juliet, a windmill, or the top of the Empire State Building. Anything or anywhere the performers tell the audience they are when atop a ladder, it can become. Whatever is used should fade from the attention of audience members when the performers' words transport them into the world of the script, for it is the setting painted with words that is most important.

The keynote is simplicity to enhance and exploit the uniqueness of the material. A setting really needs only something to stop the eye and define a neutral space wherein the action and moods may be evoked. What form shall this simplicity take? Gordon Craig, opposed to the realistic set, has substituted masses of light and shade with different planes that provided a more adequate view of the actors, using suggestive shapes rather than illusionistic details.[4] Terence Gray wanted masses of simple planes constructed of cubes of different sizes fitted together in varied scenic shapes, because to him the set "could be vested with significance only when the business of the stage was in action before and upon it."[5] Norman Bel Geddes contended that the designer should think only of abstract solids and voids. For readers theatre, if more than one level is needed to illuminate the text, one could well follow Bel Geddes' concept of space, shapes, platforms, and voids around them, and thus gain verticality.[6] Christie A. Logan sees the stage space as a globe, and she charts the journey to the diverse locales in relief. She suggests "magnetizing" areas

A simple set effectively represented the town of Milk Wood in this scene from Dylan Thomas' *Under Milk Wood*.

of the stage space and designating places where power sources are most intense. She writes:

> These "magic spots" in the playing area are repositories of tensions that accumulate rather than dissipate as the journey progresses. Magic spots are places where the terrain is charged—for instance, characters revitalize there, sensory experience for the audience is most intense there (because of language, character, action, lights, sound, color, etc). These may be recurrent areas where the most intense actions take place, where the atmosphere is most dense. The audience can come to intuitively expect another visit there; this action can unify their experience of disparate environments because the stage area accumulates meaning and density as the performance unfolds.[7]

An example of the use of simplified, suggestive, abstract space staging is *You're a Good Man, Charlie Brown*, the first professional readers theatre-style musical. After an introductory series of solo remarks by various characters in the cast, punctuated by bits of music, the lights came on. "The stage is suddenly filled with light and we at last can see its contents: several oversized, brightly painted objects in simple geometric shapes, and six undersized, simply dressed people of straightforward, uncomplicated characters."[8] As the musical continues, those shapes and areas of the stage become various locales as we are told what they are or see them used in a suggestive way. The largest object on the stage could easily be mistaken for a doghouse, and we know it is just that when Snoopy enters wearing a white turtleneck sweater, black pants, and sneakers. But if we don't, Patty's first line after he enters tells us: "Oh, Snoopy, you're such a sweet doggy." Pools of light direct our attention from one area of the stage to another, as they dim in one section and come up in another. The dialogue identifies the scene as we enter it. If the mood changes, the lights change: *The scene is dimmed and spotted with evening colors, and airy music is heard. Linus and Lucy wander on, looking at the sky.*[9] This playground was conceptually realized from the playscript. In a presentation of the children's script *Charlotte's Web* by E. B. White, a huge spiderweb constructed of white rope was suspended behind the performers. In a production of Feiffer sketches, four reversible freestanding screens suggesting the panels of a comic strip stood behind the performers. On one side were the names of the stories to be performed; on the other was a cartoon sketch of the leading character in that story. As the story began, the screen was revolved to reveal this other side. For a moment the attention went to the drawing, returning then to the world of the story.

Another approach to staging is the use of symbol or **metaphor**. If a character is mentally hemmed in on all sides, for example, the metaphorical setting could be a large box. A character bound by tradition, for example, might be physically bound by ropes. Frustration could be revealed in a similar way. The more frustrated the character, the more ropes would be added. A verbal struggle between two characters could be physicalized as a game of tug of war. If a character is treated like a caged animal, the remaining cast members could become this cage and "prod" the character with their words and actions. In one production of Samuel Beckett's *Endgame*, the characters wore heavy books around their necks with chains to suggest the presence of the author and the weight of his words and voluminous stage directions. In Beckett's play *Happy Days*, a woman is buried up to her waist in something (what she is buried in is not defined) in the first act, and is buried up to her neck in the second act. In addition to this limitation, the performer is constantly bombarded by stage directions dictating what little movement she can do and directing her delivery and pauses. One director used a metaphor and placed the production in a laboratory setting where the woman (and her husband) become human experiments. The stage directions were embodied by performers who suggested laboratory scientists, they spoke the stage directions (e.g., "pause," "long pause," "longer pause," etc.), and then observed the specimens and took notes on their behaviors.

EXPERIMENT

Choose a short scene from any conventional play and see what happens when you stage it employing economy and suggestion instead of literalization.

Staging

The productions discussed so far have been staged in proscenium-type facilities, ones in which the audience is seated in front of and distanced from the playing area. What happens if the audience is on two sides (alley staging), three sides (thrust), or all sides (in-the-round)?

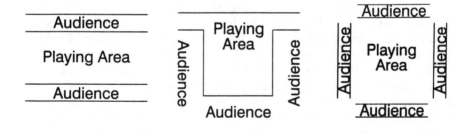

Figure 3-5 Alley Stage   **Figure 3-6** Thrust Stage   **Figure 3-7** In-the-Round

In alley staging, set pieces are put at either end as the performers move back and forth between them. In a production of *Cinders* by Janusz Glowacki, which tells the story of oppression in a Polish reform school for girls, one end of the stage was the principal's office and represented "administration." The other end suggested the girls' dorm room and represented confinement. The center was a neutral place which provided the space necessary for the girls to stage their version of the Cinderella tale while a government deputy and TV crew eavesdropped on their project.

If a three-quarter or thrust stage is used, tall furnishings can be placed next to the back wall so that they do not interfere with the view of the audience. Thrust staging is very similar to proscenium staging, except that there is an extended area downstage to use for important moments or characters. The major characters, for example, could play downstage, while a chorus stands upstage of them. If all performers are to remain onstage throughout, chairs could be set up across the back wall, and performers can move down into scene, and then exit back to their chairs.

If in-the-round staging is employed, great care has to be exerted not to block areas of the stage from any part of the audience. Low stools and benches without backs are usually needed. These should be out from the center, around the periphery of the playing space. If all aisles are not used for exits or entrances, the furnishings can be located in front of them. The major problem for directors is to place performers so that all audience members can see someone's face at all times. The key to movement is to play with backs to the aisles, and performers should employ the "shouldering" method. In shouldering, two characters facing each other will have the left shoulder of one on line with the left shoulder of the other. Standing in this way, the performers do not block each other. Half of the audience sees one performer's face, and the other half sees the other performer's face. With in-the-round productions, it is wise to keep the performers separated rather than bunched together. Keeping them at some distance from each other (approximately four feet when possible) opens them up to the audience. Not holding any one position for an overly long time helps, and having faces turned in to the center allows more people to see them. Avoid high levels in the center that would block from view any action behind the levels. If a script demands height, it is better to use three-quarter round rather than in-the-round staging. When a director employing theatre-in-the-round communicates with the cast, the clock designation works well. Place 12 o'clock at one spot and then move in equal increments around to 1, 2, 3, and so on, with 6 o'clock directly across from 12 o'clock. Instead of telling an actor XDR (cross downright), you tell them to X to 8 o'clock.

The problem with staging readers theatre productions in either alley or in-the-round formations is that offstage cross focus is almost impossible to use since the audience is not in one place where the imaginary scene may be said to occur. Performers may still address the audience directly using offstage audience focus, and, of course, onstage focus may be employed.

Space in churches with altars, long narrow store buildings, outdoor areas, classrooms without platforms, and other such "found spaces" present specific and different problems. Keep in mind that the major goal is to allow the audience to see the faces of the performers and to hear their words. Design your setting to facilitate this. K. B. Valentine, an innovator in varied uses of readers theatre, writes:

> Where can I find space for performance? If I wish to reach a neighborhood audience, I walk around until I find a cul-de-sac or other section of rarely used pavement that can be turned into a performance area. I look for a "pocket-park" or vacant lot, a front lawn or stoop that can serve. I look for places where neighborhood people gather. In a school or campus setting, I look for a speaker's platform outside, or any slightly raised surface inside. I look for steps or slopes leading to an area that can be opened up for performance. As with the neighborhood search, I look for areas where people tend to collect. In the more restrictive atmosphere of the correctional or other institution, I look for the recreation room, the eating space, or the library. In a business or factory, I look for the place people go for their breaks.[10]

To sum up, directors have more than one alternative in staging readers theatre productions. They may use a comparatively bare space with a few set pieces to provide places to sit, to elevate the action, and to make meaningful stage pictures that help communicate what is occurring. They may employ a metaphor in staging, or may choose a full, more realistic setting. The choice should be influenced by the style and form of the script and by the mood it requires, for the goal is to illuminate the complexities of the text through performance.

Lighting

Speaking of illumination, lighting can focus attention on different areas of the performing space, produce dramatic effects, project images on surfaces to aid in pictorial composition, help establish mood, and make key performers stand out from others in a scene. Many directors believe that light is the most important single factor in production other than the performers and the literature itself.

The presentational nature of readers theatre, demanding as it does interaction with and the cooperation of the audience, suggests a further employment of light—light in the audience area. Occasionally, the house lights are left on or are only slightly dimmed. Since the audience is often addressed and its imaginative participation is required, keeping the house lights slightly up increases the audience's sense of involvement. This principle may be carried even further. Just as lights are subtly manipulated onstage to brighten, dim, and change colors and areas, the degree of light within the audience may vary with the degree of direct communication within a specific scene. Scenes composed primarily of descriptive narration would utilize more audience illumination than scenes enacted onstage with little or no descriptive narration.

Readers theatre light is of two kinds, as is regular stage lighting: **specific illumination**, or shadow-producing light, and **general illumination**, or light which does not produce shadows. The problem of the lighting designer (should you be fortunate enough to have a lighting designer) is to proportion and manipulate these two kinds of light during a performance. Hunton D. Sellman divided the functions of stage lighting into five: (1) selective visibility, (2) revelation of form, (3) illusion of nature, (4) composition, and (5) emotional and psychological effects. These same divisions are valid for readers theatre lighting. Let us look at each of these five lighting functions.

Selective visibility is illumination provided so that an audience is able to see clearly everything the director intends it to see. It is used to light an area either more brightly, or exclusively, in order to focus attention on a portion of the playing area and the performers occupying it.

Revelation-of-form light is modeling light, added to give highlights, shadows, and variety in the distribution of light. General illumination tends to give performers, properties, and settings a flat, uninteresting quality. Form is revealed by shadow-producing light, light from specific directions balanced by shadow, and areas of varying degrees of brightness.

Illusion-of-nature lighting creates atmosphere with beams of light through windows and doors—imaginary or otherwise—accenting thereby important playing areas and objects, or spotlighting the performers. Some illusion can be provided by making use of the angle of the sun or moon, getting normal shadows from the performers and natural shadows from window bars and other architectural units.

Pictorial composition can be enhanced through a combination of specific and general illumination. This is accomplished by providing light sources that properly highlight objects and performers and produce shadows to form part of the design. It involves ensuring that everything is lighted from the best angle. Such lighting aids design, and is useful in focusing attention.

Backlighting silhouettes the performers in *Under Milk Wood* while the narrators who are downstage left and downstage right are lit from the front.

Emotional and psychological effects involve the symbolic use of colored lights, light and shade, variations in shadows, and the speed with which light changes are made. Lighting can also help suggest transitions from one part of the script to another. We spoke in chapter two about the various structures of collage compilation scripts. One way to make those shifts between sections clear is to darken one area, and then bring the lights up on another area to suggest a change in time, mood, attitude, locale, and so on.

Although general illumination, that is, light that does not make appreciable shadows, is the most commonly used method of lighting in conventional readers theatre, more elaborate lighting effects are becoming common as more and more theatricality is added. Areas of the stage are picked out of the void to draw attention by dimming the illumination on one portion of the stage as light is brought up on another portion. Individual performers are given total attention with pinpoint spots. Projected scenery, such as an oriental pagoda for *The Mikado*, or a symbolic cross of light can indicate locale. Motor-driven "effects discs" on projectors create water ripples, fire, smoke, falling leaves, moving clouds, and other such effects. It should be said, though, that these can easily become distracting, and should be approached carefully.

To emphasize the timeliness of Edna St. Vincent Millay's *The Murder of Lidice*, the performers stood for a moment in silhouette at the beginning while a swastika was thrown on the scrim (a curtain with an open weave which can be lit from behind or in front for different effects; slides, videos, film, etc. can be projected on it) behind them; then, at the end, the silhouette was repeated, but this time the hammer-and-sickle emblem was projected onto the scrim. In a production of *One Flew Over the Cuckoo's Nest* the effect of shock treatment on the mind of an inmate of a mental institution was enhanced by a blinding white strobe light flashing on and off for the moment of contact, followed by a dull red glow to suggest the aftereffects of a muddled mind. In a production of Alan Ayckbourn's *Woman in Mind*, lighting altered drastically to differentiate the main character's "real" family from her "fantasy" family. In *The Glass Menagerie*, lighting enhanced the mood as Laura and her "gentleman caller," Jim, danced. A revolving mirror ball of light which was supposed to be coming from the Paradise Dance Hall across the alley filtered into the Wingfield living room. As soon as Jim and Laura were comfortable dancing, another mirror ball filled the room they were in so that they became, for a moment, part of that "Paradise."

If you have the ability to experiment with lighting, feel free to try some of the effects described in this section. If not, remember that the main requisite of lighting is to illuminate the faces of the performers (and occasionally the audience). If this is achieved, often the language will do the rest.

Costumes

What the performers wear must be given careful consideration because it can be very useful in reinforcing characterization and in helping to convey your theme or intention. As Milly S. Barranger explains:

> Costumes etablish period, social class, economic status, occupation, age, geography, weather, and time of day. They help to clarify the relationships and relative importance of various characters. Ornament, line, and color can tie together members of a family, group, faction, or party. Changes in costume can indicate alteration in relationships among characters or in a character's psychological outlook. Similarities or contrasts in costumes can show sympathetic or antagonistic relationships.[11]

Notice how costumes depict class and status in this production of *Jane Eyre*.

In many readers theatre productions, however, costumes cannot be literalized to the extent that Barranger suggests. Often in readers theatre, performers play more than one role, or play someone whose character may span an entire lifetime. Trying to literalize these changes in character would be impossible. Consequently, **suggestive costuming** may be required. For example, in a production of Edgar Lee Masters' *Spoon River Anthology* on Broadway, basic costumes were used and were changed by simply adding scarves, shawls, and hats; by wearing blouses and dresses with adaptable necklines that could be low for one character and high for another; by quickly altering hemlines by tucking up the skirts; and by using shawls, either as a head-covering, or as something to be thrown lightly across the shoulders.

If elaborate costuming is not required or possible, then consider what you can do with the performers' own clothing. Consider the choice of somber or dark colors for very serious or heavily dramatic presentations; bright, cheerful colors for light or humorous programs. If the production is formal, performers may wear suits or long gowns; if the production is more informal, casual clothing like jeans, sweatshirts, etc. may be used.

The only real requirement is that the performers' clothing supplements and supports the production and does not distract or call attention to itself.

Properties

To use or not to use properties is another question whose answer depends on the particular script being presented. Will the use of a literal prop help illuminate the script? Will it be in the way with frequent shifts in locale? Will a literal prop fit into the overall production plan? Will the use of a real prop add significance to the production if no other prop is literalized?

Since much is left up to the imagination in readers theatre, most properties are imagined, too. This does not mean that no literal props may be employed. Rather, use only what will best serve to illuminate, clarify, and animate the script being presented. In a readers theatre production of the John Dennis play, *Hannah*, the only literal prop was a pillow that the two orphaned girls used to suffocate the unwelcome new girl, Hannah.

If the literal use of a property helps convey your production concept, by all means use it. There is, of course, a practical reason for not using a real property. If it is not needed in subsequent scenes and there is no logical means of getting it offstage, it will be in the way. It might be better to mime it. When Baby in *The Death of Everymom* says about her breakfast, "it's on the floor," and then pantomimes picking up her plate and throwing it on the floor, the audience knows and reacts to what has happened. The imagination is a wonderfully creative faculty. With the use of proper behavioral synecdoches, most properties will be clearly envisioned by the audience even though they are not actually on stage.

Media

Many readers theatre productions are enhanced by the use of music, sound effects, projections, electronic sounds, tapes, and other such devices. Too often, however, enthusiasm over mixed-media effects results in their taking over a show instead of adding dimension to it. The general rule is: if in doubt, do without. In readers theatre, as we have emphasized, the performer and the script should carry the ball.

A few samples of how music and sound have been used in various scripts will be useful. In Norman Corwin's radio script, "My Client Curley," a popular tune of the time with which the comedy deals, "Yes, Sir, That's My Baby," is heard many times, sometimes as a harmonica solo and once even with a full orchestra. In a production mentioned in chapter two—"The Gladdest Things in the Toyroom," a compiled script on the destruction of a relationship—the main characters are called Jack and Jill. As the show begins and the couple first meet as young children, the song "Jack and Jill went up the hill to fetch a pail of water . . ." is played with joyous simplicity. At the end of the show, once Jack and Jill's relationship has dissipated, the song is heard again, this time in a minor key and with complex chords.

Like lighting, music can help reinforce scene changes or transitions from one section of a script to the next. Think about appropriate music to include to make transitions clear.

Slides are often useful in creating time and place. In "The Parade's Gone By," a compiled script on old-time radio from the turn of the century to the 1950s, Winston Jones employed period music and slides to point up the years involved. The slide sequence included recognizable political personalities, clothing styles, automobile styles, and other memorabilia accompanied by characteristic songs and sound effects over the sound system. In the opening moments of the production of *The Glass Menagerie* mentioned earlier, as Tom, the narrator of the play, returns home after years as a merchant seaman, slides of significant moments of the life he led with his mother and his sister were projected on a scrim to help motivate his opening monologue. One of Tom's most important memories is his father, who left the family years earlier. To highlight the importance of this memory to Tom, oversized pictures of his father appeared at various places on the stage walls in three-dimensional frames.

Vocal sounds such as humming or the sounds of a crowd muttering or exclaiming often add a dimension to the scene. When used, exercise great care and judgment in selecting the appropriate effects and then proceed to integrate them skillfully and subtly into the presentation as a whole.

Other mixed-media devices include film, artwork, projections, modern dance, electronic sounds, tapes, or whatever media comes to mind and is purposeful. Care must be exercised, as has been emphasized, to avoid blurring the impact of the script with these elements of spectacle. An example of effective use of dance was in the production of Lorca's poem "Lament for Ignacio Sanchez Mejias," in which a dancer symbolically danced the bullfight and, on the lines describing the blood on the sand, let the black, red-lined cloak sink to the floor, red side revealed.

These, then, are the physical elements of a readers theatre production: settings, lighting, costumes, properties, and mixed-media devices. Whatever is done in the way of using and combining costuming, music, lighting, and set pieces should be done in harmony with the script, and should provide insight into the material. The suggestive rather than the explicit, the nonrealistic rather than the realistic, should be employed as the nonrealistic often allows more options for creativity and greater use of the imagination.

Evaluating Your Script and Production

Once your script has been produced, ask yourself the following questions:

Script Analysis
1. Is the theme or purpose of the script clear?
2. If you are dealing with a compiled script, is the assertion clear?
3. If you are dealing with a collage compiled script, is the structure clear?
4. What is the mode of your script?
5. On what basis were lines assigned to particular voices?
6. Examine the dynamics of the script. Does it have builds and releases? Is there a climax? What contributes to the dynamics of the script?
7. Are the relationships between or among the characters clear?

Production Analysis
1. Is your production concept clear?
2. Is there a theatrical complement?
3. Does your staging underscore the important themes or images in your script?
4. How will focus be used?
5. What conventions will you use to underscore the presentational nature of this medium?
6. How will spectacle elements be added?

Post-Production Analysis
1. If you had it to do again, what would you do differently? How would you change the script, and why? How would you change the production, and why?

2. For an expanded program compiled script, how are the selections organized? Is it clear why we moved from one selection to another? How might they have been ordered differently?

3. For a collage compiled script, how might the materials have been structured in another way?

4. What special problems did you have orchestrating, compiling, or directing this readers theatre production? How did you solve them? What would you do differently next time?

Summary

In this chapter, we described the physical necessities of producing readers theatre scripts. When casting readers theatre, type casting is not recommended. The nonrealistic nature of readers theatre allows for flexibility in casting.

Blocking in readers theatre involves moving the performers in relation to each other and to any furniture or set pieces that may be included. Downstage is a stronger position on stage than upstage, and strong crosses should be made downstage of furniture and other performers. Blocking varies depending on whether you are working on a proscenium stage, where the audience sits in front of the performers and usually at some distance, an alley stage, an in-the-round stage, or a thrust stage.

Focus is a complicated matter in readers theatre. The most common type of focus employed is offstage audience focus, where the audience is directly addressed, or offstage cross focus where performers imagine seeing each other in and directly above the audience members' heads. Another focus option is onstage focus where performers look at each other, playing profile to the audience.

Action and movement in readers theatre depend on economy and suggestion. Literalizing movement is often not possible, and consequently action must be symbolic rather than realistic to keep the scene in the audience's imagination.

As with action and movement, setting and set pieces are often symbolic rather than literal. Synecdoche—using a part to represent the whole—is often true of setting requirements, and stools, benches, ladders, blocks, and so on, may be used to suggest many other things.

Lighting is important in readers theatre not only to illuminate the faces of the performers, but to enhance mood, help with transitions, and suggest where the audience's focus should be at any given time.

Costumes also may be suggestive rather than literal. Adding shawls, collars, hats, and the like may help a performer quickly switch from one character to another. Properties may be literalized if very significant to the scene, or mimed if literalization is not necessary.

Such media as slides, music, film, and video may be employed as long as their inclusion adds to the production's impact and does not interfere with the audience's comprehension of the language.

Notes

[1] Edwin Wilson, *The Theatre Experience* (New York: McGraw-Hill, 1975), pp. 282–284.

[2] Marion and Marvin Kleinau, "Scene Location in Readers Theatre: Static or Dynamic?" *The Speech Teacher* 14, no. 3 (September 1965), p. 198.

[3] See Leslie Irene Coger and Sharon Pelham, "Kinesics Applied to Readers Theatre," *The Speech Teacher* 24, no. 2 (March 1975), pp. 91–99; Leslie Irene Coger, "Kinesics in Interpreters Theatre," *Readers Theatre News* (Spring 1975), pp. 6–7; and Ray L. Birdwhistell, *Kinesics and Context: Essays on Body Motion Communication* (Philadelphia: University of Pennsylvania Press, 1970).

[4] Allardyce Nicoll, *Development of Theatre*, 3rd ed. (New York: Harcourt Brace Jovanovich, 1946), p. 202. Also see Arnold Rood, "After the Practice the Theory: Gordon Craig and Movement, *Theatre Research* 11, nos. 2 & 3 (1971), pp. 114–132.

[5] Nicoll, *Development of Theatre*, p. 203. Also see Graham Woodruff, "Terence Gray and Theatre Design," *Theatre Research* 11, nos 2 & 3 (1971), pp. 114–132.

[6] Also see Willard F. Bellman, *Scenography and Stage Technology* (New York: Thomas Y. Crowell, 1977) for trends in staging; particularly good on the "master symbol," pp. 9–11.

[7] Christie A. Logan, "Form and Rhythm in Compilation Productions: Progressing the Audience's Field of Experience." An unpublished manuscript presented at the Speech Communication Association Convention, Boston, MA, Nov. 1987.

[8] From Charles Schultz, *You're a Good Man, Charlie Brown* (New York: Random House, 1967, 1968). Copyright ©1967, 1968 by Clark Gesner.

[9] Ibid.

[10] From "Found Space," unpublished essay by K. B. Valentine, Arizona State University, Tempe.

[11] Milly S. Barranger, *Theatre: A Way of Seeing*, 3rd ed. (Belmont, CA: Wadsworth, 1991), p. 146.

Chapter Four

Chamber Theatre:
Creating the Script

Chamber theatre is a technique for staging prose fiction texts: short stories and novels. In this chapter, we will concentrate on those elements of a prose fiction text that must be analyzed in preparation for a staged adaptation. The first half of this chapter concentrates specifically on understanding the complex role of the narrator and the narrator's point of view. The second half of this chapter focuses on adapting prose fiction texts for the stage. In chapter five, we focus on staging your adapted scripts.

As we discussed in chapter two, you must understand your selection before you can begin to adapt it for the stage. The type of analysis that reveals the most pertinent information for performance is the dramatistic analysis, which attempts to answer the following seven questions: who is speaking, to whom, about what, where, when, how, and why. The answers to these essential questions will provide you with the basic information you need to begin your adaptation and to devise your production concept—your particular approach to the material.

Robert S. Breen developed the idea for chamber theatre in the 1940s as a way to feature the narrative voice. In chamber theatre, you focus on the narrator as he or she is responsible for creating every aspect of the story. Breen considered the narrator the most important element in a prose fiction text, and believed that the strongest performer should be cast in this important role. He originated chamber theatre as a technique for staging prose fiction texts—especially epic-mode prose fiction texts where there is a strong interplay between narrators and the characters they re-create.

Breen defined chamber theatre as follows:

> [Chamber Theatre] is a method of preparing and presenting undramatized fiction for the stage, as written, the only changes being those to accommodate the limitation of time, physical stage set-up, or number of actors. . . . What an audience sees in a Chamber Theatre production bears some resemblance to a traditional play—there are characters speaking dialogue, expressing emotions in a plotted action, and giving all the evidence of vital immediacy. What distinguishes the production from a conventional play, however, is the use of the author's narration to create setting and atmosphere and more important, to explore the motivations of the characters at the moment of action.[1]

Chamber Theatre and Conventional Theatre

Breen's definition suggests that there are similarities between chamber theatre productions and conventional theatre productions. A story is told, place and time are indicated, and characters speak dialogue and interact with each other. As we pointed out in chapter one, many times audiences view productions such as *Nicholas Nickleby, The Grapes of Wrath, A Clockwork Orange, Les Miserables, Dr. Jekyll and Mr. Hyde, The Trial* and never realize that they are seeing adaptations of narrative fiction.

What differentiates chamber theatre from conventional theatre productions?

The major differences may be summarized as follows:

- Chamber theatre stages epic-mode prose fiction (fiction that features a strong interplay between narrator and characters) rather than plays.

- Chamber theatre maintains the narrator as the central and major "character."

- Chamber theatre stages stories that have already happened; stories written in the past tense rather than in the present tense of most plays. Chamber theatre deals, then, with "vicarious experience" rather than "witnessed event."

In conventional theatre adaptations of many stories and novels, the mode becomes dramatic (defined characters speaking to each other). The narrator is often eliminated, and the story is rewritten so that only characters speak as if the events were happening now for the first time. Therefore, the narrator's particular stance, way of speaking, inside views and privileged information about characters and their motivations are also eliminated. As Breen writes, "Chamber theatre is not interested in the problems of transforming fiction into drama: it resists the temptation to delete narrative descriptions and rewrite summaries as dialogue. No effort is made in Chamber Theatre to eliminate the narrative point of view which characterizes fiction; indeed, the storyteller's angle of vision is emphasized through physical representation on the stage."[2] Frank Galati, a former student of Breen's and a Tony Award-winning adapter and director for *The Grapes of Wrath*, agrees. In an interview in *The New York Times* before his adaptation was to appear on public television's "American Playhouse," Galati said, "It was never my purpose to 'turn' this novel into a play, to change its modality. I sought to find out what the novel itself would feel like if it took to the stage."[3] In chamber theatre, then, we feature the narrator and we are told not only what characters said and did, but also how they thought and felt and what motivated them. This has to do with the difference between "telling" and "showing."

Conventional theatre ordinarily concentrates on "showing" us experiences that seemingly are happening now. We are to believe that the actors are speaking their lines and hearing their cues for the first time. There is an element of spontaneity. Chamber theatre, on the other hand, deals both with "showing" and "telling." The narrator *tells* us directly some parts of the story including, as Breen writes, "the motivations of the characters," and at other times the narrator allows the characters to *show* us what happened. Remember, though, that in chamber theatre, we stage narrative memory; we see only what the narrator remembers or wants us to see. The narrator is the only one who exists in the **virtual present**—the time in which the narrator tells us the story. He or she tells us a story about an equally **virtual past**—the time in which the events of the story took place. We say *virtual* "because it is 'embodied' and 'objectified' in the literary work, has a sharable public presence and 'a kind of "permanent presence" not possible in any case of actual experience.'"[4] In chamber theatre then, we deal with both the now and the then, the present and the past, telling and showing. Much of this is determined by understanding the narrator's perspective or **point of view**.

Narrative Point of View

First, it is important to point out that although the author of a story is extremely important, we must differentiate between the author who is the speaker *of* the story and the narrator who is the speaker *in* the story. When adapting and staging a fiction text, we are not concerned with trying to impersonate authors onstage, but rather the narrators they create. (There are exceptions to this, though. In some stories and novels, especially in some postmodern texts which we will discuss later, the authors cannot resist putting themselves inside their stories. Kurt Vonnegut, Jr., for example, often creates himself as a character in his works. In his novel *Breakfast of Champions*, for example, he disguises himself, enters the Holiday Inn where his two major characters will have their climactic confrontation, and ultimately sets one of his characters "free." These are special cases, though, not the norm.) The narrator may be like the author, may share a similar perspective or attitude, but the narrator is a fictive creation, someone who lives and breathes only in this work, and adapters are free to interpret them through their particular vision. As you begin to tackle adapting a story for the stage, discover first the narrator's point of view—the perspective he or she takes on the story. Understanding the point of view will guide you in determining the role of the narrator and his or her relationship with the characters in the story. There are three general categories of points of view: first person, third person, and the less common second person.

First-Person Narrators

First-person narrators tell their own, personal stories, and refer to themselves using the pronouns "I" or "we." They are participants in the events they relate as well as the narrator of them—they are both in and out of the action. There are three kinds of first-person narrators: **first-person major character, first-person minor character**, and **nonparticipating witness**.

A first-person major character narrator is a major participant in the story and relates events in which he or she played a major role in the past. These narrators are usually fully developed characters, and in production they are fully dramatized. Character-narrators include Mark Twain's Huckleberry Finn, Charlotte Brontë's Jane Eyre, Holden Caulfield in Salinger's *The Catcher in the Rye*, and Sister in Eudora Welty's short story "Why I live at the P.O."

First-person major character narrators, on first analysis, may seem highly reliable and credible since they were actually there at the time the events occurred. This, though, is what makes their stories not quite as believable as one might think. Since these narrators are central to their tales, they may not have the distance or objectivity of someone not as closely involved. The driver of a car involved in an automobile accident, for example, may not be the most reliable witness of the events that occurred during the accident. Unreliability is a complex term that has many manifestations. Narrators may be considered unreliable if they:

- distort the truth in order to persuade us to believe their versions of the stories,
- are too young or inarticulate to turn impressions into accurate expressions,
- are mentally incapacitated, or
- are just unaware or unconscious of the reality of their situations.

Some first-person major character narrators are outright liars or at least misleaders. In "Why I Live at the P.O.," for example, Sister exhibits paranoid tendencies, and interprets threats which originate from inside her own mind as coming from members of her family. She exaggerates details beyond the realm of possibility, and occasionally recounts incidents which occurred when she was not present. Holden Caulfield misrepresents the truth because he does not understand or appreciate the real motivation behind his actions. He tries to appear intelligent and suave to hide his teenage confusion and lack of self-confidence.

Some first-person major character narrators are unreliable because a disparity exists between the events and their ability to describe them— possibly because of youth, inexperience, limited vocabulary, or naïveté. Huckleberry Finn, for example, is a young boy telling of experiences he really does not have the language or vocabulary to relate accurately. The narrator in Joyce Carol Oates' short story "The Molesters" also is unable to understand or articulate the experience she undergoes. Some first-person major character narrators are incapable of explaining their situations because they are mentally incapacitated; for example, Benjy, the thirty-year-old narrator in Faulkner's *The Sound and the Fury*.

In other cases, first-person major character narrators' accounts are inaccurate, skewed, or just plain wrong. A dramatic series on television entitled "My So-Called Life," featured a major character, Angela, who was a fifteen-year-old unreliable narrator. She was blinded by love for an unresponsive hunk named Jordan Catalano. In one episode, we heard her voice-over narration, "Our conversations are really deep and meaningful." Then, we hear one of their conversations:

Angela: There's a tiny leaf in your hair.
Jordan: A what?
Angela: A leaf.

Not particularly deep or meaningful, but it is to Angela. She is an unreliable narrator because she is unable to perceive the inaccuracy of her perceptions.

A second type of first-person narrator is a minor character rather than a major participant. These narrators tend to be more reliable than first-person major character narrators because they are somewhat outside the core of the story and therefore are more objective. Since they maintain some distance, they tend to inspire the audience's trust and identification with their believable, first-hand accountings. (Although reliable narrators seem objective, even these narrators have opinions, prejudices, and attitudes that color their storytelling.) Ishmael in Herman Melville's *Moby Dick*, Nick Carraway in *The Great Gatsby*, and Dr. Watson in the Sherlock Holmes stories are first-person minor character narrators.

The third type of first-person narrator is the nonparticipating witness. Unlike most first-person narrators, we often know very little about the nature of these narrators. Often they are unnamed. They are less subjective than the other two types because they merely observe the action and report what happened. The narrator of William Faulkner's "A Rose for Emily" is such a narrator. The narrator in this story never refers to himself or herself, and uses "we" as if speaking for the entire town.

The narrator's point of view is not always consistent throughout a story. A first-person major character narrator could at moments in the story become a first-person minor character narrator if he or she shifts the focus of attention to someone else. A first-person minor character narrator may become major if the story seems to revolve around him or her at any particular time.

Third-Person Narrators

While first-person narrators are called this because they refer to themselves with the first-person pronoun "I," there is no parallel construct with third-person narrators. While they do use the third-person pronouns "he" and "she" when telling their stories, they are not referring to themselves but to the characters. Third-person is, therefore, really a misnomer. Third-person narrators are really first-person narrators who do not refer to themselves but instead concentrate on the characters and their exploits. This does not mean that the narrator is not important or central, it just means that these narrators are undramatized, and were not involved in the past actions they relate.

There are two kinds of third-person narrators: **third-person omniscient** and **third-person observer**. The all-knowing omniscient narrators see into the minds and hearts of the characters. They know what everyone thinks and feels, and they know *why*. There are two kinds of third-person omniscient narrators. While omniscient narrators know what every character is thinking or feeling, for various reasons they may not reveal this information to us. They may want to keep some elements a surprise or they may want to withhold information in order to encourage us to identify with one character rather than another. If a narrator reveals what every character thinks and feels, this is called **total omniscience**. If a narrator only reveals what one or two characters think or feel, this is known as **limited omniscience**. Henry James speaks of this limited omniscient narrator as being the "center of consciousness." He or she is a *reflector* of the major character.

Omniscient narrators have God-like abilities: they can bridge large expanses of time and space and reveal information no mortal could reveal. Why, then, do we say that third-person omniscient narrators are unreliable? We've already mentioned that such narrators may not always reveal everything they know. This is one aspect of their unreliability. Another aspect deals with what they *do* reveal. Often what omniscient narrators share with us are the direct thoughts of a character. The narrator, for example, could say:

> Mary Roberts was aware of her amazing beauty. She realized every man in town was totally enamored of her and would give anything to spend just one evening with her. She could have her choice, but which one would she choose?

While what the narrator tells us Mary Roberts is thinking is true, Mary's thoughts may not accurately reflect reality. Mary may have an inflated opinion of herself. The narrator reliably conveys what Mary is thinking, but the unreliable aspect is that what Mary is thinking is subjective and skewed and creates an impression that may not be accurate.

Works with omniscient narrators include Twain's *Tom Sawyer*, every story by Flannery O'Connor, and James Joyce's "The Boarding House."

A second type of third-person narrator is the impersonal, objective observer, who can see no more than a camera can. Objective observers are interested in telling us only what the characters in the story said or did. Objective observers, like omniscient narrators, are outside the stories they tell and were not involved in the action. These are probably the most reliable narrators, although even these objective observers have opinions, a vested interest in the stories they tell, and a rhetorical purpose in telling them. An objective observer narrator, for example, could tell us that "Brian walked through the doorway," or "Brian flitted into the room," or "Brian fell over the threshold as he entered the room." Each of these phrases is told by an observer narrator, but each reveals a different attitude toward Brian. The attitude of all narrators is an extremely important element to project in performance. Check the language closely—especially the adjectives and adverbs—for clues to the narrator's attitude.

Works with third-person observer narrators include "A Clean, Well-Lighted Place," and "The Killers" by Ernest Hemingway and "The Third Prize" by A. E. Coppard.

Again, point of view is not always consistent. On occasion, a third-person omniscient narrator may seem to be observing events without revealing interior thoughts. Notice when the narrator is omniscient, and when the narrator is observing.

Second-Person Narrators

The second-person point of view is rare, but is becoming more and more prevalent, especially in contemporary, postmodern literature. In second-person stories, the narrator uses the pronoun "you." This technique, says Irene Kacandes, "presumes to efface the boundary between fiction and reality by talking directly to the reader."[5] We are invited to become part of the work, to become more actively involved in the creation of the events.

The difficulty and complexity of these stories surround the identification of this slippery "you." Is the "you" the reader? Is the "you" the narrator? Is the "you" the author? Is the "you" some character in the story? The answer varies depending on the work. In Italo Calvino's postmodern novel *If on a Winter's Night a Traveler*, for example, Calvino consciously reflects on this confusion when his narrator says:

From *If on a Winter's Night a Traveler* by Italo Calvino

(Don't believe that the book is losing sight of you, Reader. The you that was shifted to the Other Reader can, at any sentence, be addressed to you again. You are always a possible you. Who would dare sentence you to loss of the you, a catastrophe as terrible as the loss of the I. For a second-person discourse to become a novel, at least two you's are required, distinct and concomitant, which stand out from the crowd of he's, she's, and they's.)

While second-person stories are rare, they are becoming increasingly popular. Readers enjoy these works because they present a kind of game to be played between the author and the reader. We get involved in the story because we feel a part of it, and because there is often an intriguing puzzle to solve. This presents interesting possibilities for performance which we will consider in chapter five.

EXPERIMENT

While it is difficult to analyze the point of view without reading the entire story, see if you can determine the point of view of the passages below and identify the distinguishing characteristics of the narrators.

1. He was always busy, Toshiko's husband. Even tonight he had to dash off to an appointment, leaving her to go home alone by taxi. But what else could a woman expect when she married an actor—an attractive one? No doubt she had been foolish to hope that he would spend the evening with her. And yet he must have known how she dreaded going back to their house, unhomely with its Western-style furniture and with the bloodstains still showing on the floor. (From "Swaddling Clothes" by Yukio Mishima.)

2. She was a beautiful baby. The first and only one of our five that was beautiful at birth. You do not guess how new and uneasy her tenancy in her now-loveliness. You did not know her all those years she was thought homely, or see her poring over her baby pictures, making me tell her over and over how beautiful she had been—and would be, I would tell her—and was now, to the seeing eye. But the seeing eyes were few or nonexistent. Including mine. (From "I Stand Here Ironing" by Tillie Olsen.)

3. You are about to begin reading Italo Calvino's new novel *If on a Winter's Night a Traveler*. Relax. Concentrate. Dispel every other thought. Let the world around you fade. Best to close the door; the TV is always on in the next room. Tell the others right away, "No, I don't want to watch TV!" Raise your voice—they won't hear you otherwise—"I'm reading! I don't want to be disturbed!" Maybe they haven't heard you, with all that racket; speak louder, yell: "I'm beginning to read Italo Calvino's new novel!" (From *If on a Winter's Night a Traveler* by Italo Calvino.)

4. I got another barber that comes over from Carterville and helps me out Saturdays, but the rest of the time I can get along all right alone. You can see for yourself that this ain't no New York City and besides that, the most of the boys works all day and don't have no leisure to drop in here and get themselves prettied up.

You're a newcomer, ain't you? I thought I hadn't seen you round before. I hope you like it good enough to stay. As I say, we ain't no New York City or Chicago, but we have pretty good times. Not as good, though, since Jim Kendall got killed. When he was alive, him and Hod Meyers used to keep this town in an uproar. I bet they was more laughin' done here than any town its size in America.

Jim was comical, and Hod was pretty near a match for him. Since Jim's gone, Hod tries to hold his end up just the same as ever, but it's tough goin' when you ain't got nobody to kind of work with. (From "Haircut" by Ring Lardner.)

Narrator and Time

One of the responsibilities of the narrator is to manipulate time. If the amount of time which elapsed in the virtual past was 24 hours—**story time**—the narrator is free to decide what part of that 24-hour story will be told in the virtual present, and how much time each part of the story will take—**discourse time**. In prose fiction, the rhythm of the story is primarily determined by the narrator's manipulation of time in terms of summary, scene, and description. Since the narrator already knows the ending of the story before retelling it, the narrator has the option of condensing some details that may not seem important, **summary**; maintaining the actual time frame in which an event occurred, **scene**; or stretching out some events to give them added significance, **description**. Because the events of the story have already taken place, the narrator decides how to retell them, which elements to stress, and which elements to minimize or eliminate based on the point of view.

When the narrator shortens events or capsulizes long sequences of time, he or she uses summary, and discourse time is faster than story time. If the narrator says, "She woke up early, went to work, got fired, drove to the bar, had two vodkas on the rocks, and went home," the narrator uses summary. Summary lines are usually epic in mode and are usually spoken by the narrator.

Scene occurs when discourse time is equal to story time. Scene exists when the narrator's use of time in telling the story is equal to the actual amount of time needed for the events to occur. Scene, then, would exist when characters are engaged in dialogue since it would take as long for the characters to say those lines in the present as it did in the past, or any time the narrator's retelling of an action takes as long to say as it did to enact, as in, "She took two steps forward," or "She picked up the bottle of wine." Dramatic-mode moments, then, are usually scenic.

When narrators elaborate on the narrative line, making events take longer and seem more detailed than they actually were, the narrator uses description, and discourse time is slower than story time. An example of a descriptive line is, "Her hair was long and blond, tied back with an ornamental barrette, which glimmered in the sunlight like an oriental doll." The example just cited is a descriptive line in the epic mode.

When a narrator goes into the mind of a character and tells us what he or she is thinking or feeling (often lyric-mode moments), these mental narratives may also be told in scene, summary, or description. If the narrator says, "She thought about the man she saw on the beach," it would be *lyric scene. Lyric summary* would sound like this: "She thought about the man on the beach, the groceries she needed to buy, the house that needed cleaning, and the deposit she needed to make at the bank." If the narrator were to say, "She thought about the man in the white trousers, blue shirt, brown sandals, and metal-framed glasses who had smiled at her so alluringly that sunny, Monday morning," it would be *lyric description.*

Narrative Style

When analyzing the "how" of a story—the manner in which the narrator tells the story—you are dealing with matters of style which involve diction (language) and syntax (the way words and sentences are linked). Studying narrators' diction and syntax will help you determine the attitude and personality of undefined, third-person narrators, in particular, who are not characters defined in the story.

If "language makes the man [or woman]" then analyzing the language in a story can help you make important decisions about the kinds of narrators you are dealing with. Look first at the words the narrator uses. Are they short and simple ("The woman walked down the street") or are they more complex and unusual ("The woman pranced down the avenue like a prized colt")? Are the words charged with emotion ("He despised everything about her") or are they more tempered and controlled ("There were things about her which he did not appreciate")? Does the narrator tend toward judgment ("She could never make up her mind") or description ("She thought about what he said")? Does the narrator employ the vernacular of the character ("bidnis" for "business"), jargon (language of a specific group, for example actors talk of "scrims" or "backlighting") or slang ("ain't" for "is not")? Word choice may include regionalisms ("aw, shucks"), idioms ("like water off a duck's back"), or old-fashioned words ("dollop"). Word choice, then, is a good place to begin to differentiate specific types of narrators.

Syntax is the second major element of style that can be analyzed to help you understand the personality of the narrator. Normal syntax involves subject, verb, direct object or predicate adjective: "She handed him the spoon," "She wore a blue dress." When narrators use convoluted or unusual syntax ("Home is where he always desired to go" or "The dress in which she was attired was pale blue"), they may be revealing a poetic inclination. When narrators create cause-effect patterns, employing such words as "because" or "therefore," they usually are displaying a careful reasoning process. Types of sentences are also indicators of personality. Long or complex sentences give an impression of formality, whereas short exclamations tend to suggest speed and informality, or perhaps an impulsive nature. Narrators who use rhetorical questions often foster a closeness or intimacy between themselves and their audiences.

If you can describe the narrator's style, you often can describe the narrator. In a text entitled *Tough, Sweet and Stuffy: An Essay on Modern American Prose Styles*, Walker Gibson describes the three title styles as exemplars of specific authors. According to Gibson, Marvell's "To His Coy Mistress," an editorial in *Sports Illustrated*, a letter from Raymond Chandler, and the writings of Gertrude Stein are "mostly tough." Novels by Hayden Carruth, articles in *Glamour* magazine, and United Air Lines instructions for emergency escape are "mostly sweet." Jerome Bruner, Paul Tillich, and a newsletter from the New Jersey State Division on Aging are "mostly stuffy." Mixed styles are exemplified in works by William James, Henry James, Erich Fromm, William Faulkner, and Jack Kerouac, among others.[6]

How an undefined narrator speaks, then, is an important indicator and often is the only insight you have to determine that narrator's personality and attitude.

Narrative Roles

Narrators are as varied and diverse as human beings. The study of the narrator's function or role is essential in the adaptation and staging of prose fiction texts. Narrators are responsible for determining which events to tell and in which order, and for controlling the audience's view of these events and the characters in them in accordance with their unique perspectives or points of view. The performer cast in the challenging role of the narrator needs to be given tangible cues to help in performance.

Some narrators are defined characters, such as Sister in "Why I Live at the P.O." or Huckleberry Finn or Nick Carraway or Holden Caulfield, and consequently clues for performing them can be found in the text and analyzed accordingly. These narrators speak dialogue as well as narration, and we learn about them from what they say and do. Some narrators, however, are outside the story, and are undefined—not "characters" in the stories they tell. They do not speak dialogue, as they are not participants in the story. The gender, for example, of these narrators is not even specified. (Thus, knowing whether to cast a man or a woman to play these roles is often a difficult matter. The general rule is if the author and major character are female, cast a woman. If the author and major character are male, cast a man. The assumption being that women are better able to know other women, and men are better able to know other men—even though this might not always be true!) When performing undramatized narrators, the performer must depend on a close study of the narrator's language and syntax to help define the narrator's "role." It is not enough to know that the narrator is third-person omniscient or third-person observer. As Wayne C. Booth explains, point of view alone tells "us nothing of importance unless we become more precise and describe how the particular qualities of the narrators relate to specific effects."[7] Joanna Hawkins Maclay says that it is necessary to find a role relationship for the narrator—a relationship that the narrator has to the story, to the audience, and to the characters within the story. Maclay says that when staging chamber theatre productions, we must translate the psychological relationship between narrator and character into social terms—find social roles as metaphors for psychological roles.[8] Think of all the plays you have seen with narrators in them. What do all these narrators have in common? They are all defined characters. Audiences expect to see identifiable characters onstage. They are not accustomed to seeing a third person narrator talking to them—a narrator who doesn't play a social role in the story. (One musical with an undefined narrator is *Into the Woods*, and he is summarily killed and returns as a defined character!)

Ascribing a specific role to a third-person narrator gives the performer something tangible to work with. When defining these roles, though, we do not turn them into characters, instead we are dealing with metaphoric equivalences. In Saki's "The Open Window," for example, the narrator is depicted as a "butler" in the home of Mrs. Sappleton (see the adaptation of this story in chapter eight). He is not literally a butler, though, since Saki did not make this clear in the story. The actor assaying this role, however, acts "like" a butler. He opens the door for Framton, takes his coat and "letters of introduction," announces him to Mrs. Sappleton, serves refreshments, etc. We interpret him in this way because he seems to be a fixture in the home; he knows the niece is lying but keeps quiet and remains loyal to the family. (By keeping quiet, he also keeps the ending a surprise.)

There are many potential roles that narrators can play based on discoveries in a text. In addition to the metaphoric social roles of butler (narrator may seem servile or eager to assist), or lover (narrator may seem enamored or attracted to a character), or confidant (narrator assumes the role of friend or advisor), etc., there are more generalized roles narrators may assume. Three of these potential roles are narrator as moralizer, narrator as double, and narrator as camera eye.

Narrator As Moralizer

Narrators assume the role of **moralizer** when they openly or subtly comment on or judge the characters to sway audience response. Moralizers establish our sympathies as well as determine the degree of distance we should feel. Whatever "moral" message the writer wants to convey, the moralizer-narrator normally makes the point clear through commentary to the audience. The narrators in Aesop's fables and in the contemporary fables by James Thurber, for example, are moralizers who give us "the message" in a moral at the end. One way to play the moralizer is to adopt a ministerial demeanor, but there are a wide range of moralizing equivalents, some loaded with negative connotations! Some metaphoric equivalences are narrator as "teacher" (especially an extremely didactic one), or "preacher" (especially one bent on constant sermonizing), all-knowing "counselor" or "psychiatrist," etc. In general, moralizers tell us exactly how and what to feel, evaluate the situation, and often are self-righteous people who believe they have all the answers. Writers like O. Henry, Saki, and Guy de Maupassant write stories with ironic reversals—usually involving moral dilemmas. In the following passage from O. Henry's "The Gift of the Magi," the narrator begins by ridiculing and patronizing the poverty-stricken newlyweds.

From "The Gift of the Magi"
by O. Henry

Three times Della counted it. One dollar and eighty-seven cents. And the next day would be Christmas. There was clearly nothing to do but flop down on the shabby little couch and howl. So Della did it. Which instigates the moral reflection that life is made up of sobs, sniffles, and smiles, with sniffles predominating.

O. Henry's commentary continues in much the same manner through-out the story until, at the end, the narrator gives the "moral," reduces the distance and the irony, and, by contrast, allows the audience to get emotionally close to the sacrificing couple:

But in a last word to the wise of these days let it be said that of all who give gifts these two were the wisest. Of all who give and receive gifts, such as they are wisest. Everywhere they are wisest. They are the magi.

Narrator As Double

Another role narrators may assume is the major character's **double**. The double narrator has also been called the "alter ego" or "mirror image" or "second self." These narrators are often first-person major characters who manifest two separate personalities, or third-person omniscient narrators privileged with inside information about the major character. The double narrator usually has a twofold function: (1) to help the audience understand the complexity of characters' minds and personalities, and (2) to enable characters to come to clearer understandings of themselves by improving, or in some cases, destroying self-concepts, or by making characters aware of parts of themselves that have been denied. Claire Rosenfield asserts that with Freud's stress on human irrationality, the double became a more forceful and inescapable reality. We are compelled to admit "the possibility that each of us has within us a second self dwelling inside the eminently civilized, eminently rational self."[9]

Double narrators often act as the major character's best friend or confessor; but they may also act as the major character's evil side depending on the text. Think, for example, of two of the most famous double novels: *The Picture of Dorian Gray* by Oscar Wilde and *Dr. Jekyll and Mr. Hyde* by Robert Louis Stevenson. *Dorian Gray* is a duplicate double story. The first self, the forever young Dorian, faces his reflected second self which is represented by a hideously aging portrait. In *Jekyll and Hyde*, we are introduced to a divided self. Here the double underlines the division of good and evil in one person. Chamber theatre literalizes this duplication/division in human nature by employing the convention of bifurcation—casting two performers to play the same role. (There is a sense that the narrator is always "bifurcated" in chamber theatre productions. Since the narrator is really the only speaker in a prose fiction text, anytime characters are created as separate entities as they are in chamber theatre productions, the narrator has been split or divided.) Consequently, these doubles can be creatively realized in chamber theatre adaptations.

The appearance of the double is often signaled by the presence of long narrative passages (interior monologues) as characters question their goals, actions, past experiences, and so on. These passages may be adapted for chamber theatre as dialogues with the self. As discussed in chapter one, in Conrad Aiken's "Impulse," the narrator may be portrayed as Michael Lowes' double—in this case, his reversed mirror reflection—to magnify a division in Michael's personality. Breen suggests that when staging "Impulse" in chamber theatre, the opening passage could be adapted to read like an internal dialogue between the narrator, who represents Michael's "spontaneous and impulsive side," and Michael, who is basically "cautious, calculating, and shrewd."[10]

Initially, the double in literature was a representation of the immortal soul—a beneficial part of the self. Later views of the double interpret it as an evil, tempting, demonic apparition representing the accumulated malignancy in humans. C. F. Keppler delineates six specific types of doubles: Twin Brother, Pursuer, Tempter, Vision of Horror, Saviour, and Beloved.[11] In "Impulse," for example, the narrator could be portrayed as Michael's Tempter double, encouraging him to stray from his calculating, conservative ways.

In the following passage from Poe's "The Tell-Tale Heart," the first-person major character narrator is bifurcated into two selves: a submerged self (Narrator 1) and a projected self (Narrator 2). Narrator 1 is confused, nervous, and frightened. Narrator 2 is angry, defensive, but pretends to be calm and self-assured.

Chamber Theatre Adaptation
From "The Tell-Tale Heart"
by Edgar Allan Poe

Narrator 1 (*pacing, listening to an imaginary psychiatrist in the audience speak*): True!—nervous, very dreadfully nervous I had been and am

Narrator 2 (*seated center, speaks to audience as psychiatrists*): but why *will* you say that I am mad? (*He stands, seats Narrator 1 in chair he has vacated.*) The disease had sharpened my senses—not destroyed—not dulled them. Above all was the sense of hearing acute. I heard all things in the heaven and in the earth.

Narrator 1 (*to self*): I heard many things in hell.

Narrator 2 (*to doctors, frustrated with Narrator 1*): How, then, am I mad? (*Pacing, angry*) Hearken! and observe how healthily—how calmly I can tell you the whole story. (*Tries to get Narrator 1 to participate in the re-creation of the past scene with him.*)

Narrator 1 (*to Narrator 2*): It is impossible to say how first the idea entered my brain;

Narrator 2 (*to Narrator 1, as encouragement*): but once conceived, it haunted me day and night.

Narrator 1 (*to Narrator 2, as reasons why the deed should not have been done*): Object there was none. Passion there was none. (*Turns Narrator 2 to face him.*) I loved the old man. He had never wronged me. He had never given me insult. For his gold I had no desire.

Narrator 2 (*smiling, to psychiatrists*): I think it was his eye! Yes, it was this! (*Narrator 1 is despondent.*) He had the eye of a vulture—a pale blue eye, with a film over it. Whenever it fell upon me, my blood ran cold; and so by degrees—very gradually—I made up my mind to take the life of the old man, and thus rid myself of the eye forever.

Narrator As Camera Eye

Film has a great narrative potential and it therefore shares a close bond with prose fiction. Many narrators function in a similar manner to the camera in film in that the narrator, like the camera, filters experience through a particular lens. On the surface, the camera may seem to be an "innocent bystander," objectively recording what happens. In reality, however, it is this seeming objectivity that gives the camera its subtle ability to manipulate perception. Since it is assumed that the camera is objective and accurately reflects what it sees, this objectivity is often taken for granted. But the camera can shoot down on people making them seem small and insignificant; it can shoot up on people making them seem gigantic; it can zoom in, forcing us to perceive certain details; or it can distort images. As Breen writes, ". . . the narrator in certain novels can be seen profitably as a camera, not, however, simply as an objective eye, impersonal and lacking any capacity for interpreting surface events."[12]

Some of the characteristics that might signal that the narrator is assuming the role of the camera eye are:

1. *Minimal narrative intrusion.* There is a sense of scene seemingly without a narrator even though his or her presence is apparent in shot selection and arrangement. The unfolding of the story rather than the narrator's personality predominates. Many stories by Ernest Hemingway display camera-type narrators.

2. *Simultaneous action.* Although prose fiction is written serially (one thing happens and then another thing happens, etc.), a camera narrator can use the filmic technique of **crosscutting**—quick scene shifts from one locale to another—to give us this sense of simultaneity. Read Stephen Crane's story "The Bride Comes to Yellow Sky" for an example of the crosscutting technique as the narrator cuts back and forth from one parallel story line (town Marshall Jack Potter bringing his new bride home to Yellow Sky) to another (Scratchy Wilson getting progressively more intoxicated while waiting for a showdown with Potter).

3. *Attention to detail, angle, perspective.* The narrator acts like the camera when he or she focuses attention on certain images and "shoots" things from various angles and distances, both of which determine audience perception. The narrator's intense interest in detail, angle, and perspective is obvious in Robbe-Grillet's novel *Jealousy.* In Breen's production of *Jealousy,* for example, he conceived of the novel as a film being shot. In this concept he called the narrator the camera man, the one who selected the details to be filmed. In a similar way he gave all the narration that described what the characters wore to a narrator called the costumer. In this way, the division of the narration helped to convey his concept of the production as a film being shot.

Think, too, of the camera in terms of scene, summary, and description. When the narrator uses summary, the camera position is "panorama." The narrator is some distance from the events and sees the entire landscape of a situation. When the narrator uses scene, he or she moves in for a "close up" with an audible sound track. In this position, we see and hear dialogue between characters. When the narrator reveals detailed descriptions of people or objects, for example, this is an extreme close up and the narrator moves in even closer. The manipulation of time, then, can indicate narrative position and placement as well.

EXPERIMENT

Read the passages below and see if you can determine a social role to define the narrator's relationship with the characters. Stage these passages so that the narrator's relationship with the characters and with the audience is clarified.

1. The Crutchmans were so very, very happy and so temperate in all their habits and so pleased with everything that came their way that one was bound to suspect a worm in their rosy apple and that the extraordinary rosiness of the fruit was only meant to conceal the gravity and the depth of the infection. Their house, for instance, on Hill Street with all those big glass windows. Who but someone suffering from a guilt complex would want so much light to pour into their rooms? And all the wall-to-wall carpeting as if an inch of bare floor (there was none) would touch on some deep memory of unrequition and loneliness. And there was a certain necrophilic ardor to their gardening. Why be so intense about digging holes and planting seeds and watching them come up? Why this morbid concern with the earth? (From "The Worm in the Apple" by John Cheever.)

2. The waiter took the brandy bottle and another saucer from the counter inside the cafe and marched out to the old man's table. He put down the saucer and poured the glass full of brandy.

    "You should have killed yourself last week," he said to the deaf man. The old man motioned with his finger. "A little more," he said. The waiter poured on into the glass so that the brandy slopped over and ran down the stem into the top saucer of the pile. "Thank you," the old man said. The waiter took the bottle back inside the cafe. He sat down at the table with his colleague again. (From "A Clean, Well-Lighted Place" by Ernest Hemingway.)

3. Below Oldmeadow, in the green, shallow, soddened hollow of fields, lay a square, deep pond. Roving across the landscape, the doctor's quick eye detected a figure in black passing through the gate of the field, down towards the pond. He looked again. It would be Mabel Pervin. His mind suddenly became active and attentive. . . .

    He followed her minutely as she moved, direct and intent, like something transmitted rather than stirring in voluntary activity, straight down the field towards the pond. There she stood on the bank for a moment. She never raised her head. Then she waded slowly into the water.

    He stood motionless as the small black figure walked slowly and deliberately toward the centre of the pond, very slowly, gradually moving deeper into the motionless water, and still moving forward as the water got up to her breast. Then he could see her no more in the dusk of the dead afternoon. (From "The Horse Dealer's Daughter" by D. H. Lawrence.)

The Narrator's Rhetorical Voice and Audience

As we stated earlier, regardless of the narrator's point of view or role, all narrators are to some degree rhetorical. They have specific intentions when they tell their stories. Their primary intention, however, is to persuade audiences to view the stories from their particular points of view. Narrators are rarely, if ever, neutral about the stories they tell. Why would they bother recounting tales which they care little about, which left no impression, or which did not move them one way or the other? Decide, then, what the narrator's reason is for recounting this story. Ask yourself, "What is the theme or central idea of this story? What moral or concern is the narrator trying to share?" Let the answers to these questions affect how the narrator speaks and to whom.

In addition to the narrator's intentions in telling the story, decide also *to whom* this story would ideally be told. Since narrators in chamber theatre productions normally address the general audience, they must establish a relationship with audience members. Characterizing this audience is an important issue. While the identification of the audience is rarely literalized in a text, determining the nature and composition of this audience is a primary consideration in chamber theatre productions. Authors have "ideal audiences" in mind when they write their stories. Some readers may like a story because they fit that "ideal audience" profile; some readers may not because they do not fit the profile.

Occasionally, the nature of the narrator's audience may be identified in the story. In Ring Lardner's story "Haircut," the narrator, a barber, is talking to an unidentified customer. In "Why I Live at the P.O.," we know that when Sister is telling the story in the virtual present, she is in the China Grove, Mississippi post office. Since this is a small town where everyone already knows everyone else's business, it is unlikely that Sister's audience is composed of townspeople. Most likely she is addressing strangers—perhaps travelers who are passing through town and want to purchase postcards or stamps or mail a letter. The audience is probably not composed of people who expect to hear the postmistress' life story. How would that affect Sister's performance?

In most stories, though, the nature of the audience is a matter of individual interpretation. To assist you in discovering who the audience *might* be in any given text, consider the following:

1. *The subject matter of the story.* Stories about marriages, childrearing, love, hate, war, etc., might be more appropriate for some groups of people rather than others.

2. *The diction and syntax the narrator uses.* If the narrator uses highly sophisticated language, this might indicate a particular type of audience and exclude others. Stories for children often use a vocabulary that corresponds with the age level of the audience.

3. *The ending of the story.* Sometimes the ending of the story will indicate where the narrator must be at the beginning. Holden Caulfield in *The Catcher in the Rye*, for example, is in a mental hospital at the end of the story. So, since the story is in the past tense, in the virtual present telling of the story Holden is already in the institution. This helps limit the potential audiences Holden could be addressing. The audience could be composed of other institutional residents or perhaps psychiatrists. Whatever you decide, this decision must be incorporated into the narrator's performance. (Although the audience may not be able to assume or even realize the role that it has been ascribed, the narrator is still affected by this decision.) While the characters have a dialogue with each other, the narrator has a dialogue of sorts with this defined audience—who audience members are influences the way the narrator addresses them.

The discussion so far has dealt primarily with understanding the major element of prose fiction texts: the narrator. We are now ready to delve into the process of adapting prose fiction texts for the stage.

General Techniques for Adapting Prose Fiction Texts for the Stage

In chapter one, we spoke of the characteristics of lyric-, dramatic-, and epic-mode texts. Let us clarify each mode in relation to prose fiction texts. A lyric-mode text features an undefined narrator who uses more narration than dialogue. A dramatic-mode text features a defined narrator and more dialogue than narration. An epic-mode text features equal amounts of narration and dialogue. In chamber theatre, epic-mode prose fiction texts work best because epic-mode texts feature a strong relationship between narrator and characters. When we examine a text in terms of the nature of the speaker, the type of experience, and the elements of time and place we are dealing with the **external mode**.

Let us take this discussion one step further and discuss mode in terms of who is being addressed in any given line. This is called the **internal mode**. If you understand external and internal modal distinctions, you will be able to solve the initial considerations of who is speaking and to whom in prose fiction texts—the most modally-mixed of all the genres of literature. There are three internal modes: epic, dramatic, and lyric.

Epic Mode

In general, **epic-mode lines** are lines that are intended to further the story line, establish time and place, summarize information, provide transitions, and present information to audience members that they do not already have. Epic-mode lines are usually spoken by narrators directly to the audience. Some epic-mode lines are:

Mary walked to the store and bought two pounds of chocolate candy.

Tom took off his coat and hat, hung them on the coat rack, and read the paper.

The sky was a beautiful azure blue as it always was at the height of summer.

The house was newly painted, but the areas around the eaves needed to be touched up. The downspouts had been replaced two years previously, but they seemed to be hanging on by aluminum threads.

The time was almost midnight, and there was loud shouting from the pub across the street. Three hours later Tom arrived at his town-house and confronted Mary whom he hadn't seen for weeks.

Teresa wore a slightly faded red dress, and did not realize her slip was showing.

Dramatic Mode

Dramatic-mode lines are lines of direct discourse (or indirect discourse). **Direct discourse** is dialogue—the exact words of the characters, usually enclosed in quotation marks. Direct discourse resembles dialogue exchanges between characters in plays. **Indirect discourse** is a more complicated consideration. Indirect discourse is when the narrator tells us what characters said rather than shows us with the use of direct discourse. "Mary said that she didn't want to go to the store with Tom" is a line of indirect discourse. If the line were directly conveyed, it would read "'I don't want to go to the store with you, Tom,' said Mary." There are four options for the delivery of indirect discourse.

First, the narrator may deliver the line, conveying his or her attitude. In this option, the adapter decides the line is epic in mode, and thus the narrator delivers it to the audience.

But, a convention of chamber theatre is allowing characters to talk of themselves in the third person and in the past tense, thus presenting another option. Remember that since the narrator is literally the only one in the virtual present telling the story, the actress playing Mary could say "Mary said that she didn't want to go to the store with Tom," as if it were dialogue—dramatic mode—because she is not really Mary, but is "presenting" what Mary said then. As Breen explains, ". . . the actors and characters are separated so that the audience is allowed to see the artist at work demonstrating his or her character consciously and conscientiously."[13] When a performer "demonstrates" these lines of indirect discourse, the character's perspective not the narrator's, is featured. More will be said about this "actor/character" separation in chapter five.

A third option in deciding how to assign lines of indirect discourse is to have the narrator take the line, imitating Mary's voice and body, but revealing his or her attitude toward Mary. With this option, you get the sense of Mary simultaneous with the narrator's point of view. As Judith C. Espinola makes clear, ". . . one very important function of all kinds of indirect discourse is to effect the simultaneous presentation of narrative point of view with character personality and vision."[14]

One last option is to allow both the narrator and the character to say the line. For example, the narrator delivers the line to the audience, while Mary says the line to Tom in a soft voice under the narration.

Ultimately, your decision as to whom to assign lines of indirect discourse depends on your interpretation of the story and on whose attitude you want to prevail at any given time. Remember, there is no right or wrong way to adapt. Look, for example, at these four different, but equally acceptable adaptations of a passage from "The Third Prize" by A. E. Coppard, which we referred to in chapter one. In the first adaptation, the narrator gives all the narration and the characters give their direct dialogue.

Chamber Theatre Adaptation 1
from "The Third Prize"
by A. E. Coppard

Narrator: George Robins, a cute good-looking clerk, devoted his gifts of gallantry to Margery, and none the less readily because she displayed some qualities not commonly associated with demureness.

George: From London you come!

Narrator: exclaimed George.

George: How'd you get here?

Narrator: the young lady crisply testified that she came in a train—did the fathead think she had swum? They were jolly glad when they got here, too and all. Carriage full, and ructions all the way.

George: Ructions! What ructions?

Margery: Boozy men! Half of 'em trying to cuddle you.

Narrator: Mr. Robins intimated that he could well understand such desires. Miss Margery retorted that then he was understanding much more than was good for him. Mr. Robins thought not, he hoped not. Miss Margery indicated that he could hope for much more than he was likely to get. Mr. Robins replied that, he would do that, and then double it. And he asserted, with all respect, that had he but happily been in that train he too might have, etc. and so on. Whereupon Miss Margery snapped, would he? and Mr. Robins felt bound to say Sure!

In the next adaptation, the characters say all the narration, speaking of themselves in the third person and the past tense (a convention of chamber theatre).

Chamber Theatre Adaptation 2
from "The Third Prize"
by A. E. Coppard

George: Mr. Robins intimated that he could well understand such desires.

Margery: Miss Margery retorted that then he was understanding much more than was good for him.

George: Mr. Robins thought not, he hoped not.

Margery: Miss Margery indicated that he could hope for much more than he was likely to get.

George: Mr. Robins replied that, he would do that, and then double it. And he asserted, with all respect, that had he but happily been in that train he too might have, etc. and so on.

Margery: Whereupon Miss Margery snapped, Would he?

George: and Mr. Robins felt bound to say Sure!

When the characters give their own narration as in the previous example, they seem to portray their outside selves as well as their inner selves. They know what they did but they are also aware of the motivations for their actions, as Breen suggests.

Here the characters give the indirect dialogue while the narrator gives the tag lines or lead-in portion of the narration.

Chamber Theatre Adaptation 3
from "The Third Prize"
by A. E. Coppard

Narrator: Mr. Robins intimated that

George: he could well understand such desires.

Narrator: Miss Margery retorted that

Margery: then he was understanding much more than was good for him.

George: Mr. Robins thought not, he hoped not.

Narrator: Miss Margery indicated that

Margery: he could hope for much more than he was likely to get.

Narrator: Mr. Robins replied that

George: he would do that, and double it.

Narrator: And he asserted, with all respect, that

George: had he but happily been in that train he too might have, etc. and so on.

Narrator: Whereupon Miss Margery snapped

Margery: Would he?

Narrator: and Mr. Robins felt bound to say

George: Sure!

We include one additional adaptation possibility that underscores the concept of simultaneity. As we said earlier, prose fiction is written serially, with one action following another. In reality, though, actions often happen simultaneously. In the phrase "'Oh my gosh, it's the gift I've always wanted,' Mary said opening the Christmas present," Mary is opening the present and speaking simultaneously, but this cannot be realistically represented on the page whereas it can be represented on the stage. Look how the passage from "The Third Prize" can be written so that the characters are engaged in dialogue as the narrator speaks.

Chamber Theatre Adaptation 4
from "The Third Prize"
by A. E. Coppard

Narrator: Mr. Robins intimated that he could well understand such desires. Miss Margery retorted that he was understanding much more than was good for him. Mr. Robins thought not, he hoped not. Miss Margery indicated that he could hope for much more than he was likely to get. Mr. Robins replied that, he would do that, and then double it. And he asserted, with all respect, that had he but happily been in that train he too might have, etc. and so on. Whereupon Miss Margery snapped,

Margery: Would he?

Narrator: and Mr. Robins felt bound to say

George: Sure!¹⁵

George: I can understand that.

Margery: Then you understand much more than is good for you.

George: I think not, I hope not.

Margery: You can jolly well hope for more'n you're likely to get.

George: I'd do that, and double it. And I'll tell you, if I'd have been on that train, I'll tell you what I'd've done. (*He continues to improvise until narrator cues in Margery.*)

EXPERIMENT

Here is a passage from Katherine Anne Porter's story "The Rope," which abounds in lines of indirect discourse. Read the selection several times, and decide how you would divide the lines. Stage your finished product in class.

From "The Rope"
by Katherine Anne Porter

On the third day after they moved to the country he came walking back from the village carrying a basket of groceries and a twenty-four-yard coil of rope. She came out to meet him, wiping her hands on her green smock. Her hair was tumbled, her nose was scarlet with sunburn; he told her that already she looked like a born country woman. His gray flannel shirt stuck to him, his heavy shoes were dusty. She assured him he looked like a rural character in a play.

Had he brought the coffee? She had been waiting all day long for coffee. They had forgot it when they ordered at the store the first day.

Gosh, no, he hadn't. Lord, now he'd have to go back. Yes, he would if it killed him. He thought, though, he had everything else. She reminded him it was only because he didn't drink coffee himself. If he did he would remember it quick enough. Suppose they ran out of cigarettes? Then she saw the rope. What was that for? Well, he thought it might do to hang clothes on, or something. Naturally she asked him if he thought they were going to run a laundry? They already had a fifty-foot line hanging right before his eyes. Why, hadn't he noticed it, really? It was a blot on the landscape to her.

Lyric Mode

Lyric-mode lines are those lines usually found within the narration that reveal characters' thoughts and feelings in the characters' vocabulary and syntax. Stephen King, for example, is a master of conveying interior thoughts to the audience. The convention he often employs is to italicize these lines to signal to readers that they are receiving inner thoughts. In this passage from King's novel *Misery*, a kidnapped writer, Paul Sheldon, reacts to his captor's use of language:

From *Misery*
by Stephen King

The oogiest part, he thought. *Save that one for the Annie Wilkes lexicon in your memoirs—if you ever get a chance to write your memoirs, that is. Along with dirty birdie and fiddle-de-foof and all the others which I'm sure will come up in time.*

The italicized lines indicate Paul's lyric thoughts, and could be performed by the actor playing Paul speaking aloud to himself or addressing the narrator. While King makes lyric lines very obvious by italicizing them, his style of shifting the pronoun from "he" to "I" and changing verb tense from past to present for lyric thought lines is not typical of other writers. Look at this passage from Flannery O'Connor's short story "Good Country People." In this passage, the underlined words could be considered the thoughts of the main character, Hulga, as she ponders her relationship with the Bible salesman, Manley Pointer.

From "Good Country People"
by Flannery O'Connor

She smiled looking dreamily out on the shifty landscape. She had seduced him without even making up her mind to try. "How?" she asked, feeling that he should be delayed a little. He leaned over and put his lips to her ear. "Show me where your wooden leg joins on," he whispered.

In this passage, the narrator has a very different knowledge of the events than does Hulga since the narrator knows what will happen. The narrator knows, for instance, that Hulga only thinks she had "seduced him." In reality, Manley premeditatedly seduces her. By allowing the performer playing Hulga to say this "seduction" line, you allow the audience to hear what Hulga is thinking and the narrator, who would have to deliver the line quite differently, keeps Manley's intentions a surprise. The second underlined phrase, "feeling that he should be delayed a little," could also be Hulga's line as she thinks she is coyly delaying Manley's satisfaction.

Before we consider specific information on adapting prose fiction texts, let us consider one last aspect of prose fiction selections: tag lines.

Tag Lines

The adaptation from "The Third Prize" brought up the problem of what to do with tag lines. **Tag lines** are the "he saids" and "she replieds" that writers use to indicate to the silent reader who is speaking. When the dialogue is spoken on stage by the character, however, the tag lines may not be necessary. It is rash, though, to cut the tag lines without careful consideration. Often the tag lines give us information in addition to who is speaking. In "The Third Prize," for example, the narrator uses terms like "intimated," "indicated" and "asserted" to describe the rather simplistic and unsophisticated speech of Cockney children. The tags in this story help the narrator create a formality, a distance, and help him communicate a superior self-impression. Often the tag lines contribute to the rhythm of a selection. Much of Dorothy Parker's story "Here We Are" is dialogue, and the narrative tags create a natural rhythm between these lines of dialogue.

Let us describe four different kinds of tag lines: simple, action, descriptive, and interior. Simple tags are the "he saids" and "she saids" that are primarily for the eye. These may be cut—unless the story is told in the third-person observer point of view, in which case they should usually be kept because they remind the audience that the story is in the epic mode and in the past tense.

Action tags like "she replied walking to the door" or "he asked as he got into his car" may be cut if the action can be realized or suggested on stage. The character may do the action while the narrator takes the line, or the character may take the line and do the action simultaneously.

Descriptive tags usually include adverbs which suggest how something was said or done and often indicate the narrator's attitude. A descriptive tag that just gives information like "he said loudly" may be cut since "he" can say the line "loudly." A descriptive tag like, "Shannon awkwardly entered the room" gives us the narrator's attitude toward Shannon's entrance. (If descriptive tags are kept and a character does not do the action described [does not speak loudly, does not enter awkwardly], the reliability of the narrator may be called into question.)

Interior tags are often indications that the narrator is going into a character's mind. For example, interior tags like "she felt," "he sensed," and so on should be kept as they indicate omniscience. Either the narrator or the character may say these tags.

In general, if the tag lines do nothing other than make clear who is speaking, they may be cut. If they give us more information than that, keep them, and decide if the narrator should say them with his or her attitude, or if the characters can take them to indicate a conscious awareness of the way they are speaking or behaving.

Let's now consider specific information for adapting first-person narrator texts into chamber theatre scripts.

Adapting First-Person Narrator Texts

As with all texts, begin with a dramatistic analysis which will help you define and analyze the narrator and his or her point of view. Narrators of first-person texts are characters in the stories they tell, were participants in the action, so one of the first considerations you should make is to decide if the narrator telling the story in the virtual present is *psychologically* or *emotionally* different from the person he or she was in the virtual past. If there is an obvious difference between the way the narrator seems as he or she tells the story as opposed to the way he or she seemed in the past, or if the narrator seems to want us to perceive him or her differently in present and past, then the convention of bifurcation (or even trifurcation), discussed in chapters one and two, may be employed. When you bifurcate, you cast one performer to play the narrator in the virtual present, and another performer to enact the past scenes. With trifurcation, three performers may be cast to accentuate the differences in the narrator.

A time differential alone, however, is not enough to warrant bifurcation or trifurcation. Since most stories are told in the virtual present about the virtual past, casting one performer to play the narrator in the present and another to play the character in the past would always be necessary. The questions to ask are: Has time psychologically or emotionally changed the narrator? Does the narrator feel differently now about the events in the past? Does the narrator desire us to see him or her differently? If two performers are cast to play the same role, would each have a different motive or intention to play? If the answer to any of these questions is yes, then two performers (or three) may be cast to highlight this change or difference. In "Why I Live at the P.O.," for example, only five days have elapsed between the virtual present and the virtual past, consequently bifurcation is not necessary as there wouldn't be anything different for the two actresses to play. In Frank O'Connor's "My Oedipus Complex," however, the language in the story indicates that the narrator in the virtual present is a grown man who in the virtual past when he was a child suffered from an Oedipus Complex. In this case, bifurcating the narrator—one actor playing the adult narrator in the virtual present with a rather humorous attitude and another actor playing the narrator as a young boy in the past suffering from the dreaded complex—effectively shows the change time has wrought.

Look at this passage from Charlotte Brontë's *Jane Eyre*. Here the narrator is bifurcated to show the difference between Jane Present, the woman which is happily married with a child, and Jane Past, the frightened orphan child.

Chamber Theatre Adaptation
from *Jane Eyre*
by Charlotte Brontë

Jane Present (*to audience*): I remember but little of the journey to Lowood. When I arrived at the school, I stood and warmed my numbed fingers at the fireplace in the room I had been left in, then I looked round;

Jane Past (*to Jane Present*): there was no candle.

Jane Present (*to Jane Past, trying to reassure her*): but the uncertain light from the hearth showed, by intervals papered walls, carpet, curtains, shining mahogany furniture: it was a parlour,

Jane Past (*to Jane Present*): not so spacious or splendid as the drawing-room at Gateshead,

Jane Present (*to Jane Past*): but comfortable enough. (*Miss Temple enters with candle, Miss Miller is close behind her.*)

Miss Miller (*to Miss Temple*): This is the new girl, Miss Temple.

Miss Temple (*to Jane Past as she crosses to her*): The child is very young to be sent alone.

Miss Miller (*to Miss Temple*): She certainly is, Ma'am. (*Miss Temple puts candle down and considers Jane attentively, helping her take off her coat, etc.*) She had better be put to bed soon; she looks tired: are you tired? (*She places her hand on Jane Past's shoulder.*)

Jane Past (*to Miss Temple*): A little, Ma'am.

Miss Temple: And hungry, too, no doubt. Is this the first time you have left your parents to come to school, my little girl?

Jane Present (*to audience*): I explained to her that I had no parents. She inquired how long they had been dead; then how old I was, what was my name, whether I could read, write, and sew a little; then she touched my cheek gently with her forefinger, and saying

Jane Past (*to Miss Temple*): I have no parents.

Miss Temple (*to Jane Past*): How old are you, my child.

Jane Past: I'm 10-years-old.

Miss Temple: What is your name?

Jane Past: Jane Eyre, Ma'am.

Miss Temple: Can you read, my dear?

Jane Past: Yes, Ma'am.

Miss Temple (*touching Jane Past on cheek*): I hope you will be a good child

Jane Present (*to audience*): dismissed me along with Miss Miller.

This adaptation establishes a maternal relationship between Jane Present and her younger self, indicates how some narrative information can be used as stage directions and become action, shows how lines like Jane Present's description of the room "papered walls, carpet, curtains, shining mahogany furniture" can create the spectacle for the audience in language, and illustrates the convention of simultaneity as Miss Temple and Jane Past converse under Jane Present's lines to the audience.

In general, if you bifurcate the narrator, lines that maintain a present perspective should go to the performer telling the story. Lines that suggest minute physical details, indicate how the character felt then, or imply that the character is reliving the past should go to the performer playing the character in the past.

If time has not changed the narrator in any observable way, then one performer plays the narrator in and out of scene. This technique is employed in the play *The Glass Menagerie*, for example, as Tom Wingfield tells us in the opening monologue that he is both the narrator of the play and a character in it. The convention of speaking in and out of scene can be very difficult, and the performer playing this difficult role must understand his or her relationship both with the audience and with all of the characters in the remembered scenes. This is the case in the following adaptation of F. Scott Fitzgerald's *The Great Gatsby* as Nick Carraway, the first-person minor character narrator, visits his "second cousin once removed" Daisy Buchanan at her "white palace" in fashionable East Egg.

Chamber Theatre Adaptation
from _The Great Gatsby_
by F. Scott Fitzgerald

Daisy (*to Nick*): I'm p-paralyzed with happiness. (*Daisy laughs again, and looks into Nick's face.*) This is Jordan Baker. (*Jordan nods at Nick, and tips her head back as if balancing something.*)

Nick (*to audience*): I looked back at my cousin who began to ask me questions in her low, thrilling voice. There was an excitement in her voice that men who had cared for her found difficult to forget: a singing compulsion, a whispered "Listen," a promise that she had done gay, exciting things just a while since and that there were gay, exciting things hovering in the next hour.

Daisy (*to Nick*): Where have you been Nick? I haven't seen you in such an age.

Nick (*to Daisy*): I stopped off in Chicago for a day on my way east and a dozen people sent their love through me.

Daisy (*to Nick*): Do they miss me?

Nick (*to Daisy*): The whole town is desolate. All the cars have the left rear wheel painted black as a mourning wreath and there's a persistent wail all night along the North Shore.

In this adaptation, Nick shares his remembrances about Daisy with the audience, perhaps colored by the attitude he has of her in the virtual present. He must also behave as the outsider/newcomer in the scene as he becomes reacquainted with Tom and Daisy and meets Jordan seemingly for the first time.

Let us now look at the technique of dividing third-person prose fiction texts for chamber theatre.

Adapting Third-Person Narrator Texts

Whereas first-person narrators are identified and characterized in the stories they tell, as we've said before, this is not true of third-person narrators. Third-person narrators are not characters—they are undefined storytellers with attitudes! Adapters often find these types of narrators difficult because the only clue to identifying them or their attitudes is gained by a close examination of the language they use. Third-person omniscient narrators, in particular, display qualities beyond those of most mortals—they are able to read minds and indicate the motives behind the behavior of the characters. If narrators use words such as *felt, thought, seemed, imagined, believed, reminisced,* or *hoped,* for example, they are showing omniscience. The adapter tries to establish the nature of the relationship the narrator has with the character(s) with whom he or she is omniscient by establishing a social or psychological role for the narrator to play, as we delineated earlier. We described the role of the third-person omniscient narrator in "Impulse," for example, as the main character's reverse mirror image—someone who seems to be like Michael but is, in reality, his mirror opposite. The narrator shares lines with Michael, and the staging would suggest their close relationship. "Close relationships," though, are not necessarily agreeable. In other words, narrators are often omniscient with characters they do not approve of or admire. Some narrators are omniscient with characters to help the audience see more than just what the characters say or do—they allow us to hear the characters' thoughts to reveal the characters' failings, prejudices, or faults. In many Flannery O'Connor stories, for example, the narrator is often omniscient with the characters who need the most spiritual guidance. O'Connor's narrators usually hold attitudes very similar to O'Connor, who was a devout Roman Catholic. The intention of both is to reveal the inner thoughts of the main character—often the character who needs God's grace the most—so that the audience will see how misguided he or she is. We normally learn the most about the character(s) with whom the narrator is omniscient. The more we know about a character, the more we seem to identify with him or her. Consequently, O'Connor's narrators encourage the audience's identification with those characters who O'Connor believes are most like her audience. O'Connor wrote that she was aware that her audience did not share her beliefs; she felt she had to make her vision apparent by shock. Something horrifying usually happens to her main characters—something that horrifies us as well. Do not assume, then, that narrators must necessarily like or feel positively about those characters with whom they are omniscient.

In the following adaptation of Saki's (H. H. Munro's) third-person omniscient story "The Open Window," the adapter has used many of the ways of dividing lines that may be used in chamber theatre. This story illustrates how prose fiction can reveal the complex motivations of characters, the elements that describe action, and the attitudes and emotions that can be conveyed through a combination of descriptive narration and direct discourse (dialogue). Note that some of the narrator's lines that indicate omniscience are spoken by Framton Nuttel and reveal Framton's thoughts. To the right of the adapted lines, we have indicated when the lyric, epic, and dramatic modes are heard.

Chamber Theatre Adaptation
from "The Open Window"
by Saki (H.H. Munro)

Narrator (*to audience*): Framton Nuttel endeavoured to say the correct something

Epic-mode narration, summary

Framton (*to Narrator*): which should duly flatter the niece of the moment

Lyric-mode, character thoughts

Narrator (*to Framton*): without unduly discounting the aunt that was to come. (*He steps down to talk to the audience.*) Privately he doubted more than ever whether these formal visits on a succession of total strangers would do much towards helping the nerve cure which he was supposed to be undergoing. (*Framton's sister, who has been hiding behind Framton's chair, appears and stands above Framton.*)

Epic-mode, description

Sister: I know how it will be

Dramatic-mode, dialogue, scene

Narrator: his sister had said when he was preparing to migrate to this rural retreat.

Epic-mode, tag line, summary

Sister: you will bury yourself there and not speak to a living soul, and your nerves will be worse than ever from moping. I shall give you letters (*She drops letters on Framton, which the narrator picks up and puts in his pocket.*) of introduction to all the people I know there. Some of them, as far as I can remember, were quite nice.

Dramatic-mode, dialogue

Framton (*to no one in particular*): Framton wondered whether Mrs. Sappleton

Lyric-mode, character thoughts

Narrator (*to audience*): the lady to whom he was presenting one of the letters of introduction

Epic-mode, description

Framton: came into the nice division.

Lyric-mode, character thoughts

In this adaptation, dramatic-mode lines are delivered to the character being addressed, the epic-mode narrative lines are delivered to the audience and the narrator conveys the attitude he or she has regarding the situation conveyed. Framton Nuttel delivers his lyric-mode lines either to himself or to the narrator, conveying Framton's attitude regarding the situation.

Bifurcation or trifurcation can be effectively employed in the adaptation of third-person texts if either the narrator or a character exhibits an emotional or psychological split. In James Joyce's story "Eveline," for example, two actresses may be cast to play the title role as she struggles with the notion of running off with the man she loves or remaining home to care for her father. In stories where the narrator is omniscient with more than one character, this may be suggested in the adaptation by having one narrator for each character. In Edith Wharton's "Roman Fever," for example, only one narrator was cast to share the inner thoughts of Mrs. Slade. If the narration had indicated an omniscient relationship with Mrs. Ansley as well, then two performers could be cast: one to play Mrs. Slade's narrator, and one to play Mrs. Ansley's narrator.

Stories with third-person observer narrators, like Hemingway's "The Killers" or "A Clean, Well-Lighted Place," are a bit easier to adapt because the narrator only tells us what characters said and did—although these narrators also display attitudes. Because many of these stories seem to be dialogue with minimal narration, they tend to adapt most easily into a conventional play script where the characters say the dialogue, and the narrator's lines are converted into stage directions. These stories often are not particularly suitable for chamber theatre because there usually is not a strong relationship established between the narrator—who often seems to want to remain effaced—and the characters who enact the scenes without much narrative intervention.

Miscellaneous Techniques

Sometimes an adapter will use a mimed scene or a dance/ballet as a background to amplify and enrich the narration. In Leslie Irene Coger's adaptation of *A Woman in the Sky*, as the narrator stood on a level above talking to the audience, Brigid and Lena crossed to the postmaster and mimed signing for a letter. Then they crossed in a circular motion to center stage, returning to stage left to enter the pub. The women smiled at each other and were content. This mimed scene was essential to the story to reveal the happiness of these two women who were able to live their lives as they pleased. In "The Use of Force" by William Carlos

Williams, there is an examination going on of a child suspected of having diphtheria. The doctor seems to have an overwhelming attraction to this child, and the "force" he uses could be a metaphoric rape. In one production of this story, the doctor and the little girl were bifurcated—one pair enacted the scene in dialogue while two dancers suggested the rape in choreographed dance.

We discussed using a chorus in chapter two in reference to readers theatre. A chorus may be employed in chamber theatre productions as well. A group of performers can be created to take narrative lines. This technique was employed in the eight-and-a-half hour production of Dickens' *Nicholas Nickleby*. The narration became a community of voices telling the story. A chorus may speak in unison (indicating their single-ness of attitude or purpose), or the lines may be divided among the chorus members (indicating their individual points of view). In a recent production of Kafka's *The Trial*, a cast of thirteen played a total of nineteen different characters. The central character, Joseph K., was played by one actor, and the remaining twelve cast members often spoke as a unified group and at other times took on individual roles. In an adaptation of *The Scarlet Letter*, a chorus of ten performers represented the evil of the forest in which Hester and her young daughter, Pearl, lived. Here is an excerpt from that script.

Chamber Theatre Adaptation
from *The Scarlet Letter*
by Nathaniel Hawthorne

Hester (*to God*): O Father in Heaven,—if You are still my Father,—what is this being which I have brought into the world? (*Pearl overhears, turns and smiles at her mother. Pearl then runs to her mother with the flowers she has picked and flings them one by one at her mother's bosom. She dances up and down like an elf whenever she hits the scarlet letter.*)

Hester (*half-playfully*): You are not my child! You are no Pearl of mine! Tell me, then, what you are, and who sent you here?

Pearl: Tell <u>me</u>, mother! (*Pearl comes up to her mother and presses herself close to her knees.*) Do you tell me!

Hester: Your Heavenly Father sent you!

Pearl (*touching the scarlet letter with her forefinger*): He did not send me! I have no Heavenly Father!

The chorus in this scene from *The Scarlet Letter* suggests the haunts of the witch, Mistress Hibbins.

Hester (*suppressing a groan*): Hush, Pearl, hush! (*Chorus now makes a "sh" sound.*) You must not talk so! He sent us all into this world. He even sent me, your mother. Then, much more, you! or, if not, you strange and elfish child, from where did you come?

Chorus (*repeating softly*): Tell me! Tell me!

Pearl (*no longer serious, laughing*): Tell me! Tell me! It is you that must tell me! (*Chorus members assume aspects of the evil forest, and when not saying a line keep softly repeating "tell me" under the following:*)

Chorus 2: Tell me! Tell me!

Chorus 4: A demon offspring!

Chorus 6: Tell me! Tell me!

Chorus 3: A brat

Chorus 5: Of a hellish breed

Chorus 8: To promote some foul and wicked purpose!

Chorus 9: Tell me!

Chorus 7: Tell me!

Chorus 1: The child should be taken from her.

Chorus 10: Christian interest in the other's soul

Chorus 7: requires that this stumbling-block

Chorus 1: be removed from her path. (*Chorus exhales.*)

Another technique is to have inanimate forces speak in a work. These forces not only speak, but may move. In *A Woman in the Sky*, the cold, the darkness, and the wind materialized as wraith-like beings and danced as described in the narration.

One last technique to keep in mind deals with telling and showing. Although Breen warns us not to rewrite the story, there may be long passages of narration that could effectively be turned into dialogue without much sacrifice of the narrator's attitude or point of view. The following dialogue from *The Great Gatsby* is created from a long expository passage spoken earlier in the novel.

Chamber Theatre Adaptation
from *The Great Gatsby*
by F. Scott Fitzgerald

Gatsby: What happened Daisy? Why didn't you wait for me?

Daisy: I was young, Jay, only 18, and I was surrounded by men. You were gone, and I had my choice of the Louisville elite.

Gatsby: Why didn't you come to New York to say goodbye to me before I went overseas?

Daisy: I planned to, Jay, my bags were packed, but my parents refused to let me leave. I didn't speak to them for several weeks after that.

Gatsby: Why did you have to marry Tom Buchanan?

Daisy: Oh Jay, please don't do this to me. (*pause*) Rich girls don't marry poor boys. Rich girls don't marry poor boys.

If you do turn some narration into dialogue, work to maintain the flavor of the writer's style and the character's language.

Cutting

The length of your finished production may depend upon some prescribed time limit. Often an entire short story can be adapted and presented, but a novel often presents a larger problem. Novelists, unlike playwrights, do not write with the idea of "two hours traffic on the stage." When adapting a novel for the stage, therefore, cutting will probably be necessary. Before you begin to adapt the novel, read it over several times and devise a production concept. A production concept is the premise or overall idea that you wish your script to convey. Your production concept helps you decide what to keep and what to cut. In a production of *As I Lay Dying*, for example, fifteen different first-person narrators tell the story of the Bundren family's journey to bury their wife/mother and at the same time, search for significance in their everyday lives. As the journey proceeds, we hear from the Bundren family as well as neighbors, friends, and strangers they meet along their way. When Breen adapted this production for chamber theatre, his production concept was to focus only on the Bundren narrators. Often in long works, there are several threads that can be followed to make a unified script. *Dandelion Wine*, by Ray Bradbury, is a novel that relates a series of incidents that occur during one summer in a small town. A number of episodes in the novel deal with machines: the time machine, the happiness machine, the fortune-telling machine, the trolley car, the Green Machine, and the machine for making dandelion wine. These threads, only, could be adapted to make a unified production.

Often long passages of narration may be cut if that narration can be realized in the technical design of the production, e. g., costumes, props, set, and so on. Likewise you may cut unessential scenes or scenes that can be summarized in narration for the sake of brevity. Often minor characters can be cut if the narrator can assume these roles, or if what they say is not necessary to your production concept.

Use the following guidelines for cutting a novel or even a short story that exceeds your prescribed time limit:

1. Read the piece several times before cutting.

2. Analyze the selection applying the dramatistic analysis described earlier. Let this analysis help shape your production concept and help you decide those sections that must be retained and those which can be omitted.

3. Outline the plot or story line you will retain.

4. Decide which characters will be left in the script and understand why they must be retained. Watch for minor characters that may be dropped or played by other characters.

5. Write summary narration (transitions) as needed. If you search carefully, you may be able to find lines to use from the cut sections.

6. Keep variety in what is retained. One often has to forfeit a serious scene and add a light one to contrast mood. If need be, rearrange scenes to keep variety.

7. Occasionally, lines can be cut that can be presented by physical action or by spectacle elements (set, lights, costumes, props, etc.).

Whether you are working with a short story or novel, your goal in preparing the script is to illuminate and vivify the literature so that it becomes a meaningful aesthetic experience for the audience.

Let us now review some of the primary considerations to keep in mind as you adapt narrative fiction for the stage. Begin by studying the literature carefully, and select among these ways of assigning lines:

1. Give all the narration to the narrator and only the dialogue to the characters. This places emphasis upon the narrator and his or her control of the story.

2. Give narration to the characters when it seems to express their thoughts and feelings, or reveals their awareness of their motivations.

   A. Often this is in a dependent clause, sometimes marked with a colon (see James Joyce's "The Boarding House").

   B. Indirect discourse that reveals the character's thoughts in the character's vocabulary.

   C. The diction of the narrator might suggest the character. If the narrator would normally say "business" but instead says "bidnis," this could indicate the **vernacular**—the idiom or jargon which characterizes someone's language—of the character, not the narrator.

3. Allow characters to improvise dialogue said under narration.

4. Have characters mime the action described by the narrator.

5. Divide the narration among a chorus of people.

6. Divide the narrator's and/or character's lines among two or more actors to reveal facets of personality: youth versus age; naive versus sophisticated; female versus male characteristics; id, ego, and superego traits; and so on.

7. Allow narrator and characters to say some lines together. This will reveal the closeness of the two.

8. Occasionally, narration and indirect discourse can be turned into dialogue.

In chapter five, we will concentrate on how to stage your finished chamber theatre adaptations. Traditionally, adapters are also the directors of their own scripts. Despite this, try to write your adaptation so that another director will have some idea of your production concept. Include, for example, descriptions of the narrator and each character, what you envision the set to look like, time and place, and so on.

EXPERIMENT

Here is Mark Hillenbrand's contemporary version of a well-known fairy tale. Using the information you have learned from this chapter, adapt this passage for chamber theatre, and then stage your script in class.

Jack and the Beanstalk
by Mark Hillenbrand

Once upon a time, there was a poor widow who had a son named Jack and a cow named Milky White. All they had to live on was the milk the cow gave every morning, which they carried to the market and sold. But one morning, Milky White gave no milk. Jack's mother concluded that they must sell Milky White, and start their own small business.

On his way to the market, Jack met a long-bearded old man whose jacket and trousers were two times too big.

"Good morning," said Jack. "I'm off to market to sell Milky White."

"How about a trade," said the old man. "Your cow for these five magic beans. I'll give you a cow-back guarantee good for thirty days from today. Son, these beans will grow up to the clouds, through the ozone hole, and beyond. They're hybrids."

Jack put on his thinking cap and concluded that this was a pretty good deal. They shook hands and traded.

"Back so soon?" said Jack's mother. "How much did you get for Milky White?"

"Five magic beans."

"How could you be so foolish?" demanded Jack's mother as she threw the five beans out the window. Jack was sent to his room with no supper.

But as they slept, the amazing hybrid beans sprouted, growing a foot for every night minute that ticked by. At day break, the beanstalk was interfering with air traffic control radar signals.

As soon as Jack saw the amazing stalk, he climbed out his bedroom window, hopped on the stalk, and began to climb skyward. He climbed and climbed and climbed, growing slightly dizzy due to the lack of oxygen. Jack eventually reached the kingdom of Mr. Giant and Mrs. Giant, zip code unknown.

As Jack walked along he came to the Giant's home and at the doorstep stood a woman three times as tall as Jack.

"Good morning, Ma'am. Could you give a small boy something to eat for breakfast?"

"Little boy, be off! My old man sits in front of the television and eats small boys for snacks during the commercials."

"Well, I'm willing to risk it for some food," replied the famished Jack.

The Giant's wife took Jack in through the back door and into the kitchen and made a stack of pancakes as tall as Jack.

"Fee-Fi-Fo-Fum
I smell the flavor of strawberry gum.
Boys with bubble gum are as good as dead
That bubble-burstin' pop goes right to my head."

The entire house shook with every word. The Giant's wife hid Jack away in her oven just before the Giant entered the kitchen.

"Deary," explained the Giant's wife, "you just smell leftovers from yesterday's dessert."

The Giant had his breakfast, and soon fell fast asleep as he counted his gold. Jack leapt out of the oven, grabbed a bag of gold, and was down the beanstalk before the Giant woke.

Jack and his mother lived off the gold for some time, but their spendthrift attitude left Jack and his mother broke in eight months. Thus, Jack made up his mind to try the beanstalk again.

On his second trip, Jack slipped by the Giant and stole the hen that produced solid gold eggs on command. Jack returned home, and soon after his mother purchased a condo in Sarasota, Florida.

But Jack soon got bored counting his gold day after day, and he decided to try his luck a third time.

"Three times a charm," he said to himself as he put on his brand new beanstalk climbing boots. Jack returned to the Land of the Giant and snuck into the Giant's home. This time, Jack spied a magic musical harp that gladly took requests. But as Jack tried to make his way out with the magical instrument, the harp suddenly launched into an interpretation of the Beatles' classic "Help!"

The Giant woke and was furious! He chased Jack out of the house and down the beanstalk. Jack reached the ground first and grabbed a chainsaw. All came tumbling down, and the Giant broke his crown.

Jack was wealthy, he married a princess and they both lived happily ever after.

That is, after Jack served ten long years in San Quentin for grand larceny.

MORAL: Today, you need a good lawyer for a storybook ending.

Commercial, Non-Academic Chamber Theatre

As we suggested earlier, adaptations of short stories and novels are proliferating all over the United States. Theatre companies are seeking the challenge of adapting and staging stories, of widening the potential material available for presentation. Commercial adaptations, however, are not as interested in maintaining an integrity or fidelity to the original text as Breen was when he created chamber theatre as a "technique for staging prose fiction in the classroom." Contemporary audiences want to understand who is who. They expect to see only characters, they want to be *shown* more than *told*; they often do not know what to make of someone "omniscient" onstage who is not a participant in the action. Of all the chamber theatre adaptations that are doing well or have done well on commercial stages (e. g., *Les Miserables, A Clockwork Orange, The Grapes of Wrath, As I Lay Dying, The Trial, The Secret Garden, Nicholas Nickleby, The Scarlet Letter, Jane Eyre*), not one of them includes an undefined narrator who shares inside thoughts. If there are narrators at all, they are either defined (as they are in most plays and musicals) or eliminated, with characters taking their own narration. Often passages of narration are converted into dialogue exchanges. Although many may decry the liberties these scripts take, these liberties do allow for a certain artistic freedom. After all, we are dealing with two different art forms—the literature on the page and the script on the stage. They are different mediums. How then do we judge the worth of an adaptation? On its own merits—on how well it communicates the adapter's view of a work. As Michael Bowman writes:

> By question of its [chamber theatre's] own intentionality; by posing as a self-less servant of the text, chamber theatre hopes to avoid any close scrutiny of its own axiological orientation to the world. It banks on our longstanding inability to explain the moral aspects of "technique" to preserve its posture of distance, neutrality, objectivity, impartiality. Chamber theatre effectively rewrites the literature in the adaptation and staging . . . Adaptations of literature for performance do not just "happen," of course, as if by accident or chance. Neither do they bear a "natural" or an ideologically neutral relation to the texts on which they are based or to the audiences they address. They are constructed to project a certain point of view, to promote various aims or interests, and to encourage a particular range of responses. In chamber theatre, as in most performed adaptations, these matters receive very little attention, however, because the interpretive coding that surrounds the practice of adapting and performing literature tends to restrict criticism, when it occurs at all, to questions of fidelity: Was the production faithful to the original? Did it respect and convey the author's meanings and intentions? Leaving aside the question of whether it is possible to recover an author's meanings and intentions, the question of whether performed adaptations should strive to be faithful rarely arises.[16]

What Bowman is getting at is allowing the script creator the moral right to interpret a text as he or she sees fit, and permitting a group performance to exist as a separate entity, perhaps related to but not exclusively bound by some prescribed meaning of the source text. This more liberal, experiential viewpoint is most clearly expressed in chapter five where "metonymic" group production types are discussed—productions that do not intend to uphold the perceived integrity of the original source material. This allows the script creator to feel that he or she is doing more than serving the literature—instead a new entity is produced which is capable of being judged on its own merits. An example of this kind of script is Michael T. Downey's adaptation of "A Wife's Confession" by Guy de Maupassant. While Michael's adaptation may have been prompted by the original story, his script departs drastically from the one-woman confession revealed in de Maupassant's story. We include both the original story and Michael's adaptation so that you can see what he has done to make his script a unique creation.

"A Wife's Confession"
by Guy de Maupassant

My friend, you have asked me to relate to you the liveliest recollections of my life. I am very old, without relatives, without children, so I am free to make a confession to you. Promise me one thing—never to reveal my name.

I have been much loved, as you know; I have often myself loved. I was very beautiful; I may say this today, when my beauty is gone. Love was for me the life of the soul, just as the air is the life of the body. I would have preferred to die rather than exist without affection, without having somebody always to care for me. Women often pretend to love only once with all the strength of their hearts; it has often happened to be so violent in one of my attachments that I thought it would be impossible for my transports ever to end. However, they always died out in a natural fashion, like a fire when it has no more fuel.

I will tell you today the first of my adventures, in which I was very innocent but which led to the others. The horrible vengeance of that dreadful chemist of Pecq recalls to me the shocking drama of which I was, in spite of myself, a spectator.

I had been a year married to a rich man, Comte Hervé de Ker—a Breton of ancient family, whom I did not love, you understand. True love needs, I believe, at any rate, freedom and impediments at the same time. The love which is imposed, sanctioned by law and blessed by the priest—can we really call that love? A legal kiss is never as good as a stolen kiss. My husband was tall in stature, elegant, and a really fine gentleman in his manners. But he lacked intelligence. He spoke in a downright fashion and uttered opinions that cut like the blade of a knife. He created the impression that his mind was full of ready-made views instilled into him by his father and mother, who had themselves got them from their ancestors. He never hesitated, but on every subject immediately made narrow-minded suggestions without showing any embarrassment and without realizing that there might be other ways of looking at things. One felt that his head was closed up, that no ideas circulated in it, none of those ideas which renew a man's mind and make it sound, like a breath of fresh air passing through an open window into a house.

The château in which we lived was situated in the midst of a desolate tract of country. It was a large, melancholy structure, surrounded by enormous trees, with tufts of moss on it, resembling old men's white beards. The park, a real forest, was enclosed in a deep trench called the ha-ha, and at its extremity, near the moorland, we had big ponds full of reeds and floating grass. Between the two, at the edge of a stream which connected them, my husband had got a little hut built for shooting wild ducks.

We had, in addition to our ordinary servants, a keeper, a sort of brute, devoted to my husband to the death, and a chambermaid, almost a friend, passionately attached to me. I had brought her back from Spain with me five years before. She was a deserted child. She might have been taken for a gypsy with her dusky skin, her dark eyes, her hair thick as wood and always clustering around her forehead. She was at the time sixteen years old, but she looked twenty.

The autumn was beginning. We hunted much, sometimes on neighboring estates, sometimes on our own, and I noticed a young man, the Baron de C—, whose visits at the château became singularly frequent. Then he ceased to come; I thought no more about it, but I perceived that my husband changed in his demeanor toward me.

He seemed taciturn and preoccupied; he did not kiss me, and in spite of the fact that he did not come into my room, as I insisted on separate apartments in order to live a little alone, I often at night heard a furtive step drawing near my door and withdrawing a few minutes later.

As my window was on the ground floor, I thought I had also often heard someone prowling in the shadow around the château. I told my husband about it, and, having looked at me intensely for some seconds, he answered:

"It is nothing—it is the keeper."

Now one evening, just after dinner, Hervé, who appeared to be extraordinarily gay, with a sly sort of gaiety, said to me:

"Would you like to spend three hours out with the guns, in order to shoot a fox who comes every evening to eat my hens?"

I was surprised. I hesitated, but as he kept staring at me with singular persistency, I ended by replying:

"Why, certainly, my friend." I must tell you that I hunted like a man the wolf and the wild boar. So it was quite natural that he should suggest this shooting expedition to me.

But my husband, all of a sudden, had a curiously nervous look, and all the evening he seemed agitated, rising up and sitting down feverishly.

About ten o'clock he suddenly said to me:

"Are you ready?"

I rose, and as he was bringing me my gun himself, I asked:

"Are we to load with bullets or with deer shot?"

He showed some astonishment; then he rejoined:

"Oh, only with deer shot; make your mind easy! That will be enough."

Then after some seconds he added in a peculiar tone:

"You may boast of having splendid coolness."

I burst out laughing.

"I? Why, pray? Coolness because I go to kill a fox? What are you thinking of, my friend?"

And we quietly made our way across the park. All the household slept. The full moon seemed to give a yellow tint to the old gloomy building, whose slate roof glittered brightly. The two turrets that flanked it had two plates of light on their summits, and no noise disturbed the silence of this clear, sad night, sweet and still, which seemed in a death trance. Not a breath of air, not a shriek from a toad, not a hoot from an owl; a melancholy numbness lay heavy on everything. When we were under the trees in the park a sense of freshness stole over me, together with the odor of fallen leaves. My husband said nothing, but he was listening; he was watching; he seemed to be smelling about in the shadows, possessed from head to foot by the passion for the chase.

We soon reached the edges of the ponds.

Their tufts of rushes remained motionless; not a breath of air caressed them, but movements which were scarcely perceptible ran through the water. Sometimes the surface was stirred by something, and light circles gathered around, like luminous wrinkles enlarging indefinitely.

When we reached the hut, where we were to lie in wait, my husband made me go in first; then he slowly loaded his gun, and the dry crackling of the powder produced a strange effect on me. He saw that I was shuddering and asked:

"Does this trial happen to be quite enough for you? If so, go back."

I was much surprised and I replied:

"Not at all. I did not come to go back without doing anything. You seem queer this evening."

He murmured:

"As you wish." And we remained there without moving.

At the end of about half an hour, as nothing broke the oppressive stillness of the bright autumn night, I said in a low tone:

"Are you quite sure he is passing this way?"

Hervé winced as if I had bitten him, and with his mouth close to my ear he said:

"Make no mistake about it! I am quite sure."

And once more there was silence.

I believe I was beginning to get drowsy when my husband pressed my arm, and his voice, changed to a hiss, said:

"Do you see him there under the trees?"

I looked in vain; I could distinguish nothing. And slowly Hervé now cocked his gun, all the time fixing his eyes on my face.

I was myself making ready to fire, and suddenly, thirty paces in front of us, appeared in the full light of the moon a man who was hurrying forward with rapid movements, his body bent, as if he were trying to escape.

I was so stupefied that I uttered a loud cry, but before I could turn round there was a flash before my eyes; I heard a deafening report, and I saw the man rolling on the ground, like a wolf hit by a bullet.

I burst into dreadful shrieks, almost going mad; then a furious hand—it was Hervé's—seized me by the throat. I was flung down on the ground then carried off by his strong arms. He ran, holding me up, till he reached the body lying on the grass, and he threw me on top of it violently, as if he wanted to break my head.

I thought I was lost; he was going to kill me, and he had just raised his heel up to my forehead when, in his turn, he was gripped, knocked down before I could yet realize what had happened.

I rose up abruptly and I saw kneeling on top of him Porquita, my maid, clinging like a wildcat to him with desperate energy, tearing off his beard, his mustache and the skin of his face.

Then as if another idea had suddenly taken hold of her mind, she rose up and, flinging herself on the corpse, she threw her arms around the dead man, kissing his eyes and mouth, opening the dead lips with her own lips, trying to find in them a breath and the long, long kiss of lovers.

My husband, picking himself up, gazed at me. He understood and, falling at my feet, said:

"Oh, forgive me, my darling. I suspected you, and I killed this girl's lover. It was my keeper that deceived me."

But I was watching the strange kisses of that dead man and that living woman, and her sobs and her writhings of sorrowing love, and at that moment I understood that I might be unfaithful to my husband.

Chamber Theatre Adaptation
"A Wife's Confession"
by Guy de Maupassant
Adapted by Michael T. Downey

Scene: A bus station in Buffalo, New York. Late afternoon hustle and bustle.

Characters: Five people are seated in various sections of the station: A young girl (YG), a portly middle-aged man (PMM), an American veteran in a wheelchair (VET), a Krishna priest (PRI), and an old woman (WOM).

Voice: Buses twelve and fourteen bound for Whitesands now boarding at terminal "A" and "L." Please have tickets and baggage ready for pre-boarding. Thank you for riding Brown Wolf Bus Lines, serving the United States, Canada, and Northeast Mexico since 1954.

(*The portly middle-aged man rises with bag in hand. There is a brief moment before a full cord sounds and a bright light flashes. After a second moment, an over-light comes up on him and he subsequently drops his case before speaking.*)

PMM (*acting as Narrator and as if possessed at first, then settling into this language*): My friends (*He speaks to the other people in the station*), you have asked me to relate to you the liveliest recollections of my life. I am very old, without relatives, without children, so I am free to make a confession to you. Promise me one thing—never to reveal my name. I have been much loved, as you know; I have often myself loved. I was very beautiful; I may say this today, when my beauty is gone. Love was for me the life of the soul, just as the air is the life of the body. I would have preferred to die rather than exist without affection, without having somebody always to care for me.

(*The people are paying attention, but growing more and more perplexed with this overweight gentleman's verbal explosion.*)

VET (*rolling over to the PMM*): Hey man, what the hell's the . . . (*There is a similar cord sounded with a flash and then an over-light on the Veteran. He begins to act as a character directed by PMM. He speaks to the Priest.*): You mustn't put me off any longer. I must have an answer.

PRI (*The same cord sounds, a flash, and an over-light sequence. The Priest is now a character directed by PMM.*): But I've told you, we must be patient and wait. You must believe that I love you with my whole heart and will forever.

VET: Why must we wait? I often feel that you are just pretending to love me. This has all been another of your games—your husband must still hold some attraction for you.

PRI: That isn't true. I've told you over and over how I feel. *(pause)* A legal kiss is never as good as a stolen kiss.

PMM *(to audience)*: Women often pretend to love only once with all the strength of their hearts; it has often happened to be so violent in one of my attachments that I thought it would be impossible for my transports ever to end.

PRI *(slowly)*: Be patient . . . and wait . . . I'll love you forever.

PMM *(to audience)*: However, they always died out in a natural fashion, like a fire when it has no more fuel. I will tell you today the first of my adventures, in which I was very innocent but which led to others. *(He pauses, preparing to start story.)*

Voice *(breaking in, returning all to normal)*: Last call for Whitesands, last boarding call!

(The Krishna Priest, Middle-Aged Man, and Vet, all a little dazed, leave their spots and go to the bus offstage left. The Old Woman and Young Girl have been watching this and are equally dazed.)

WOM *(calling offstage left)*: Drug addicts! *(A flash of light, cord, and over-light comes up on Old Woman and Young Girl.)* A legal kiss is never as good as a stolen kiss.

YG: My husband was tall in stature, elegant, and a really fine gentleman in his manners.

(Fade to black.)

Summary

This chapter covered the basic techniques for analyzing and adapting narrative fiction for the stage. Robert S. Breen defined and developed chamber theatre as a technique for staging prose fiction.

Chamber theatre differs from conventional theatre in three primary ways: it stages narrative fiction not plays—as a result, the narrator is always considered the central or major character; the epic not the dramatic mode is represented; and the production occurs in the past tense, not the present tense of most plays.

In a chamber theatre adaptation, the narrator is engaged in both telling and showing. In the virtual present, the narrator "tells" his or her story to the audience. The scenes from the virtual past are "shown."

The first element of a text to consider when adapting is the narrator's point of view. There are five basic points of view from which a story may be seen and told: first-person major character, first-person minor character, first-person nonparticipating witness, third-person omniscient (limited or total), and third-person observer. In addition, more and more contemporary writers are creating second-person storytellers, who employ the slippery "you."

First-person narrators are characters in the stories they tell and consequently their roles are defined (the exception is the nonparticipating witness narrator who is not clearly defined). Third-person narrators are undefined and they must be given a "role" to play. The study of the narrator's function or role is essential in the adaptation and staging of prose fiction texts.

All narrators have a certain vested interest in the stories they tell. They are usually trying to convince a particular audience—which adapters must identify and define—that their rendition of the story is the true one. Narrators, then, are rhetorical and are trying to persuade a particular group to believe their versions of stories.

An internal modal analysis helps in assigning lines in chamber theatre adaptations. Epic lines are usually said by the narrator to the audience, dramatic lines are dialogue lines and are said by the characters. Lyric lines are the most complex and may be taken by the narrator or the character depending on the language used. Lyric-mode lines are usually the spoken thoughts of a character. Indirect discourse are lines where the narrator tells us what someone said or thought. These lines may be said by the narrator or by the character.

Tag lines are the identifying markers writers use so that the reader will know who is speaking. Since we are putting a story on stage, who says what is clarified. There are times when tag lines should be maintained, however.

When adapting stories with first-person narrators, look closely at the narrator to see if there is a difference between the virtual present telling and the virtual past showing. If a great deal of time has elapsed and there is a psychological or emotional difference in the narrator, bifurcating this role may be useful in showing this split or difference.

When adapting stories with third-person narrators, look closely at the language the narrator uses to determine the narrator's attitude and role. Examine long narrative passages and decide if the narrator's attitude and language prevail in any line or whether the character's attitude and language are suggested.

Examining the narrator's diction and syntax can be helpful in determining attitude and personality, especially of undefined narrators who are not characters in the story. If you can define the style of the narration, you can often define the style of the narrator.

Undefined narrators often may be given "social roles" to play which help define their responsibilities as storytellers. Three of these social roles are narrator as moralizer, narrator as double, and narrator as camera.

Some miscellaneous techniques include adding mime, dance, or a chorus; characterizing inanimate forces; and turning narration into dialogue.

Often a work may have to be cut to fit a prescribed time limit. Cutting should be based on a thorough understanding of the work and should occur only after devising a production concept, which helps you know what to retain and what to eliminate.

Commercial chamber theatre adaptations often alter a text to meet the needs and expectations of a contemporary audience. They are not concerned about a perceived integrity to the original text.

Notes

[1] Robert S. Breen, "Chamber Theatre," Supplement VII, *A Course Guide in the Theatre Arts at the Secondary School Level*, rev. ed. (Washington, DC: American Theatre Association, Inc., 1968), pp. 107, 108.

[2] Robert S. Breen, *Chamber Theatre* (Englewood Cliffs, NJ: Prentice-Hall, 1978), p. 4.

[3] John J. O'Connor, "Steppenwolf's 'Grapes,' As It Was on Broadway," *The New York Times*, October 11, 1992, p. H2.

[4] Don Geiger, "Poetic Realizing as Knowing," *Quarterly Journal of Speech* 59 (October 1973), p. 314.

[5] Irene Kacandes, "Are You in the Text?: The 'Literary Performative' in Postmodernist Fiction," *Text and Performance Quarterly* 13 (1993), pp. 139–153.

[6] Walker Gibson, *Tough, Sweet and Stuffy: An Essay on Modern American Prose Styles* (Bloomington: Indiana University Press, 1966), pp. 142–43.

[7] Wayne C. Booth, *The Rhetoric of Fiction* (Chicago: University of Chicago Press, 1961), p. 149.

[8] This material comes from a lecture delivered by Joanna Hawkins Maclay at the Ozarks Spring Oral Interpretation Festival at Southwest Missouri State University in April 1977.

[9] Claire Rosenfield, "The Shadow Within: the Conscious and Unconscious Use of the Double," *Daedalus* 92 (Spring 1963); reprinted in Albert J. Guerard, ed. *Stories of the Double* (Philadelphia: J. B. Lippincott Co., 1967), p. 311.

[10] Breen, *Chamber Theatre*, p. 93.

[11] See C. F. Keppler, *The Literature of the Second Self* (Tucson: University of Arizona Press, 1972).

[12] Breen, *Chamber Theatre*, p. 58.

[13] Breen, *Chamber Theatre*, p. 71.

[14] Judith C. Espinola, "The Nature, Function, and Performance of Indirect Discourse in Prose Fiction," *Speech Monographs* 41, no. 3(August 1974), pp. 193–204.

[15] This adaptation was made by Joanna Hawkins Maclay at a workshop for the Ozarks Spring Interpretation Festival.

[16] Michael S. Bowman, "'Novelizing' the Stage: Chamber Theatre After Breen and Bakhtin," *Text and Performance Quarterly* 15, no. 1(January 1995), pp. 1–23.

Chapter Five

Chamber Theatre:
Staging Your Adaptation

Chapter four presented many different ideas for the analysis of prose fiction scripts to create chamber theatre adaptations. This chapter will focus on how to make those adaptations work on stage. As with readers theatre, choices in staging chamber theatre scripts are determined by the material itself—what will best illuminate the interaction of characters, their psychological makeup, the symbolic action of the text, and so on. Chamber theatre, though, unlike readers theatre, borrows much from conventional theatre staging. The director must choose the type of focus, the type and degree of movement, and the visual and aural aspects such as setting, lighting, costuming, properties, and multimedia enhancements according to the needs of the script. Since directing chamber theatre productions is not that different from directing conventional theatre productions, we will begin with some basic directing concepts that apply to both mediums.

Directing in Chamber Theatre

As we stated in chapter one, we must not forget that chamber theatre is a "theatrical" art form which demands a certain appeal to the visual sense. (Famed acting teacher John Houseman required his students to read novels by Dickens because he believed this was the best way to learn about the theatre!) This means that performers do not merely stand and recite their lines, they must move to underscore their relationship to each other and to the audience. The scenes in chamber theatre must be "blocked"—which involves arranging the characters in relationship to the scenic elements (tables, chairs, benches, stools, etc.). Let us now detail some specific directing techniques.

We clarified the nine areas on a stage in chapter three, but you may want to review that now. Some directors pre-block a show, determining ahead of time where and when performers will move. Some directors wait until they have a cast to work with before making these decisions. Whether you pre-block or block with the cast present will probably be based on the amount of directing experience you have, and how much time you have to get the show on its feet. Before you can block, though, you must decide what the set will look like and where the set pieces or furniture will be placed on that set. (Remember, don't put anything onstage that you will not use.) Whereas in readers theatre productions the entire cast often stays on stage the entire time, in chamber theatre, the characters acting in scenes may make literal entrances and exits. The director must decide ahead of time where entrances and exits will be, and what is in the "offstage world." Decide where characters come from when they enter, where they will go when they enter, how they will move, and where they will go when they exit. Try to block characters reasonably close to exits several lines before their exit line. Try to avoid assigning long movement on short speeches. Consider stage picture and composition. Variety in stage pictures is important. Try to use a variety of levels and planes.

Performers may cross in a straight line or in a curved line. Normally, a performer should end movement and a line of dialogue at the same time. If movement comes before the line, the line is emphasized. If the movement comes after the line, the movement is emphasized. In general, keep the following in mind—but remember that these are only conventional blocking norms and need not be adhered to.

1. Crosses should usually be made downstage of people and furniture.
2. Do not move or cross while someone else is speaking. Audiences will follow the movement of the moving character and may not listen to what the speaking character is saying.
3. Performers should usually take the shortest path when making a cross.
4. Try to stage scenes so that they take place downstage of furniture and set pieces.

5. Try to avoiding upstaging. Upstaging occurs when the performer who should receive the focus must turn upstage in order to address someone. To avoid this, put the two performers on the same level.

Special problems occur with love scenes (How much do I literalize? Do I suggest the behavior?) and fight scenes. Fight scenes must be choreographed, like a dance. Safety must be the first consideration, and someone skilled in stage combat should be called in to help. If no one is available to choreograph the fight, find a way to suggest rather than literalize it. If appropriate, stylized movement and gestures may be employed such as those appropriate for melodramas, musicals, and parodies. Stylized movement includes walking backwards, side-stepping, exaggerated gestures, slow motion (useful to convey that the narrator is using description), and speeded up motion (useful when the narrator is using summary).

As we mentioned in chapter four, the degree of telling versus showing employed in a script will help you know how much movement is required. If there is more telling than showing, then the narrator's major responsibility may be to interact with the audience. If there is more showing than telling, the narrator is engaged in recreating scenes—in which case directors must decide how involved the narrator is in the stories he or she shows us. Much will be determined by the production concept which we discussed in chapter four. An adapter/director (again, we are assuming that this is the same person) begins with a production concept that informs all other decisions. If you decide to do *A Midsummer Night's Dream* in a traditional Elizabethan style, this will be a very different production than one staged in a white gymnasium as if the characters were circus performers!

Rehearsals should begin with blocking the show. If the show has been pre-blocked, give the performers their blocking and ask them to write it down IN PENCIL! If blocking is to occur while performers are on their feet, encourage them to pause to write their blocking down. Then, run the show several times while performers hold their scripts so that they can get used to saying their lines while moving. This way, performers tend to learn their lines and blocking simultaneously. Eventually, scripts should be put down (if they are not to be used in the production), necessary props added, and the scenes reworked, adjusted, or, if necessary re-blocked, and eventually polished.

Focus

The scenes in chamber theatre—the dramatic-mode dialogue between characters—are staged conventionally. The characters look at and address each other using onstage focus. Onstage focus means that the performers relate to each other on the stage as is true in representational theatre. If characters speak epic lines, they may then use offstage focus and address the audience. (Refer to the diagrams in chapter three to review the differences between onstage and offstage focus.) If characters speak their lyric thoughts, three different options are possible depending on your analysis of the text: the characters may speak their thoughts aloud to themselves (much like Hamlet does in "To be or not to be"), characters may address the audience (if they are conscious of an audience), or the characters may address the narrator (depending on the relationship you wish to establish between the narrator and characters).

Notice how the actress portraying Myrtle Wilson in this production of *The Great Gatsby* receives focus. She is higher than the other actors in the scene and she faces full front while everyone else is angled to some degree.

Narrators use both offstage and onstage focus. When they relate to the audience, they use offstage audience focus, and look directly into the eyes of the audience members. As the narrator addresses audience members, he or she addresses them keeping in mind who the adaptor has decided they are. In chapter four, for example, we discussed the novel *The Catcher in the Rye*, and stated that at the end of the novel we learn that Holden Caulfield is in a mental institution. This knowledge reduces the possible audiences Holden could be addressing. Holden would probably speak differently if you decide he is addressing other residents rather than psychiatrists, for example. Remember, the narrator "dialogues" with the audience just as the characters share dialogue with each other. In addition to offstage audience focus, the narrator also relates to the characters onstage. The narrator may warn, encourage, assist, lecture, and so on, the characters on stage. The way the narrator addresses each character helps to indicate the kind of relationship the narrator shares with that character.

Narrator/Character Relationship

In chapter four, we cited various types of social roles the narrator (especially third-person narrators) could assume during a production, including moralizer, double, and camera. When this relationship is put on stage, you must find a way to make it clear to your audience. The following is a list of some of the actions and movements of narrators that will help to reveal their relationships with the story and the characters. In general, narrators:

1. May assist characters by moving them to certain spots, holding properties for them, opening doors, placing a prop, etc.
2. May play the role of minor characters.
3. May play the role of **director** or **reporter** of characters' behavior. (These two roles concern the relationship the narrator shares with the characters in terms of power or control. If, for example, the narrator says "Bob took off his hat," and then Bob takes off his hat, the narrator is a director. If Bob takes off his hat, and then the narrator says the line, the narrator is reporting. A narrator who is eager to dictate what the characters do and when may act as a director. If you remember what Breen did with his production of Robbe-Grillet's novel *Jealousy*, the narrator was depicted as a movie director dictating character movement, costumes, etc. A narrator who is more self-effacing

or who wishes to allow the characters to act seemingly independent of the narrator may act as a reporter. Many narrators in Hemingway's stories allow the story to unfold with minimal narrative intrusion. They could assume the role of reporters.)

4. May become a property, such as a coat rack, or a mirror (as in "Impulse").

5. Can control the focus of the audience by moving close to a character or by moving to another area.

6. Can set the rhythm and tempo with movement.

7. May show empathy with a character by assuming that character's stance, gestures, etc.

8. May move into the audience to invite them into the story.

9. May move close to characters when omniscient to relate their thoughts and feelings and show empathy, or may maintain some distance, if required.

10. May stand or sit away from characters when describing them physically or when acting as objective reporters, like a camera pulling away for the panoramic view. (Ordinarily, omniscient narrators do not sit with the characters in scenes. This participatory behavior seems to suggest that they are characters in the scenes and lessens their ability to be perceived as omniscient.)

11. May move in and out of the scenes when alternating between objective reporting and subjective omniscience.

12. May move to a higher level than the others if their language is elevated or if they look down on the characters.

13. May speak to the audience directly and not watch the scene (at times) or may watch the scene and talk.

14. If they are first person, may stand away from the scene they describe if the story indicates their present whereabouts as separated from the events they recall.

15. May move into the scene after establishing a distinct time and place, placing themselves close to the main character.

16. May see the characters or see what the characters see.

Staging Omniscience

How does a director go about directing a performer to play someone who has abilities that exceed those of most humans? The third-person omniscient narrator poses such a problem. These narrators read minds, span large periods of time, and move from country to country in a few paragraphs. Directors must devise their own conventions for making this kind of ability clear on stage.

The best way to explain how to go about conveying that a narrator is omniscient is to give you an example of what was done in a production of "The Comforts of Home" by Flannery O'Connor. To show the narrator's omniscient relationship with Thomas—the protagonist in the story—the performer playing the narrator often played scenes as Thomas saw them rather than as the narrator perceived them. Thomas, for example, thinks of the young woman Thomas' mother tries to help as a "little slut," whereas the narrator is less judgmental. To illustrate the difference between these two points of view and to magnify Thomas' bigotry, the scene where Thomas first meets the girl (her real name is Sarah Ham but she likes to be known as Star Drake), was played twice; the first time from Thomas' point of view and the second time from the narrator's. In the first rendition, Star was vulgar and coarse. In the second version, the narrator's version, she seemed meek and rather pathetic. In addition, the story dealt with how Star had invaded the "comforts" of Thomas' "home," so the layout of this home was important. Without literalizing real walls or doors, the characters walked around on the stage maintaining the dimensions of each room and miming the doors. The narrator, on the other hand, was not bound by space restrictions and walked wherever he needed to go despite imaginary walls or doors. This convention underlined the narrator's omniscient abilities.

Omniscient narrators normally stay close to the character or characters with whom they are omniscient, but often the relationship demands distance. As we pointed out in chapter four, just because a narrator is psychologically close to a character does not mean that he or she must be physically or emotionally close. The type of relationship the narrator shares with each character will determine whether they are close or distant. It is also possible, as we have previously pointed out, for the narrator to engage in a dialogical relationship with characters. Look, for example, at the narrator-character exchange in the adaptation of "Impulse" in chapter one. In that short excerpt, the narrator, playing the role of Michael Lowes' mirror double, looks at and talks to Michael as Michael is shaving, and Michael, thinking aloud, talks to him.

Creating Conventions

Often directors of chamber theatre productions are confronted with situations in texts that present unique challenges. The conventions of traditional theatre do not suffice, and the director must find creative solutions. Since prose fiction writers rarely write with a staged production in mind, they may include some difficult situations to translate onstage. How does one span large periods of time and varied locales? How does one stage fires, floods, wars, and so on? Basically, directors must create their own conventions, and find ways to suggest rather than literalize situations. There is always the tendency to want to do everything representationally, but this is not always possible or best. Let me describe how some directors have solved some of the problems that texts present.

Since literalizing all locales in a full-length novel, like *Gone with the Wind*, is not possible, allow the narrator's language and selected pieces of furniture to help create different locales. In a production of *The Great Gatsby*, for example, the various locales were established by Nick's descriptions and by selected furniture pieces that were carried in and placed by four tuxedoed servants in full view of the audience: white wicker for Tom and Daisy's home; red velvet furniture with a grand piano for Gatsby's mansion; gas pumps, trash cans, and dusty benches for Myrtle and George's garage; a love seat, two chairs, and a coffee table for the Plaza Hotel, and so on.

One director had to find a way to suggest characters wading into a pond in a production of "The Horse Dealer's Daughter." Two performers stood on either end of the stage and held large pieces of blue cloth. At the appropriate time, they manipulated them to suggest the movement of water as the characters walked between them.

One director was confronted with the task of directing an adaptation of *Sybil*, the true story of a woman who suffered from multiple personalities. Her solution was to create a convention called **depletion**. Sixteen performers were cast to play Sybil and Sybil's other selves. In reality, though, Sybil is really the only one ever present as the other selves are *part* of her not *separate* from her. To suggest that Sybil was really the only one there, the actress playing the original Sybil was always onstage when her other selves made appearances, but unless she was speaking she was "depleted"—seated lifelessly onstage. When two selves appeared simultaneously, only one would speak while the other (and Sybil) were depleted. For example, one of Sybil's male selves, Mike, entered with his shoes untied. He tied his right shoe, but then Sid, the other male self,

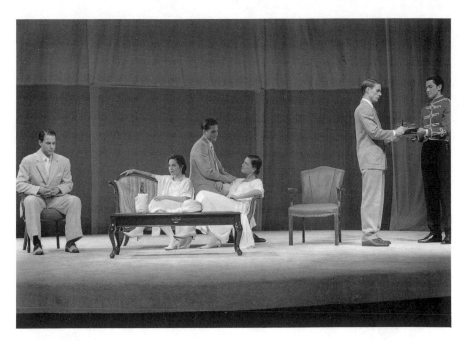

Suggestive set pieces were used in this production of *The Great Gatsby* to establish
the convention of various locales. This picture depicts a scene which took place
in the Plaza Hotel.

wanted to make an appearance. Mike depleted, and Sid appeared with
his right shoe tied, and tied his left shoe.

To suggest a fire in Isaac Bashevis Singer's "Henne Fire," the director
brought in a choreographer who gave the performers red scarves and
choreographed a "fire dance."

We spoke in chapter four about authors who occasionally enter their
stories because they can't resist sharing the stage with their characters.
In two such productions, the author-characters competed with the
narrators they had created to tell their stories. In a production of John
Fowles' *The French Lieutenant's Woman*, the contemporary author often
interrupted the Victorian narrator's attempts to tell the story, and the
narrator tried to cope with this intrusion. This distinction between them
was magnified by spatial and temporal differences. The author-character
was dressed in a contemporary costume and moved in and out of a
contemporary setting. Everyone else was dressed in Victorian costumes
and moved on a set that suggested the Victorian period.

On the far right is the surrogate author (in contemporary attire), who interrupts the Victorian narrator's (far left, in Victorian garb) attempts to tell the story in this scene from *The French Lieutenant's Woman.*

In Vonnegut's *Breakfast of Champions*, the "author" constantly intrudes, directing the audience's attention to him and away from the story. The "author," for example, continually draws pictures which are found throughout the book. The director wanted to find a way to reproduce these visual distractions onstage. In one production of this novel, the character of the "author" was on a raised platform attached to two ladders at either end of the stage where a clothesline was hung. On one side sat the author-character with an oversized copy of *Breakfast of Champions*. Inside this large tome was an artist's sketch pad on which the performer drew his illustrations, attached them with clothespins to the clothesline, and sent them across the stage. This device served to distract the audience in the same way that the illustrations in the book distract the reader.

Second-person texts, as we mentioned in chapter four, encourage audience participation and involvement. Several techniques could be employed to involve the actual audience—in addition to looking at and talking directly to them. The audience could be a "you" participant in the story. Try placing some of the performers in the audience, and have the narrator beckon them to come out of the audience to perform in the scenes. Another possibility is to have the actual audience participate. Have the narrator hand them scripts with their cues and lines clearly indicated, but be prepared for all the ramifications that could develop once unrehearsed performers enter your production. This performance possibility demands creative flexibility on everyone's part. If conditions permit, consider staging a script of this kind in the round, with the audience in the center of the circle while the text unravels itself around them.

In general, look for creative solutions for the special problems posed by some prose fiction texts. Some directors decide not to work with a story that is too difficult, or they cut sections that seem too difficult to translate onstage. Try, instead, to develop and define your own conventions. Make sure, though, that the audience understands what you are doing. Since your intention is to find a way to communicate a text to the audience, you must make some changes if the audience doesn't understand what you are doing. Once you get your production staged, take a step back. Put yourself in the place of an innocent audience member who does not know the story or understand what chamber theatre is. This perspective may help you to modify, alter, or completely rework your conventions.

Use of Scripts

Although the presence and use of scripts during a performance have been traditions of readers theatre and chamber theatre productions for years, as we stated in chapter three, scripts do not seem to serve the same symbolic function they once did. At one time, the presence of the script indicated an integrity to the text, and suggested that the performers were not making their lines up as they went along. The script was usually present even though the material was memorized. When audiences today see manuscripts used during performances, they usually think that the performers are not prepared or did not memorize their lines.

Breen suggests that only the narrator carry a script during a chamber theatre production, and then only if the narrator is a nonparticipating witness or a third-person observer uninvolved in the scenes. The more involved the narrator is and the more personal the story, the less need there should be for a manuscript to be present. Whether or not the script is held, the material must be completely mastered. Although narrators may glance at the script occasionally, they must use their eyes to create items in the imaginary scene, and to establish contact with the audience or characters onstage. They cannot keep their eyes glued to the page nor can they grope for the words that come next.

If scripts are used, they can effectively be used as props in the production, e.g., newspapers, fans, weapons, proclamations, and so on. If scripts are used, less physical movement is usually possible or expected. If scripts are not used, more physical movement is possible and expected.

Since there is usually more representational movement in chamber theatre than in readers theatre, the presence of the script—while reminding us of the presentational nature of the form—often gets in the way and lessens the narrator's ability to interact. Ultimately, the decision to use scripts is up to the director. Whatever decision is made, it should be based on the production concept and not on the fact that some performers need scripts because they are less prepared than others. If some performers use scripts and others do not, this inconsistency could confuse some audience members who try to discover its significance.

Spectacle Elements: The Visual and Aural Aspects

Setting and Set Pieces

Unlike many play scripts, prose fiction texts rarely keep the unities of time, place, and action in mind. Aristotle theorized that plays should take place in one twenty-four-hour period, in one locale, and with one plot line. Prose fiction texts may span years, take place in a variety of locales, and often have more than one through line of action. What does one do, then, about creating an appropriate set for a prose fiction script that may make such great demands?

There are two answers: rely on the author's words and on synecdoche. The language in a text—especially the descriptive passages—often can create in our imaginations a more spectacular set than could ever be literalized onstage.

Listen to the undefined narrator's description of her room in Charlotte Perkins Gilman's story "The Yellow Wall-Paper":

From "The Yellow Wall-Paper"
by Charlotte Perkins Gilman

It is a big, airy room, the whole floor nearly, with windows that look all ways, and air and sunshine galore. It was nursery first and then playroom and gymnasium, I should judge; for the windows are barred for little children, and there are rings and things in the walls.

The paint and paper look as if a boys' school had used it. It is stripped off—the paper—in great patches all around the head of my bed, about as far as I can reach, and in a great place on the other side of the room low down. I never saw a worse paper in my life.

A set designer would find it difficult to reproduce this room as complete and detailed as the narrator describes it. Her language, though, creates the images in the minds of the audience members, and they

The challenge of re-creating one of Gatsby's parties was solved in this production with a more detailed set. Multi-colored lights adorned a tent which was lowered onto a carpeted white oval. The actors could be seen downstage or upstage of the tent. Notice also the period costumes.

create the setting. Of course, performers cannot perform on a set of words alone. In "The Yellow Wall-Paper," the room and the paper in it take on a personality of their own. The narrator hallucinates about a woman trapped in that room, in that wall-paper, and this image more than the literal room may be suggested in the set design. In chamber theatre, more than in readers theatre, a more representational set is usually required but directors must choose what they use with care.

Synecdoche is a literary term that we spoke of in chapter three and which means using a part to represent the whole. If an oak tree is called for, a tree limb can be used to suggest the whole tree. A bench can suggest a bed, a chair, a coffin, a door, or held upside down, a large bucket! Breen explains:

> It would seem . . . that the best kind of setting, speaking generally, for Chamber Theatre productions, is the kind that has a minimum of standard, generalized pieces that can be fleshed out with detailed verbal descriptions provided by the author's text. Scenery for Chamber Theatre is less a painter's or decorator's art than it is a sculptor's art. The free forms of sculpture, or the more conventional structural elements of our environment, provide the best setting: ladders, stools, benches, platforms, ramps, pipes, etc. These structural forms have a nonspecific character that allows them to serve as elevation, separation of the stage into areas, centers of action, concrete objects of sufficient rigidity and physical resistance to permit the actor to use them freely without fear of exposing them as something artificial.[1]

To sum up, chamber theatre directors have more than one alternative in staging literature. They may use a comparatively bare space with a few set pieces to provide places to sit, to elevate the action, and to make meaningful stage pictures that help tell the story. They may employ a fully realistic setting or they may establish a metaphoric staging. The choice should be influenced by the style and form of the literature and by the mood it requires, for the goal is to illuminate the complexities of the script through performance. The creative imagination can suggest unique ways to stimulate the minds of the audience to new insights. Scenery is effective if it helps the audience enter the world described by the narrator, makes its impact, and then is assimilated with the total experience.

Lighting

Lighting in chamber theatre works to achieve similar effects as it does in readers theatre: to illuminate the faces of the performers and to focus attention on different areas of the stage. The narrator is usually the key performer in chamber theatre productions, and his or her presence can be featured with a special lighting effect or perhaps a spotlight.

Lighting can help in creating transitions between scenes by signaling the ends and beginnings of scenes. When narrators want focus, lights can be focused on them and dimmed on the performers in scene. When narrators, for example, reveal confidential information that they want only the audience to hear, the lights can dim out on everyone else. When narrators want the scene illuminated, they can signal for that to be done.

Emotional and psychological effects involve the symbolic use of colored lights, light and shade, variations in shadows, and the speed with which lighting changes are made.

Finally, lighting is very useful in establishing a certain mood. As Breen writes:

> Unlike scenery, which tends to particularize and therefore to compete with the spoken descriptions in the text, lighting is highly generalized and operates subtly and often indirectly on the sense. A cold, dreary light on the stage will support any particularized description of a cold, dreary atmosphere expressed in the text. Of course, it can be used in a realistic fashion to represent sunrise or sunset, or to suggest lightning but its greatest value is the creation of moods.[2]

Costumes

Often what characters are to wear in chamber theatre productions is described in the selection. The narrator, for example, may describe in vivid detail what a character wears: "Mary wore a rose-colored dress with lace up to her throat, white gloves, and a red hat with flowers on it." In this case, the costumer must find a dress, gloves, and hat that fit this description. Decisions must be made as to how realistic costumes are to be. What if Mary wears many different dresses in the production? Decide, then, if every character will literally change clothes whenever a change is called for by the narrator, or if perhaps one appropriate costume is to be used for each character and the other costume descriptions deleted. If the narrator isn't particularly concerned about what someone wore, it is up to the costumer in conjunction with the director to make this decision based on information in the text.

First-person narrators are characters in the story so ideas for their costumes can be found in the text. Third-person narrators are a more complicated matter. Often these narrators have a formal demeanor and

In an updated version of "Little Red Riding Hood," selected props and costumes were used to suggest each character.

so formal wear may be appropriate. In general, if you define the narrator's social role, this will help you to determine an appropriate costume.

As was true in readers theatre, *suggestive* costuming—items or costume pieces that can be worn to represent a character's status, occupation, mood, or state of mind—may be appropriate. Especially considering that in chamber theatre performers may play more than one role in successive scenes, a performer could wear something neutral, put an apron on to suggest a butcher in one scene, take off the apron, and add a badge and hat to suggest a police officer in the next.

As we suggested in chapter three, attention should be given to choosing appropriate colors: dark, somber colors are usually more appropriate for very serious or heavily dramatic presentations. For light or humorous productions, use bright, cheerful colors. The choice of formal or informal attire makes a statement about the material. For instance, formal attire for a folktale would negate the folksy quality needed, and informal attire for Edith Wharton's novel about upper-class society, *Age of Innocence*, would be inappropriate.

Costuming is also effective in showing differences when bifurcation is employed. When two performers play the same role, there must be something psychologically or emotionally different about them. The director must find a way to suggest that the two performers are playing the same role, but dressing them exactly alike may diminish the differences between them. The costumes could be similar, but subtle differences could be achieved with scarves or hats or shawls, for example. In Joyce's story "Eveline," mentioned in chapter four, a woman must choose between running off with the man she loves or staying home to care for her father. In one production of this story, the role of Eveline was bifurcated to suggest the psychological distinctions created by these two choices. Both actresses playing Eveline wore black dresses, but the actress playing the Eveline who wanted to run off wore a dress with a low- cut neckline and a red scarf around her neck, and the other actress wore a high-necked gown with a black scarf.

Costuming also can show the differences in time. In the production discussed earlier of *The French Lieutenant's Woman*, there is a character on stage who represents the contemporary author whereas the rest of the characters are in Victorian England. Costuming can help show this distinction. In a production of *The Scarlet Letter*, the cast first appeared in contemporary dress, and then, before the audience's eyes, manipulated their contemporary clothes to transform themselves into a Puritan community. The director of this production wished to stress that the ideas in this novel were not so different from ideas that confront us today.

Costuming was used in this production of *The Scarlet Letter* to juxtapose the Puritan versus the contemporary points of view.

Costumes, then, should only provide what is necessary to permit the audience to see attire in the mind's eye, not characters on a theatre stage in a full-fledged, costumed play. The major point to remember is that costuming should suggest the type of character and the spirit of the literature.

Properties

Whereas props are usually mimed in readers theatre, they may be employed in chamber theatre if their presence is necessitated by the material. If most props are suggested or mimed, however, and then a real prop is used, it receives added emphasis. In a production of Beth Holmes' *The Whipping Boy*, a novel about psychological child abuse, all props were mimed except for one—the knife that the father used to try to kill his son. The threat and the violence of this act were underlined by the use of a realistic prop.

Some props can be invested with symbolic overtones. In the production of *The Scarlet Letter* referred to earlier, Hester's baby was a large

Only the knife the father used to attempt to murder his son was literalized in this production of *The Whipping Boy*.

red scarf folded to suggest a child. As the child, Pearl, grew, she wore the scarf as a shawl. The same scarf was held between Mistress Hibbins and Pearl in a tug-of-war battle for Pearl's soul.

Adding Media

A production may be enhanced by incorporating other media forms. Adding such elements as slides, dance, videos, taped or live music, film, or photographs, to name just a few, turn the production into a mixed-media performance. These additions can greatly enrich the production if the media are well chosen and employed. By using other media forms, you can facilitate the audience's understanding and appreciation and increase its involvement in the production. Such forms can also help a director suggest elements that cannot be effectively staged.

Slides, for example, can be used to underscore what is going on in the production at the time, or may be used to remind the audience of important moments that have already occurred and that present ironic parallels with something occurring at the time. In the production of *The Whipping Boy* mentioned earlier, the director wanted to illustrate the way the title character felt about his mother as opposed to the way he may have behaved towards her. To convey this, slides of images of the mother were projected on a large scrim upstage of the set. The picture on the opposite page drawn by Eleanor Everett is an example of one of these illustrations. These large, distorted faces of women became Rorschach images of the protagonist's troubled mind. In a production of *The Great Gatsby*, a huge white scrim draped onto a white-carpeted oval. On the scrim were projected photographs of those people on the list of Gatsby's party guests, the eyes of T. J. Eckleburg, as well as the schedule and General Resolves Gatsby's father shows Nick.

In that same production of *The Great Gatsby*, dance was incorporated. When Gatsby tells Nick how he first met and fell in love with Daisy Buchanan, two dancers appeared—one dressed as a young Daisy and one dressed in uniform suggesting a young Gatsby. The dance was a visual illustration of Gatsby's monologue and added a romantic intensity.

Videos can be used to suggest different locales or a journey a character is taking. One clever use of video was in a production of Richard Brautigan's novel, *Sombrero Fallout*. A writer, suffering from writer's block, ripped the first page of a new story out of his typewriter, tore it into three pieces, and tossed the pieces into the wastebasket. The stage went to black, a video screen was lowered, and the audience saw a video of the inside of the wastebasket with the papers whirling around, and

In a production of *The Whipping Boy*, images like this one drawn by Eleanor Everett were projected on a large scrim in order to give the audience a sense of the protagonist's troubled feelings toward his mother.

Dance was incorporated in this production of *The Great Gatsby* to illustrate the details of the story Gatsby tells Nick about Gatsby's love affair with Daisy Buchanan.

then exploding out of the wastebasket. When the stage lights returned, those three pieces of paper were portrayed by three actors dressed all in white with the story the writer left unfinished written on their costumes. They proceeded to become narrators and to tell the story of what happened when a sombrero fell out of the sky and landed in a small town. This was a very clever way to tell this part of the story.

Music is useful to set a mood; underscore tension, emotions, or humor; and introduce different themes. In a production of *The French Lieutenant's Woman*, original themes were composed for the three main characters and the appropriate theme was played to underscore the character's presence, even if he or she was not on the stage at the time.

Once the script is adapted and staged, decide where you would like to add music. Music may be used in the interior of a scene or as a transitional device between scenes. Time the moments where you would like to use music so that you know exactly what and how much is necessary.

In an adaptation of Kurt Vonnegut, Jr.'s "Harrison Bergeron," sound effects were created on a synthesizer to represent the sounds that poor George Bergeron was burdened with hearing as a result of being too intelligent. In the future, when this story was to have taken place, anyone more intelligent than others was kept from being able to concentrate by having to wear earphones through which played an arsenal of different sounds. In this particular production of the story, a sort of "big brother" told the story from a position unseen by the audience. He delivered his lines over a microphone and created the sounds George heard.

No matter what kind of medium you use, make sure it serves one or more of the following purposes:

- to help establish the mood or theme
- to help illustrate elements that cannot be literalized onstage
- to provide subtextual reinforcement
- to build intensity
- to underline crisis and climax moments
- to help the audience visualize ambiguous moments in the production

To convey the sense that Jane Eyre and Rochester were getting married in a church, a slide of stained glass windows was projected on a scrim upstage.

Exercise care when using media. Too often, enthusiasm over mixed-media effects results in their taking over the show instead of adding dimension to it. Make sure you do not blur the impact of the literature with these media elements. Remember, much of what occurs in chamber theatre—as well as in readers theatre—is up to the creative imagination of the audience. Make sure you do not lessen the audience's creative involvement by literalizing too many elements with media. The nonrealistic often allows more options for creativity and greater use of the imagination. The goal should be to stir the audience's imagination, to create in their minds all that the words imply. The very nature of this art form—often with a few performers playing many roles and with scenes shifting as facilely as the written word—precludes rigid realism.

Staging Postmodern Texts

The challenge of staging postmodern narratives involves working with a text that often plays with language; has no causal plot line or a clear beginning, middle, or end; and rarely has closure—the work stops without supplying a satisfying ending. There is often a sense of self-reflexivity—of authors writing about authors writing. Language in these texts is a performance in itself, and audience participation is essential to complete the task of discovering what the text "means" because of unfilled gaps and indeterminacies. Postmodern writers like Thomas Pynchon, John Barth, Donald Barthelme, and Robert Coover break the rules and defy traditional storytelling conventions; as adapters/directors, you should feel free to do the same. Experiment with creative ways of presenting these texts.

Here is the opening passage of *Lost in the Funhouse* by John Barth. As you read the selection, see if you can envision a way of staging it for chamber theatre. Following the passage is one possible adaptation.

From *Lost in the Funhouse*
by John Barth

For whom is the funhouse fun? Perhaps for lovers. For Ambrose it is *a place of fear and confusion.* He has come to the seashore with his family for the holiday, *the occasion of their visit is Independence Day, the most important secular holiday of the United States of America.* A single straight underline is the manuscript mark for italic type, *which in turn* is the printed equivalent to oral emphasis of words and phrases as well as the customary type for titles of complete works, not to mention. Italics are also employed, in fiction stories especially, for "outside," intrusive, or artificial voices, such as radio announcements, the texts of telegrams and newspaper articles, et cetera. They should be used *sparingly.* If passages originally in roman type are italicized by someone repeating them, it's customary to acknowledge the fact. *Italics mine.*

Ambrose was "at that awkward age." His voice came out high pitched as a child's if he let himself get carried away; to be on the safe side, therefore, he moved and spoke with *deliberate calm* and *adult gravity.* Talking soberly of unimportant or irrelevant matters and listening consciously to the sound of your own voice are useful habits for maintaining control in this difficult interval. *En route* to Ocean City he sat in the back seat of the family car with his brother Peter, age fifteen, and Magda G_____ age fourteen, a pretty girl an exquisite young lady, who lived not far from them on B_____ Street in the town of D_____, Maryland. Initials, blanks, or both were often substituted for proper names in nineteenth-century fiction to enhance the illusion of reality. It is as if the author felt it necessary to delete the names for reasons of tact or legal liability. Interestingly, as with other aspects of realism, it is an *illusion* that is being enhanced, by purely artificial means. Is it likely, does it violate the principle of verisimilitude, that a thirteen-year-old boy could make such a sophisticated observation? A girl of fourteen is *the psychological coeval* of a boy of fifteen or sixteen; a thirteen-year-old boy, therefore, even one precocious in some other respects, might be three years *her emotional junior.*

Barth's *Lost in the Funhouse* reflects on the art of writing, which is true of many postmodern texts. The third-person narrator's story is continuously interrupted by comments on the elements and techniques of conventional fiction. Barth encourages active participation from the audience. Notice, this story is written in both the past and the present tense. The following adaptation of the opening of this story calls for nine characters: the Narrator, the Author, Ambrose, Magda, Peter, Mom, Dad, and two lovers. The set to suggest the funhouse is stage right, with a series of framed mylar mirrors. Up left is the "Author" seated at a computer with a library of books behind him. Above his head is a screen on which we see what he is typing.

Chamber Theatre Adaptation
from *Lost in the Funhouse*
by John Barth

Narrator (*to audience*): For whom is the funhouse fun?

Lovers (*they are in the funhouse, looking at themselves in a mirror and giggling, they address each other*): Perhaps for lovers.

Ambrose (*to himself, looking in another mirror*): For Ambrose it is *a place of fear and confusion.*

Narrator (*to audience*): He has come to the seashore

Mom, Dad, Peter (*to audience, gaily*): with his family

Narrator (*to audience*): for the holiday, *the occasion of their visit is Independence Day, the most important secular holiday of the United States of America.*

Author (*at computer, working on a story called "Lost in the Fun-house." Author is typing* "the occasion . . ." *as Narrator says the line*): the occasion of their visit is Independence Day, the most important secular holiday of the United States of America. (*He pauses, searches for a Style Book on shelf behind him, and reads*): A single straight underline is the manuscript mark for italic type, (*he reads the following three words with emphasis*) *which in turn* is the printed equivalent to oral emphasis of words and phrases as well as the customary type for titles of complete works, not to mention. Italics are also employed, in fiction stories especially, for "outside," intrusive, or artificial voices, such as radio announcements, the texts of telegrams and newspaper articles, et cetera. They should be used *sparingly* (*said with emphasis*). If passages originally in roman type are italicized by someone repeating them, it's customary to acknowledge the fact. *Italics mine* (*said with emphasis*).

Narrator (*has waited patiently for author to stop, grateful to pick up the narrative again. To audience*): Ambrose was

Mom and Dad (*looking at Ambrose, talking to each other, cutting Narrator off*): "at that awkward age."

Narrator (*to audience*): His voice came out high pitched as a child's if he let himself get carried away;

Ambrose (*to Narrator*): to be on the safe side, therefore, he moved and spoke with

Author (*typing*): *deliberate calm*

Ambrose: and (*tries to continue, but is cut off by Author*)

Author (*typing*): *adult gravity.*

Narrator (*trying to maintain control, to audience*): Talking soberly of unimportant or irrelevant matters and listening consciously to the sound of your own voice are useful habits for maintaining control in this difficult interval.

Author (*typing, seen on screen above him*): *En route*

Narrator (*to audience*): to Ocean City he sat in the back seat of the family car with

Peter (*to audience*): his brother Peter, age fifteen,

Magda (*to audience*): and Magda (*pause*) G_____, age fourteen,

Ambrose (*to Narrator*): a pretty girl an exquisite young lady,

Magda (*to audience*): who lived not far from them on B_____ Street in the town of D_____, Maryland.

Author (*reading from Style Book*): Initials, blanks, or both were often substituted for proper names in nineteenth-century fiction to enhance the illusion of reality. It is as if the author felt it necessary to delete the names for reasons of tact or legal liability. Interestingly, as with other aspects of realism, it is an *illusion* that is being enhanced, by purely artificial means. Is it likely, does it violate the principle of verisimilitude, that a thirteen-year-old boy could make such a sophisticated observation? (*Author nods to Ambrose, who speaks his line again.*)

Ambrose (*to audience*): a pretty girl an exquisite young lady,

Author (*typing*): A girl of fourteen is *the psychological coeval* of a boy of fifteen or sixteen; a thirteen-year-old boy, therefore, even one precocious in some other respects, might be three years *her emotional junior.*

Postmodern literature glorifies in disrupting our normal expectations, and often revels in shocking or surprising us. These texts take advantage of what has gone before, but they are also revolutionary—not content with the status quo. These writers seek new alternatives, new solutions to contemporary theories of language. It is up to chamber theatre adapters and directors to rise to this challenge and create their own solutions to the new alternatives offered in these texts.

Metaphoric and Metonymic Productions

Most of the performance possibilities we've discussed in this chapter deal with scripts and staging techniques that attempt to reproduce exactly what the adapter interprets is called for in the text. There are two additional kinds of productions that we will discuss here: **metaphoric** productions and **metonymic** productions.

If you decide to employ a metaphoric staging, look for repeated images or motifs or styles of language in the text that suggest a setting other than what is literally in the story. In James Joyce's short story "The Boarding House," for example, the literal locale is Mrs. Mooney's boarding house on Hardwicke Street in Dublin, Ireland. The story deals with three characters, Mrs. Mooney, "The Madam" of the boarding house (bawdy house?); Polly Mooney, Mrs. Mooney's daughter; and Mr. Bob Doran, a resident in the boarding house who has had an affair with Polly. Polly is now pregnant, and Mrs. Mooney has asked Mr. Doran "What reparation would he make" in both an economic and moral sense. As you read the opening passage of this story, look for images or language that might suggest an alternative setting.

From "The Boarding House"
by James Joyce

Mrs. Mooney was a butcher's daughter. She was a woman who was quite able to keep things to herself: a determined woman. She had married her father's foreman and opened a butcher's shop near Spring Gardens. But as soon as his father-in-law was dead Mr. Mooney began to go to the devil. He drank, plundered the till, ran head-long into debt. It was no use making him take the pledge: he was sure to break out again a few days after. By fighting his wife in the presence of customers and by buying bad meat he ruined his business. One night he went for his wife with the cleaver and she had to sleep in a neighbour's house.

After that they lived apart. She went to the priest and got a separation from him with care of the children. She would give him neither money nor food nor house-room; and so he was obliged to enlist himself as a sheriff's man. He was a shabby stooped little drunkard with a white face and a white moustache and white eyebrows, pencilled above his little eyes, which were pink-veined and raw; and all day long he sat in the bailiff's room, waiting to be put on a job. Mrs. Mooney, who had taken what remained of her money out of the butcher business and set up a boarding house in Hardwicke Street, was a big imposing woman. Her house had a floating population made up of tourists from Liverpool and the Isle of Man and, occasionally, *artistes* from the music halls. Its resident population was made up of clerks from the city. She governed the house cunningly and firmly, knew when to give credit, when to be stern and when to let things pass. All the resident young men spoke of her as *The Madam*.

Mrs. Mooney's young men paid fifteen shillings a week for board and lodgings (beer or stout at dinner excluded). They shared in common tastes and occupations and for this reason they were very chummy with one another. They discussed with one another the chances of favourites and outsiders. Jack Mooney, the Madam's son, who was clerk to a commission agent in Fleet Street, had the reputation of being a hard case. He was fond of using soldiers' obscenities: usually he came home in the small hours. When he met his friends he had always a good one to tell them and he was always sure to be on to a good thing—that is to say, a likely horse or a likely *artiste*. He was also handy with the mits and sang comic songs. On Sunday nights there would often be a reunion in Mrs. Mooney's front drawing-room. The music-hall *artistes* would oblige and Sheridan played waltzes and polkas and vamped accompaniments. Polly Mooney, the Madam's daughter, would also sing. She sang:

"I'm a . . . naughty girl,
You needn't sham:
You know I am."

Polly was a slim girl of nineteen: she had light soft hair and a small full mouth. Her eyes, which were grey with a shade of green through them, had a habit of glancing upwards when she spoke with anyone, which made her look like a little perverse madonna. Mrs. Mooney had first sent her daughter to be a typist in a corn-factor's office but, as a disreputable sheriff's man used to come every other day to the office, asking to be allowed to say a word to his daughter, she had taken her daughter home again and set her to do housework. As Polly was very lively the intention was to give her the run of the young men. Besides young men like to feel that there is a young woman not very far away. Polly, of course, flirted with the young men but Mrs. Mooney, who was a shrewd judge, knew that the young men were only passing the time away: none of them meant business. Things went on for a long time and Mrs. Mooney began to think of sending Polly back to typewriting when she noticed that something was going on between Polly and one of the young men. She watched the pair and kept her own counsel.

One possible metaphoric setting for this story is a courtroom where Mr. Doran is standing trial for his sinful affair with Polly Mooney. Some of the motifs or images throughout the story that suggest such a setting include: "take the pledge," "bailiff's room," "clerks," "governed," "hard case," "credit," "stern," "let things pass," "shrewd judge," "passing the time," "counsel," and "under lock and key." The third-person omniscient narrator in an adaptation of this kind could play the role of Mr. Doran's defense attorney as the narrator seems to sympathize with Mr. Doran and feels, like Doran, that he "was being had." Metaphoric productions often require that some material be cut if it does not relate to the central metaphor, and additional characters or lines may be added to make the metaphoric locale clear.

When staging this metaphoric adaptation of "The Boarding House," one would try to create the specific locale of the courtroom and the specific circumstance of the trial of Bob Doran. The stage could be arranged in a courtroom setting with the performer playing the judge upstage center, perhaps on a raised platform with the witness chair directly to his or her left. Doran sits off left of center with his "lawyer" close beside him, and Mrs. Mooney and Polly are right of center. The "lawyer" addresses both the witnesses and audience members, which he or she speaks to as if they were the jury.

Metonymic productions extend beyond an attempt to duplicate what a text says. While metaphoric productions tend to affirm, respect, or conserve the perceived integrity of a text, metonymic productions relate to, but are not exactly like the text which is their source. Metonymic productions subvert, challenge, or transgress beyond this perceived integrity, and by doing so, they often expose new ramifications. For an example of a metonymic script, see Michael T. Downey's adaptation of "A Wife's Confession" in chapter four.

Metonymic productions of Shakespeare's plays abound. One of the most famous metonymic productions is probably Peter Brook's 1970 production of Shakespeare's *A Midsummer Night's Dream*, which incorporated circus routines within a set that was a huge white box. Director Peter Sellars "reimagined" *The Merchant of Venice* in his 1994 production. Says Sellars:

> When I direct Shakespeare, the first thing I do is go to the text for cuts. I go through to find the passages that are real heavy, that really are not needed, places where the language has become obscure, the places where there is a bizarre detour. . . . And then, I take those moments, those elements, and I make them the centerpiece, the core of the production.[3]

Sellars' production, inspired by the 1992 Los Angeles race riots, utilizes a multiracial cast, relocates the play in contemporary Venice, California, and underlines the parallels between Shakespeare's time and ours. As *TIME* reviewer Richard Zoglin wrote, " . . . the production pretty much upends everything the audience has come to expect from one of Shakespeare's most troubling but reliably entertaining comedies."[4] London's Cheek by Jowl company presented their version of *As You Like It* (a production which made *TIME* magazine's Top Ten list for 1994) where all the roles were assayed by men, as in Shakespeare's day. Richard Corliss applauded the production, saying, "What could have been minimalist camp—oh, Lord, men in pearls and blond wigs!—becomes a sweet meditation on mistaken sexual appetites and identity."[5] Ben Brantley agreed, calling the production, "a sustained conjuring act that celebrates the basic power of theater to bewitch, to teach and above all to transform."[6]

Metonymic productions, though, are certainly not restricted to plays. An update of Hawthorne's *The Scarlet Letter* appeared at the CSC Theater in New York. Phyllis Nagy's script is described by Michael Feingold: "Nagy has fun with Hawthorne's people, shaping her blunt, contemporary take on their desires into not-quite nineteenth-century language . . . while weaving phrases or whole paragraphs from the novel into scenes that are eyebrow-raisingly different from anything Hawthorne envisioned."[7] Director Meryl Friedman and her collaborator, playwright-adapter Christina Calvit, reconstructed *Jane Eyre* for their Lifeline Theatre in Chicago as a female power fantasy.

Were you given an opportunity to attempt a metonymic production, be sure you have a clear vision and a reason for subverting or challenging the literal in the text. What if you perceived the "boarding house" as an AIDS hospice, for example? What are the implications of Doran's "reparations"? Metonymic performances can be very exciting, as they empower adapters/directors to speak *of* the text, not just *in* the text. Should you prepare a metonymic production, be aware of the choices you make, and know *why* you are making them. What critical stance are you assuming? What are you trying to say about this text, and why? What new elements of the text have you discovered? Will the audience be able to get the message you intend?

Acting in Chamber Theatre

The style of acting appropriate for chamber theatre harkens back to Bertolt Brecht's **epic theatre.** Brecht, under the influence of the director of many of his plays, Erwin Piscator, produced a revolutionary kind of theatre involving a narrator relating a succession of loosely related episodes interspersed with songs and commentary. Brecht did not want the audience to identify emotionally with the characters; he aimed instead for an **alienation effect** which would keep the audience coolly reflective and critical. Piscator would question actors during rehearsals and have the performers answer the questions about the characters using the third person and the past tense, e.g., "Mary walked to the door, realizing that once she walked out of that room she would never see Peter again." After all, the actors had read the play, knew what would happen, and had the luxury of reflection. The technique of having the actors talk of themselves in the third person and the past tense gave them an opportunity to be both the characters and not the characters; to be able to "demonstrate" what the characters did while understanding why and how they did it; to be able to objectify the experience for the purpose of deeper analysis and understanding.

The acting in chamber theatre takes this rehearsal technique into the performance. It is not just the audience who is to remain coolly reflective, it is the performers as well. Performers in scene with other performers are often acting in a manner similar to the manner in which performers act in conventional plays. There are moments, however, when characters may talk about themselves in the third person and the past tense. As Breen writes:

> . . . [an actor] may be called upon in Chamber Theatre to "demonstrate" as did the actors in the Brecht-Piscator Epic Theatre. . . . The Chamber Theatre actor or actress finds it congenial to be a demonstrator because the narrative text is rich in commentary, description of action, verbalized interior thoughts and feelings, and it uses the third person and past tense. It is important for the performer to realize that his or her demonstration *repeats* something that has already occurred, but that the repetition is taking place now. The demonstrator imitates the actions of the characters and we judge the characters from these imitations.[8]

Metaphorically speaking, think of the narrator as the casting director of his or her story. The cast is composed of performers demonstrating these roles for an audience. They are not the real people of the narrator's story, they are "actors." The performer playing Tonya can say, "Tonya was aware that doom was approaching" because she is not Tonya, but is a performer showing the audience *now* how Tonya was *then*.

Acting in chamber theatre productions involves a consideration of the element of time. The spontaneous, illusion-of-the-"first time"-performance expected of performers in conventional plays may not always be appropriate for chamber theatre performances which usually deal with events that have already taken place. There is a difference, then, between seeming to create the lines as you speak them, and reflecting on how something was said or done in the past and trying to re-create that in the present.

We have now covered the creating and staging of both readers theatre and chamber theatre scripts. Both readers theatre and chamber theatre stage literary texts. The next two chapters deal with nonliterary texts. Chapter six covers the creating and staging of ethnographic and conversation analysis scripts and chapter seven focuses on creating and staging personal narratives. Chapter eight includes a number of different scripts suitable for performance.

Summary

This chapter sketched out the basic principles involved in staging chamber theatre productions. Basically, chamber theatre is a presentational medium, but some representational elements may be incorporated.

The narrator and characters in a chamber theatre production use a variety of types of focus. The narrator may speak to the audience with offstage focus or may speak to any of the characters using onstage focus. Characters may speak to the narrator or to each other using onstage focus, or may speak to themselves or to the audience.

The director must stage the relationship between the narrator and the characters. The narrator may play a variety of roles including a director or a reporter of a character's behavior. In addition, the narrator has many other capabilities, including guiding audience focus and playing properties, like coat racks or mirrors.

When a narrator is omniscient, special techniques are called for to make the audience aware that this narrator has capabilities beyond the norm. Omniscient narrators, for example, do not have to confine themselves to the physical dimensions of rooms, and can seemingly walk right through (imaginary) walls.

Often prose fiction texts will require that directors create their own conventions—methods of creatively staging elements in a text that cannot be literalized.

Although a tradition of chamber theatre is that only uninvolved narrators may carry and use a script, this convention may signal to today's audiences that the performers are unprepared. If scripts are used, they should have some significance other than helping the performers remember their lines.

The spectacle elements normally associated with representational theatre may also be incorporated into chamber theatre productions. The particular demands of the script will determine how set, set pieces, lighting, costumes, and properties are utilized.

Mixed-media effects can also be incorporated into chamber theatre productions. The use of slides, film, music, video, or dance, for example, can enhance the production's effectiveness for an audience.

The last part of this chapter dealt with how to stage postmodern texts, how to create metaphoric or metonymic productions, and discussed the acting techniques appropriate for performers in chamber theatre productions.

Notes

[1] Robert S. Breen, *Chamber Theatre* (Englewood Cliffs, NJ: Prentice-Hall, 1978), p. 78.

[2] Breen, *Chamber Theatre*, p. 79.

[3] Cited in Richard Zoglin's review of Peter Sellar's production of *The Merchant of Venice*, "Shylock on the Beach," in *TIME*, October 31, 1994, p. 78.

[4] Zoglin, p. 78.

[5] Richard Corliss, "Something to Sing About," *TIME*, December 12, 1994, p. 84.

[6] Ben Brantley, "How to Call a Play Into Being By Smearing a Man With Mud," in *The New York Times*, December 4, 1994, p. H2.

[7] Michael Feingold, "Dissecting Hawthorne," in *The New York Times*, October 30, 1994, pp. H5, H36.

[8] Breen, *Chamber Theatre*, pp. 69, 71.

Chapter Six

Creating and Staging
Ethnographic Studies and
Everyday Conversations

Introduction to Ethnography and
Conversation Analysis

The experimental theatre types we have already discussed—readers theatre and chamber theatre—are presentational rather than representational because they do not attempt to represent or reproduce the illusion of "real life." There are elements (e.g., bifurcation, address to audience, unison speaking, choreographic movement, etc.) in these production types that announce their theatricality. Readers theatre and chamber theatre are also relatively traditional and familiar group performance formats which have been popular for approximately fifty years.

The two types of experimental scripts to be discussed in this chapter, ethnographic studies and everyday conversation scripts, tend toward the representational end of the continuum as they *are* interested in depicting an illusion of real life. An ethnographic study script attempts to depict a faithful (or as faithful as possible) recording of the results of field study research into a particular cultural group. Dwight Conquergood elaborates on this definition: "Ethnographers study the diversity and unity of cultural performance as a universal human resource for deepening and clarifying the meaningfulness of life."[1] (It may be useful at this point to read the ethnographic study script in chapter eight, which seeks to re-create the performative dynamics of an Alcoholics Anonymous meeting. This script will be referred to throughout this chapter.)

A script involving everyday conversation attempts to reproduce conversation *as it occurred,* paying attention to every nuance of the discourse, for example inflection, bodily involvement, paralanguage (vocal inflection which may communicate the underlying intent of an utterance), length of pause, gesture, and so on. Performers attempt to re-create this dialogue as closely as possible; speaking, pausing, and breathing as those studied. (An examination of the conversation script in chapter eight will be useful when we get to that section in this chapter.)

These two types of experimental scripts are less traditional and familiar than are readers theatre and chamber theatre, but they are gaining in popularity. As oral interpretation evolved into performance studies, there were attendant changes in the materials we sought to stage and in the importance of "performance" as a way of knowing. Bryan K. Crow makes clear this evolution from oral interpretation (interested primarily in the performance of literary texts) to performance studies (interested in all kinds of texts and in broadening our understanding of performance). He writes that there has been an

> emergence in the speech communication discipline of a significantly
> broadened conception of oral performance. The discipline's long
> tradition of the study and practice of "oral interpretation" of literary
> texts—poems, short stories, novels—has begun to evolve into a
> "performance studies" paradigm with radical new conceptions of
> performance and of performance "texts." In characterizing the emergent
> paradigm, Ronald J. Pelias and James VanOosting [two performance
> studies professors at Southern Illinois University] emphasize its
> counterelitism: all members of the culture are viewed as potential
> performers, all utterances are potentially aesthetic, all events are
> potentially theatrical. . . . The performance studies paradigm, in short,
> embraces a dramaturgical perspective on the events of everyday life, a
> view of communication as performance.[2]

Arnold Berleant's seminal work, *The Aesthetic Field,* helped us to redefine exactly what we meant by "text" and "performance." We now define text to include not just literary texts but oral texts. Personal narratives (see chapter seven), for example, are possible texts for performance. Aesthetic objects may be considered texts for study and presentation. A quilt may be viewed as a text of a particular family, time period, culture. Rituals may be viewed as social or cultural texts. Demonstrations, rallies, and sit-ins may be viewed as political texts. Everyday conversations may be analyzed and performed as dialogic texts. Text, then, is now a metaphor for all kinds of experiences, and these "texts" may be transcribed into scripts for performance. Performance has broadened to include the theatre in everyday life occurrences that may be recorded, analyzed, re-created, and evaluated to discover what Conquergood refers to as "the meaningfulness of life." The Alcoholics Anonymous meeting discussed in this chapter, for example, may be seen as ritualistic as it encompasses a series of performative and communicative events.

Both ethnographic and everyday conversation scripts, then, feature the "theatre" in our everyday existence. As opposed to readers theatre and chamber theatre, ethnographic and everyday conversation scripts deal with nonliterary material—with the experiences of daily life. Rather than discovering the "truth" as exemplified in literary texts, we now emphasize real-life truths. We move, then, from literary performance to life performance.

Ethnography in Brief

Ethnographic study—the description and analysis of the *other*—of other groups, clubs, associations, sects, cultures, and so on, is engaged in by a variety of researchers. The research emphases of anthropologists, linguists, psychologists, and sociolinguists, among others, is studying and learning about the other. Our interest in the performance of ethnography is probably most associated with anthropologists who have recently seen the advantages of looking at performance as a research methodology. Performance studies professor Dwight Conquergood, who has engaged in extensive field studies among Lao and Hmong refugees in Chicago, asserts the necessary union between performance studies and anthropology. He writes, "Anthropology, like interpretation and performance studies, is committed to the emancipatory benefits of 'a sense of the other.'"[3] The basis of Conquergood's theories arise from the dramaturgy of anthropologist Victor Turner. Turner has written of a theoretical shift in his field which now embraces performance as a legitimate object of study. Turner writes:

> If man is a sapient animal, a toolmaking animal, a self-making animal, a symbol-using animal, he is, no less, a performing animal . . . his performances are, in a way, *reflexive*, in performing he reveals himself to himself. This can be in two ways: the actor may come to know himself better through acting or enactment; or one set of human beings may come to know themselves better through observing and/or participating in performances generated and presented by another set of human beings.[4]

This dramaturgical perspective enables us to determine what cultural groups value in their lives. As Langellier writes, "Drama enables a culture to interpret itself to itself and others; and performance enables actors to interpret themselves to themselves and others."[5]

Conversation Analysis in Brief

Conversation analysis (variously referred to as discourse analysis, the analysis of naturally occurring talk or everyday conversation) is an aspect of ethnography. The ethnography of speaking as a study in itself began in the early 1960s when U.S. linguistic anthropologist Dell Hymes published a number of essays calling for ways to study language and speech. Recently, performance studies and speech communication practitioners such as Bryan K. Crow, Nathan Stucky, Phillip J. Glenn, and Ronald J. Pelias have turned recorded everyday conversations into conversational performances.

For the sake of explication and simplicity, we will first discuss ethnography and then conversation analysis even though we acknowledge that conversation analysis is a part—a very salient part—of ethnographic study.

Ethnographic Study: Five Steps

As we have already stated, ethnography is a field study which attempts to describe and analyze culture. The goal is an *emic* rather than an *etic* study—where fieldworkers learn cultures from the inside out rather than from reading about them or listening to hearsay reports. We want to get to know the other as intimately as we can because this will inform and enhance our eventual script and performance. Whereas theatre practitioners normally work from text to performance, as a performer of ethnography you will begin with observing the performance of others, then recording that performance, and ultimately [re]performing that original performance. The process is five pronged:

1. You choose a cultural group, sect, organization, etc., you are interested in studying, and gain access.
2. You concentrate on being ethical, unbiased, and open minded.
3. You employ some type of information-gathering technique to record the "performances" of "the other." These could include audio recording, video recording, participation, observation, or

personal interviews. The goal is to record both text (what is said and done) and context (nature and response of the audience, including your own; the setting; the time; the nature and reason for the event; etc.).

4. You analyze what you have learned, and transcribe this into a script.

5. You then cast, rehearse, perform, and evaluate.

Let us examine each of these five steps.

Choosing a Cultural Group to Study

When a beginning class in ethnography and conversation analysis was given the assignment to study a particular cultural group, they decided to choose local groups because they did not have the luxury of time, money, or travel that might be necessary to study a more exotic culture. One group spent eight weeks studying the performative dynamics of Alcoholics Anonymous and the other group choose for their study a spiritual camp in Chesterfield, Indiana. Granted, A.A. and a spiritual camp in Chesterfield, Indiana may not be as alien to us as would be cannibals or the rituals of the Zhuangs, but the students still had the opportunity to taste another's reality, and as Turner says:

> If we attempt to perform ethnography, let us not begin with such apparently "exotic" and "bizarre" cultural phenomena as rituals and myths. Such an emphasis may only encourage prejudice, since it stresses the "otherness of the other." Let us focus first on what all people share, the social drama form, from which emerge all types of cultural performance, which, in their turn, subtly stylize the contours of social interaction in everyday life. In practice, this means setting apart a substantial block of time to familiarize students with the culture and social system of the group whose dramas they will enact.[6]

Saville-Troike agrees and talks of the advantages of studying one's own culture. "One of the advantages of studying one's own culture, and attempting to make explicit the systems of understanding which are implicit, is that ethnographers are able to use themselves as sources of information and interpretation."[7] A graduate student at the University of Virginia had been studying marriage in the Charlottesville area, and she decided to use the entire anthropology department to simulate a fabricated contemporary Central Virginia wedding based on her research.

The important thing is to choose a cultural group you are interested in and are willing to spend much time learning about. This is not something that should be chosen quickly as the investment of time necessary should encourage you to choose wisely. In addition, you will probably be limited to groups within your geographical location.

To gain access to the group you are interested in studying, you should first have the idea for your project clearly in mind. Be able to answer any questions that might be put to you, such as how much time this will take, and how you intend to record your information. Then, find out who is in charge. Call this person, or better yet, try to set up an appointment to meet with this person. Then explain your project in detail—or in as much detail as the person in charge cares to hear. Be sure to ask about the conditions under which you will operate. Is anonymity to be maintained? Will you be allowed to participate? Will you be allowed to videotape? Are there certain questions you should not ask? What are the customs or traditions with which you should be familiar? Remember, you are a stranger invading their territory and asking for favors. Since your project depends on their cooperation and hospitality, be polite and courteous.

Ethical Considerations

One ethical consideration involves your selection of a particular cultural group to study. Your choice empowers that cultural group; makes their voices heard. Likewise, you decline to empower other voices. Make your choice with this in mind. Remember, too, that the view you give of this cultural group may be the only view your audience members (whoever they may be) will receive. You want to reproduce your group as accurately and fairly as possible.

While an objective representation or [re]performance of the events we eventually record may be the ideal, this ideal may not be possible. We must bow to our humanness and realize that we can never gain a comprehensive understanding of another cultural group no matter how familiar it becomes to us; we can only hope to reveal subjective aspects. Often, the ethnographic report becomes more a description of an encounter than a true observation of the other. As Stern and Henderson note, the script which you will write is "inventive." "The goal," they write, "of ethnographic description . . . is not an objective understanding of another unknown or little-known culture. . . . Rather, it is a subjective understanding, derived from a variety of voices, of the ethnographer's desire to experience and interpret other cultures."[8] Just as jazz musicians are capable of improvising different licks each time they play the same number, the director of ethnographic scripts can reveal different aspects in subsequent scripts or even subsequent productions of the same material. We will discuss some of the ramifications of this "inventiveness" throughout this chapter.

Despite our subjectivity, we must be aware of our own biases and prejudices, and keep them in check as much as possible. We must remain open to possibilities that are new and different from those we have ever experienced or contemplated. Even for a study of local groups, prejudice may exist. We may have certain expectations about what the participants in an A.A. meeting are like and how they behave. We may go to the spiritual camp with a skeptical or cynical perspective.

Conquergood's own field study experiences have allowed him to categorize ethnographic approaches that produce ethical problems. These four "performative stances towards the other" are: the Custodian's Rip-Off, the Enthusiast's Infatuation, The Curator's Exhibitionism, and The Skeptic's Cop-Out. Conquergood quotes Wallace Bacon as he warns, "Goodwill and an open heart are not enough when one 'seeks to express cultural experiences which are clearly separate from his or her lived worlds.'"[9] As a consequence, Conquergood articulates these four character types as warnings of the ethical pitfalls you should attempt to avoid.

The Custodian is selfish and tends toward plagiarism and detachment. According to Conquergood, "Potential performers of ethnographic materials should not enter the field with the overriding motive of 'finding some good performance material.'"[10]

The Enthusiast tends to be superficial in his or her commitment, and consequently "trivializes" the other. He or she cruises from group to group but does not stay in one place long enough to gain any real feeling for the other. Conquergood describes the problem with this performative stance: "Too facile identification with the other coupled with enthusiastic commitment produces naive and glib performances marked by superficiality. This is . . . the quick-fix, pick-up artist, where performance runs aground in the shallows. Eager performers get sucked into the quicksand belief, 'Aren't all people really just alike?'"[11]

The Curator's stance is marked by cynicism, silence, despite a strong commitment. "Whereas the enthusiast assumed too easy an identity with the other, the curator is committed to the *difference* of the other. This is the 'Wild Kingdom' approach to performance that grows out of fascination with the exotic, primitive, culturally remote."[12]

The Skeptic is a sensationalist, with "tourists' stare," and a certain amount of detachment. "This . . . is the refuge of cowards and cynics. Instead of facing up to and struggling with the ethical tensions and oral ambiguities of performing culturally sensitive materials, the skeptic, with chilling aloofness, flatly declares, 'I am neither black nor female I will not perform from *The Color Purple*.'" To Conquergood, this "is the most morally reprehensible [stance] . . . because it forecloses dialogue."[13]

We must work to be free of prejudgments so that we can, as Conquergood suggests, engage in a true dialogue with the other. This is how we learn. This is how we grow as human beings.

Information Gathering—Text and Context

There are many ways to gather data and no single method is best. We will suggest three methods of data collecting: participant/observer, observation alone, and interviewing. These collection methods are not, of course, mutually exclusive. You may be able to combine the interview with either the participant/observer or the observation technique.

Before any method is selected, though, you should do as much background study as possible. You should know the traditions and values that inform the cultural behavior in this community. You must know how to behave in an appropriate manner if you are to be invited to observe or participate.

Be sure to narrow the scope of your project so that the time you have available fits the requirements of your project. (No matter how much time you have available to you, it probably will never seem like enough.) You should begin with a general idea of your project, and then refine this general idea into a more specific, focused topic. When Bryan K. Crow, for example, decided to investigate conversational material of intimate couples for his production of *Conversation Pieces*, his particular interest was how couples engaged in long-term relationships kept the conversation going. The outline of questions in the analysis section will help you know what data to collect and how to record it.

As you gather your data, be sure to include consideration of text *and* context. Text includes what was said and done at the event under study. Context includes the occasion for this event, the setting, the time of day, the nature and reactions of the audience as well as your own responses. Although our tendency may be to value text over context, attempt to give them equal weight and emphasis. The context helps us understand and interpret text, and both are important as we prepare our script and our eventual performance. (Realize, however, that the original context will not be replicable when you [re]perform the "performance" you recorded. The time will be different, the setting will be different, the intent will be different, blacks may enact whites, whites may enact blacks, accents may be attempted, etc. You work to record the original context, and then *attempt* to reproduce that context as closely as possible. A certain amount of "inventiveness" and creativity, though, is necessary to reproduce your field study. We will say more about this when we discuss performance.) Let us now discuss the three primary methods of data collection: participant/observer, observation, and the interview.

Participant/Observer

This method of data collection is the most common and the most emic as it allows the fieldworker to be an active member of the community for a period of time. This method is liable to reveal the kind of firsthand experience and information that can most directly be translated into script form. Fieldworkers are welcomed into the community and engage in appropriate activities. In this way, the members of the studied society learn to accept you and as a consequence you learn more about the other. As Saville-Troike puts it, "The researcher can develop a deeper understanding of the culture under study by adopting a functional role and becoming a participant."[14] By becoming a participant/observer you obtain and interpret information by learning appropriate ways to communicate in a particular community. Remember, though, the community members must feel that you are not judging them, that you have no preconceptions, and that you are not filtering the experience through your own cultural perspective. Learn to live as the other and this will enrich them as well as you. As a participant-observer be sure to record data on your own behavior in relation to these others, as well as how you interacted with them.

A form of participant/observation was the method of data collection employed by the students who decided to study the Chesterfield Spiritual Camp. The students were invited into the camp and participated by having their fortunes told, palms read, and by observing spiritualist practices such as "direct trumpet," "flame reading," and "spirit writing." The students were allowed to return as often as they liked, to engage in interviews, and to record the proceedings.

Observation

Although it is recommended that you attempt the participant/observer method of data collection, on occasion this simply is not possible. There are some sites where active participation is not appreciated or allowed, and you will have to employ the observation method. Unobtrusive observation tends to allow for objectivity. Laboratories or classrooms with one-way mirrors where you would not be visible means that you would not affect the context as much as you would were you participating.

You will want to enhance your observation (or any method of data collection you employ) with a video camera. (You must be sure that the community under study has given you permission to videotape them.) In fact, a videotape is essential as a record of the experience. It will be essential to you as you write your script, and viewing the tape will benefit your performers as they attempt to portray the "characters" you re-create. Keep in mind that a video camera is limited in scope and focus by whomever is holding the camera. Saville-Troike adds:

> When filming or videotaping is feasible in a relatively fixed context, it is best to use a stationary wide-angle studio camera for 'contextual' footage as well as a mobile camera to focus on particular aspects of the situation. To obtain a visual record of interactional events in which participants are more mobile (such as children playing together out-of-doors, or scenes in a hunting or fishing expedition), a hand-held and battery-operated 8 mm., video camcorder is more suitable.[15]

The observation method was employed by the students who attended the A.A. meetings. Although they attended "open" meetings, they were not introduced nor did they feel inclined to speak. As Saville-Troike attests, "In observing group dynamics in a meeting or other gathering it is generally better for a marginally accepted observer to refrain from taking active part in the proceedings."[16]

Interviewing

Interviewing is perhaps the most etic manner of data collecting as you do not get to observe firsthand how the cultural group behaves. This methodology, then, works best in conjunction with either of the other two, since composing your script will be very difficult without direct participation or observation. With the interview technique you can flesh out your study by asking specific questions that may reveal relevant cultural details. Saville-Troike suggests that the information you might be able to get includes "collection of kinship schedules, information on important religious and community events, and elicitation of folktales, historical narratives, songs, exposition of 'how to' in relation to various aspects of technical knowledge, and descriptions of encounters among members of the community in different contexts."[17]

Keep the following in mind if you decide to employ the interview technique:

1. If possible, inform the interviewee ahead of time of the general topics to be covered.

2. If possible, conduct the interview in a room with minimal external noise.

3. Decide ahead of time how you will record the information you receive in the interview. Will you take notes? Use a tape recorder? Use a video camera? Often this decision is based on what is available to you or on what your interviewee has agreed to. If you do use a tape recorder or a video camera, become familiar with it before the interview. Practice to determine the best recording volume. (Even if you use a recorder of some kind, you should probably take notes as well. The conversation might prompt another question that can be jotted down to be asked later. It is also important to get the spellings of names and towns, etc.).

4. Record an introduction that identifies the interviewee, the interviewer, and gives the date, time, and location of the interview.

5. Be sure you know the kinds of questions you should ask and the kinds of questions you should not ask before you ask them. There may be some taboo areas that should not be broached. This should be part of your background information.

6. Gender and ethnicity often affect the interview. Saville-Troike explains, "Females are considered less threatening than males in many communities, and are thus more readily accepted as interviewers, but in other communities it is considered entirely inappropriate for women to behave in such a manner. Further, there are often limitations on what kinds of questions an interviewer of one sex may ask an interviewee of the other."[18] Likewise, members of a minority community may resent being interviewed by a member of the majority group. They may believe that the interviewer cannot be neutral or objective. You might have to prove that this is not the case.

7. Ask questions that do not have predetermined response alternatives. For example, do not ask "Do men or women work harder in raising the children?" A better question would be, "How do the roles of men and women differ in the raising of children?"

8. Impose as little structure as possible on the interview. If you have a rigid set of questions that you are intent on asking you may not allow for the spontaneous question which flows naturally out of the give-and-take of the conversation.

9. Although open-ended questions (questions that cannot be answered with yes or no, e.g., "How are birthdays celebrated?") are preferred as they allow for an open exchange with no preconceptions, close-ended questions (e.g., "Do all the women wear long-sleeved blouses?") may also be asked to elicit specific information about concerns that you have already researched. (Saville-Troike cites examples of the difficulties of asking close-ended questions without first knowing much about the culture. She writes, "When I have asked about 'marital status', for instance, a common answer has been 'yes', and questions on the 'ordinal rank' of a child have often been answered with identification of religious affiliation.")[19]

10. Be sure that the person or persons you interview are reliable sources of information. It is probably best not to rely on just one source. The reliability of the information you seek may best be achieved by asking similar questions of a number of different community members and then comparing their answers.

EXPERIMENT

Hone your interviewing skills by conducting sessions with friends or relatives. Define a specific intent of your research and compose questions that will help you fulfill that intention.

Analyzing and Creating the Script

Analyzing Your Data—The Eleven Components

Once you have collected your data, you must organize and analyze the information prior to creating the script. Review your notes numerous times, replay your audio or videotape several times. Begin your analysis by asking specific questions about the data you have collected. The questions you should ask involve those aspects of your data that will directly relate to your transcription of the information into script form. Those aspects according to Saville-Troike include the following:

1. *Genre*—or type of event (joke, story, lecture, greeting, etc.)

2. *Topic*—referential focus

3. *Purpose or function*—both of the event in general, and in terms of the interaction goals of individual parts

4. *Setting*—including location, time of day, season of year, and physical aspects of the setting (e.g., size of room, arrangement of furniture)

5. *Key*—or emotional tone of the event (e.g., serious, sarcastic, jocular)

6. *Participants*—including their age, gender, ethnicity, social status, or other relevant categories, and their relation to one another

7. *Message form*—including both vocal and nonvocal channels, and the nature of the code which is used (e.g., which language, and which variety)

8. *Message content*—surface level denotative references; what is communicated about

9. *Act sequence*—the ordering of events

10. *Rules for interaction*—what proprieties should be observed

11. *Norms of interpretation*—including the common knowledge, the relevant cultural presuppositions, or shared understandings, which allow particular inferences to be drawn about what is to be taken literally, what discounted, etc.[20]

The application of these eleven components form the basis of a type of dramatistic analysis, allowing you a richer understanding of the who, what, where, when, how, and why of this group. An understanding of how these eleven components are revealed in your data will help enrich your eventual performance. You will have a deeper understanding of the content and structure of the event as well as the intention and motivation of the participants.

Let us now apply these eleven components to the A.A. script found in chapter eight of this text.

1. *Genre*—Alcoholics Anonymous meeting

2. *Topic*—Open discussion meeting of the "Enjoying Sobriety Group." (Closed meetings are for recovering alcoholics only.) Although many A.A. meetings have designated discussion topics, this one did not.

3. *Purpose/function*—"A.A. is a fellowship of men and women who share their experience, strength, and hope with each other that they may solve their common problem and help others to recover from alcoholism." (taken from *Alcoholics Anonymous* referred to as "The Big Book.")

4. *Setting*—A church basement, chairs, tables. At the front of the room is a table with coffee, candy, cards that announce A.A. meeting times, and pamphlets. On the walls are posters titled "The 12 Steps" and "The 12 Traditions." Chairs are arranged in a circle. It is 8:00 P.M., spring, thirty people in attendance.

5. *Key*—Serious with some humorous comments. Friendly, open, warm.

6. *Participants*—The participants include recovering alcoholics who have attended several meetings as well as new members to A.A. Participants include teenagers and adults, and represent both genders, various ethnicities, and a variety of social strata and educational backgrounds;

the observers include students from a performance studies class at Ball State University. One member is in charge (P1).

7. *Message form*—Spoken English, including mostly consultative language (the norm of spoken English) with some ritualistic recitation. There is established turn taking as well as ritualistic unison responses: "Right on," "Hi, Pat," "Keep coming back."

8. and **9.** *Message content and sequence*—P1 controls the meeting. She introduces the type of meeting, and introduces herself. All respond. P1 then asks all for a moment of silence followed by the Serenity Prayer. All bow heads and are silent for a moment, then P1 begins prayer and all join in. P1 reads announcements, and asks for any announcements from the group. Then P1 asks a member to read the A.A. preamble. She does so after a formal greeting/response. P1 then asks another member to read the twelve steps, and another to read the twelve traditions. Contributions are then collected. Then the floor is open for anyone who has a problem with alcohol or for anyone who has a topic he or she would like to discuss. No response, so P1 begins sharing a personal story. Five different members share stories or comments. Another member decides the meeting is over and they all finish by reciting the Lord's Prayer. All look up and add, with clasped hands punctuating the words: "Keep comin' back. It works!" Then the meeting is over, there are general good-byes, and the people file out. In general, the meeting has a series of recognizable communicative events. (A communicative event is a bounded entity of some kind; recognizing what the boundaries are is essential for their identification. A telephone conversation is a communicative event bounded by a ring and hanging up as a close. In A.A. meetings the communicative events include greetings, leavetakings, prayers, compliments, and so on.)[21]

10. *Rules for interaction*—Only first names are used. All have a right to speak, but they must take turns, consequently there is little overlapping. Opinions are welcome, but participants are free to agree or disagree with each other. No one is allowed to give advice. Usually someone who has been in the program for a period of time is in charge, and he or she controls the meeting if tempers flare, someone monopolizes the floor, or if the situation gets out of hand. Normally, the atmosphere is conducive to sharing and free self-disclosure, and is nonjudgmental. There is no cross talking (when one is sharing, no one is allowed to talk to that person; you can have conversations only after the meeting is officially over). There are ritualistic responses, and a prescribed beginning, middle, and end to which all adhere.

11. *Norms of interpretation*—A.A. is a sanctuary for alcoholics; a safe place. All participants are equal and feel that they can speak openly and without censure. It is often difficult to tell the difference between participants and observers because 1) different people may attend each week, 2) observers are welcome at "open" meetings, and 3) introductions are not routinely done. ["Anonymity is the spiritual foundation of all our Traditions, ever reminding us to place principles above personalities." (12th Tradition)] Thus, the presence of observers does not necessarily alter the routine or make the participants self-conscious. Everyone is welcome; participants are supportive and encourage each other to share experiences.

Creating Your Script

Before you attempt to write your script, review your notes and replay your tapes. You want to keep the original experience firmly in mind as you attempt to reproduce it as faithfully as possible. You will probably have much more material than you will be able to incorporate into a script so you will have to decide just what you wish to emphasize. The assumption is that you will have a specific time limit for your performance, and this will help you determine what may be included in your script. If your data basically surrounded the study of a particular event or ceremony, this might be easier to translate into script form than would a sense of the everyday life of a community or group. Decide what you want to do in your script. Are you interested in centering in on one event or do you want to give more of a sense of the community as a whole? This decision will dictate what material to include and what to exclude.

The A.A. script, for example, represents one particular meeting that the class members found the most representative of all the ones that they had attended. The students who attended several meetings of the Chesterfield Spiritual Camp, however, decided to perform a composite account of their experiences. As a result, they compiled various events that had happened at different meetings and combined them into one script. The compilation-type script is not, then, completely faithful to your original tape. It allows for more creativity and inventiveness as a result of the editing process. Your decisions as to what to include and what to exclude must be handled with care as what you decide will affect the audience's perception and knowledge of this cultural group.

Whether you document one event or compile several, you will want your script to be a "record" of the events and not a "report." As Fine makes clear, reproducing the experience as closely as possible in your script is the ideal; not paraphrasing it or giving a report about it.[22] The goal of your script as well as of your performance of that script is to try to give the audience (as well as the performers) as similar an experience to the original performance as possible. Use the names of the participants as the names of the "characters" in your script (unless anonymity has been requested). Try to re-create the specific setting. Analyze the structure and dynamics of the event that you are attempting to reproduce. How does it begin? What causes the conflict/tension? What is the sequence of events? What is the climax of the event? How does the event end? The answers to these questions should form the outline of your script. Your detailed notes and tapes should provide you with the individual lines of dialogue that these "characters" will speak.

Performance

Although cultural groups throughout the world have been "performing" for centuries, our reproductions of their performances are much more recent. As we stated at the opening of this chapter, anthropologists are only recently beginning to see the advantage of performance as an object of study, and performance studies practitioners are now beginning to expand their interests to include the performance of anthropological field studies. As Turner attests, (re)performance of cultural performances can "aid students' understanding of how people in other cultures experience the richness of their social existence, what the oral pressures are upon them, what kinds of pleasures they expect to receive as a reward for following certain patterns of action, and how they express joy, grief, deference, and affection, in accordance with cultural expectations."[23] The performance melds body and mind and makes the experience more personal. It allows the performers to get inside the cultural group under study rather than just reading about them. In this age of multiculturalism, what is more multicultural than the performance of ethnography!

The performance's goal is to work for authenticity and fidelity to the original experience—as much as that is possible. In order to achieve this, the performance must be prefaced by sufficient rehearsal. This may take more time than the "normal" rehearsal schedule. If everyone in the cast was not able to participate in the fieldwork, then individuals who did should serve as director and dramaturg (a person who has engaged in detailed research and supplies specific background information when necessary). Share your notes and the tapes with your cast so that they will have a sense of how to reproduce the voice and the body of the "characters" they are re-creating. By doing so, you will work to insure that the experience you received as a fieldworker may be similarly experienced by your cast as well as your audience. The nonverbal aspects of the original event may be the most difficult for your performers to reproduce, especially if they were not in the field. Performers are used to working from printed record to performance, and they are usually free to decide how to interpret the subtext of the printed record—or the underlying meaning of the words. This time, however, they must rely on the fieldworkers' knowledge of this culture. We know from our own culture that much meaning is communicated not in *what* is said but in *how* it is said. The performers must be guided by the knowledge of the fieldworkers and their notes and tape when dealing with the kinesic and paralinguistic aspects of the script.

While we are interested in text as well as context, as we have stated several times, we must realize that our performance does, as we mentioned earlier, produce a shift in context. We are obviously in a different place, performing at a different time, for a different audience, and with a shift in intent. While the intent, for example, of the participants in that original A.A. meeting was healing and helping, the intent of the performers is to re-create this event as faithfully as possible. There is, then, a shift in focus. This shift involves the idea of frames.

Turner defines **frame** as "that often invisible boundary . . . around activity which defines participants, their roles, the 'sense' or 'meaning' ascribed to those things included within the boundary, and the elements within the environment of the activity . . . which are declared to be 'outside' . . . and irrelevant to it."[24] Let us examine the idea of frames in regard to the Chesterfield Spiritual Camp script. We understand, firstly, that the group turned its fieldwork study into a "playscript" and "performed" it for the class. The first frame was pedagogical—the purpose of the exercise was to teach the students a sense of the other. The frame nested within this frame was play—the students (primarily theatre majors, theatre minors, and performance studies minors) "pretended" to be spiritualists, palm readers, fortune tellers, performers in mystical shows, etc. The third frame was working for the reality of the spiritual environment. The theatre at Ball State University was turned into the camp—as much as possible. Leaves were brought in to simulate the outside environment, appropriate music was played, candles and incense were burned, and the chairs rearranged to suggest a church. Students read palms, and frightened some of the rest of the class with the accuracy of their predictions. The atmosphere was filled with an aura that students had never experienced before. The anticipation of the event filled the theatre with many who were not in the class, but who wanted to be part of something different. The final frame was the student-teacher dynamic that was still evident. Performers often singled out faculty members to give predictions or to ask for assistance. Students were eager to turn the tables and "teach." The students were keen to convince the faculty of the legitimacy of their experience at the spiritual camp. One faculty member was convinced that the spiritualists the performers were enacting were "gifted."

To aid the authenticity of the performance, it is necessary to strive for appropriate costumes and props. If a costume designer is on hand, he or she can study the videotapes and reproduce the costumes as faithfully as possible. Fieldworkers can secure many necessary props while doing their research, others may have to be constructed. Set pieces (furniture) will have to be borrowed, made, or what is available can be altered to match the original setting.

The performance may happen in class (where one group performs for another group), or could be a more public performance. In either case, a short introduction or a program note may be necessary to explain the project and to help the audience understand its role in the reproduction of the original context of the event.

After the performance, engage in an evaluation of the event. What was learned? What insights were gained into this cultural group? What insights were gained about the value of performance in capturing this group? What did the fieldworkers/scriptwriters/directors learn? What did the performers learn? What did the audience learn? A member of the audience for the Chesterfield Spiritual Camp performance who was not a member of the class was struck by how "representational" the event was, and how "realistic" the portrayals were. He described the environment as "eerie—unlike the black box theatre's normal environment. The mood was set with candles, incense, and the students were very into the characters and situations they were portraying. The others around me were startled at how detailed the setting was. The use of audience members (who were actually students portraying "characters") as participants helped make the situation even more real." A faculty member in the audience remarked that the sign posted outside the theatre door "Camp Chesterfield: A Spiritualist Community" made him curious as to what to expect. He writes:

> Upon entering the audience was greeted with candlelight and seats arranged in rows as to suggest a church. This atmosphere transported the audience into another world. I know this sounds like a cliche, but "another world" is the best description of the environment. . . . I was particularly amused when the actors portraying "the spirits" identified me, by name, as an audience member. Of course, I realized that the

performer simply recognized me as a faculty member and singled me out. But a larger question remained in my mind: is there such a place as Camp Chesterfield where clairvoyants commune with the spirits?

This faculty member was so moved by what he saw that he took notes about his experience and went to Camp Chesterfield on the following Saturday to learn about the place firsthand.

We referred earlier to the reproduction of an authentic Central Virginia wedding ceremony performed by graduate students in Victor Turner's anthropology class at the University of Virginia. Turner describes what might be revealed at the evaluation session as discovered by his students:

> Much of the emphasis will be found to be on cultural differences, and the difficulties and delights of playing roles generated by cultures often far different from our own. In these occasions of intercultural reflexivity, we can begin to grasp something of the contribution each and every human culture can make to the general pool of manifested knowledge of our common human condition.[25]

Conversation Analysis

As we stated at the outset of this chapter, conversation analysis is an important aspect of an ethnographic study. To make your ethnographic study even more detailed and complete, an analysis of the speaking of the participants could be undertaken. A conversation analysis script attempts to reproduce as closely as possible discourse between or among individuals. It is the ethnography of speaking; the discovery of the way people in a culture communicate with one another and how language is employed when people interact in social life.

In your attempt to learn about the other, you become more aware of your own speaking habits and you become more sensitive to human discourse, in general. In addition, you will increase your listening skills. We spend approximately 45 percent of our day listening, but we rarely take the time to learn how to listen well. Listening is involved in every step of conversation analysis.

The basic pattern of performing everyday conversations involves deciding on a focus for your project, selecting subjects to tape, editing the tapes, transcribing the tapes, analyzing the tapes, casting and rehearsing, performing, and evaluating. Let us look at each of these steps.

Determining Your Project Focus

Decide on a project focus that will help determine the conversations you would like to collect. Is your production to focus on the language style of specific people (e.g., priests, teachers, married couples, twins, and so on), or on specific types of discourse (e.g., joke telling, storytelling, gossiping, and so on). The answer to this will provide the focus for your particular script.

Choosing Subjects

Once you have narrowed the focus of your project, you will have to seek out subjects who are willing to be videotaped and audiotaped, and get their permission. We have found that most people are flattered when asked if you can record them for performance purposes. You must establish a sense of trust with these people, and assure them that they will remain anonymous, if that is their desire.

We suggest that you use both an audiotape and a video recorder (a digital recorder is best) so that you can document both the oral and physical dimensions of the conversations.

You could give your subjects a camera and allow them to tape themselves (which *might* allow for less self-consciousness and which could avoid the observer's paradox of not being able to observe what would happen if you were not there) or you could make frequent visits and record the discourse yourself. The goal is to gather "naturally occurring" conversation where the subjects are not self-conscious or "playing to the recorder." (We gave a tape recorder to a native Hawaiian and asked her to turn on the tape whenever she sensed that a lengthy discussion with her children or boyfriend was about to take place. We wanted to discover the characteristics of what is facetiously referred to as "Pidgin English"—a unique style of grammar that mixes English and other languages. She testified that after two or three days of turning the tape recorder on and off, there came a time when she was not aware of the recorder and had "forgotten she had it on.") You must discover a way to gather your conversations that does not alter this naturalness. For this reason, you will need to record much more than you are likely to use. In Bryan K. Crow's study of the conversations of intimate couples entitled *Conversation Pieces: An Empirical Comedy*, he reduced some twenty hours of tapes into a ninety-minute production.

Editing

Decide which parts of the tape you will use based on your topic focus. Crow, who studied six different conversations of five different couples, writes, "All five couples reported that once they got involved in a conversation, they tended to forget about the tape recorder's presence and were not conscious of any constraints it imposed on their talk. However, I chose to transcribe only the last three conversations [of the six recorded] of each couple on the assumption that the tape recorder's presence would become even less obtrusive with repeated usage."[26]

Editing your script becomes an element of the inventiveness we mentioned earlier in reference to ethnographic studies. Editing obviously affects the recorded events, their sequence, the behavior of the participants, and ultimately the audience's perception. For this reason, editing must be done with extreme caution and with the knowledge that you are altering your original record.

Transcribing

Transcribe the parts of the tape you have decided to use into script form employing Gail Jefferson's transcription symbols, which follow. (Jefferson's transcription symbols were printed in *Structures of Social Action: Studies in Conversation Analysis*, edited by J. Maxwell Atkinson and John Heritage. For an application of these symbols, see the conversation analysis script in chapter eight of this text.) This process is very time consuming, as you must slowly examine each utterance, turning the tape on and off to be sure you are seeing and hearing exactly what was recorded. Transcription helps you translate your recording into script form without losing too much in the translation. The transcription symbols will help you indicate how to represent laughter, overlapping, simultaneous utterances, intervals between utterances, vocal dynamics, changes in intonation or inflection, and so on. Employing these symbols is essential if you want your script to be a duplication—as closely as possible—of what was actually said so that it can be reproduced by your cast. Here are Jefferson's transcription symbols:

[ ]	brackets indicate overlapping utterances
=	equal marks indicate contiguous utterances, or continuation of the same utterance to the next line

(.)	period within parentheses indicates micropause
(2.0)	number within parentheses indicates length of pause in approximate seconds
ye:s	colon indicates stretching of sound it follows
yes-	single dash indicates abrupt sound cutoff
<u>yes</u>	underlining indicates emphasis or increased volume
°yes°	degree marks indicate decreased volume of materials between
hhh	h's indicate audible aspiration, possibly laughter
·hhh	raised preceding period indicates an inbreath audible aspiration, possibly laughter
ye(hh)s	h's within parentheses indicate within-speech aspiration, possibly laughter
((cough))	Items within double parentheses indicate some sound or feature of the talk which is not easily transcribable, e.g., ((in falsetto))
(yes)	parentheses indicate transcriber doubt about hearing of passage
^yes	caret (or arrow up) indicates upward intonation of sound that follows
ᵛyes	superscript "v" (or arrow down) indicates downward intonation of sound that follows

EXPERIMENT

Before transcribing the conversation of others, try recording one of your own dialogues and practice using the transcription symbols presented here. You might begin with a telephone conversation where nonverbal behavior, in terms of gesture and body movement, does not contribute to the exchange.

Analyzing Your Material

There are various ways to analyze your material depending on your project's focus. As Crow writes:

> Conversation analysis can focus on any number of aspects of the data: speaker intentions, utterance functions, sequential patterns, mechanisms for repairing structural problems, topical coherence, cultural taken-for-granteds, and contextual frames, among others. The goals of analysis may be thick description, feature analysis,

identification of rules or other generative mechanisms, or simply appreciation of the text as a creative achievement rivaling works of art.[27]

Since we are primarily interested in the relationship between everyday conversation and the theatrical performance of dialogue, this is our focus. We want to examine elements such as verbal strategies of speakers and listeners, and we want to discover the intent of the speakers in addition to the literal meaning of the words they use. We want to examine how others "really" talk so that we can reproduce this onstage. This will help us see the similarities and differences between the way we speak and the dialogue playwrights create.

Analyze these "characters," then, as you would characters in a play. What motivates them? Why do they say what they say? What does the way they speak tell you about them? What assumptions can be made about their relationship? Our ultimate goal, then, according to Crow, is the "appreciation of the text as a creative achievement." Since our goal is to *perform* conversation as it naturally occurs, our focus is an aesthetic presentation—a "work of art"!

Analysis also occurs after the performance is over as we reflect on and evaluate what we discovered as a result of engaging in this type of creative exercise. Our job is to attempt to document those reflections, as well.

Casting and Rehearsing

Cast your production using performers who are willing to engage in a very different type of performance experience and who are willing to work to reproduce as faithfully as possible the original conversations. The cast members will first have to be given copies of the script with the transcription symbols. They will have to learn how to read and interpret these symbols, and then memorize their "lines." Then, they will have to work with the tape. If only an audiotape is possible, Stucky recommends the following rehearsal technique:

> One technique for learning parts is to listen repeatedly to the tape while following the transcript, then to speak aloud along with the tape, and finally to speak the parts without the recorder, but still reading from the transcript. After reading his or her part aloud the performer again listens to the tape in order to make corrections and the cycle begins again.[28]

We suggest that, if possible, you use both the audio and visual tapes of the conversations in conjunction with each other as one informs and reinforces the other. Anita Rich, a performer in *Talking Relationships* co-directed by Glenn and Pelias at Southern Illinois University in 1991, reports on the importance of using both audio and video recordings early in the rehearsal process:

> . . . the directors and actors who worked with video chose to keep the aural and visual dimensions separate. They spent weeks solely with the audio tape and after the verbal features became relatively "set" they incorporated the video. Upon reflection both performers stated that the physical features were introduced too late. They had hypothesized and filled in what felt like appropriate gestures and, though some paralleled the video, some had to be removed. This stripping away took time, energy, and focus; in a sense they had to "unlearn" behaviors.[29]

Cast members have different reactions to this process. At first, there is a feeling of "why don't you just show the videos as real actors are not necessary." Some feel that their creative input is negligible as they are only trying to "imitate" not "create." Some, though, had an intense sense of the other—often for the first time. All agreed that although it was very time consuming, it was also very rewarding.

Performing

Robert Hopper testifies that "using ELP [everyday life performance] procedures, even inexperienced actors achieve dramatically interesting performances that retain surprising fidelity to the details in recordings."[30] This, of course, is our goal, but we must also keep in mind what we said earlier in regard to ethnographic performances. Just like the perform-ance of ethnography, the performance of everyday conversation "neces-sarily involves a shift in context."[31] Whereas the intent of the taped dialogue may have been to share reminiscences, for example, the intent of this [re]performance is to indicate a sense of the other.

Other alterations may be required in the performance. We spoke earlier about the inventive nature of ethnographic scripts—that they cannot be totally faithful representations of what was recorded. The same is true of conversation scripts. We cannot remain steadfastly faithful to our taped version, for example, if the pace is too fast or the volume too low for intelligibility. Consequently, some alteration of the original may be necessary. Deleasa Randall, a performer in *Talking Relationships*, attests to the problems encountered when trying to maintain fidelity to the tape recording:

Both directors and performers worked for a balance between the quest
for fidelity to the original talk and the demands placed upon all aesthetic
performance. We struggled with decisions of clarity, volume and rate,
worrying about our audience's comprehension. . . . I wondered whether
our work was understood and appreciated in its accuracy and
fidelity—or whether our competence as performers was questioned. To
my chagrin, several audience members admitted uncertainty as to
whether or not we had sometimes "messed up" lines.[32]

Randall's admonition to strike a "balance" is our suggestion. Work for
fidelity, but realize that a certain inventiveness is required. If the audience
were to compare the taped version with the performance, then less
inventiveness may be necessary as the intent would be to show the
audience how faithfully the original was reproduced. If, however, your
intention is to provide a separate performative event meant to entertain,
instruct, persuade, move, etc., then you may have to move toward the
inventive side of the continuum.

The performance of conversation underscores Goffman's idea of the
theatricality inherent in everyday life. Whatever our intent in performing
conversation, we gain much from the experience. As Nathan Stucky
persuasively writes, "If we are to understand human diversity, and if
natural performance is to bring the full power of its art to this endeavor,
then the ways in which people perform their everyday lives will continue
to be a significant challenge for performers."[33]

Evaluating

After the performances, participants should engage in an evaluation
session so that students may share what they learned with each other.
Stucky and Glenn suggest that this evaluation should center around "the
believability of the performance, the extent to which audience members
felt they understood the participants, the features of interaction high-
lighted by the performance, and the performers' own reactions to the
exercise."[34]

We are also interested in what the performers "know" as a result of
engaging in this type of activity. Glenn and Pelias write of the importance
of documenting the performers' knowledge:

Since performance as a methodology is located in enactment, in full
vocal and bodily participation, in somatic thinking, then only performers
operate as performance methodologists. Directors and audience
members may have something to say about productions, but their

claims are not grounded in performance methodology. Hence, the researcher's task is to discover and report what those who have used the method have come to know.[35]

When this assignment was given in a performance studies class at Ball State University, the students were asked to reflect on their experiences and write their responses in their journals. Their responses testify to the values and benefits of engaging in this type of performative event. One student wrote in his evaluation of the experience:

> . . . it forces you to concentrate very carefully as an actor because you are training your ear, voice, and body to become someone else. Focusing on all of these at once with an ideal model in mind is difficult. But once the elements start working together something very strange happens—you begin to feel like someone else. I'm not talking about the usual creation of a new identity for the stage, I'm talking about becoming someone else that you've seen or, in some cases, know. It's kind of eerie, but very cool.

A professional actress who engaged in this assignment had this to say about it:

> This was one of the most challenging acting endeavors I have encountered. . . . I kept hearing from students who took this class before I did about how many hours they spent listening and watching the tape, trying to capture accurate gestures and precise inflections. The entire time I wondered what was so difficult about that that it required so much time. Well, I found out! I was amazed at how much concentration is needed to accurately perform someone else's vernacular, accent, speech habits, and the most difficult part, their thought patterns. . . . It took me a while to own her thinking. And this came only after an invested amount of time and energy.

One student wrote, "A benefit of performing everyday conversation is that it teaches you to really listen to the dynamics of conversation and how people really talk. This becomes useful not only to the actor, but also to the director, and especially the playwright. I noticed a real difference in the way playwrights write and the way people really speak."

Another confessed, "I am now continually finding myself eavesdropping in on people's conversations—not to hear what they're saying, but how. Hopefully, this will help make whatever scripts or films I write have a dialogic truth rather than just bowing to formula."

Other performers of everyday conversation have had similar reactions. Joanne R. Gilbert, professor of speech communication at The University of Texas at Austin admits, "Never had I been asked to imitate someone else in this extreme way. Never had I been asked to breathe, sigh, and giggle the other. To my surprise and delight, I found that rehearsing and performing such human minutiae allowed me to 'become an other' to an extent that I had never realized before."[36]

Deleasa Randall, one of the performers in Glenn and Pelias' production *Talking Relationships*, writes:

> My character and I became intimately connected. The simultaneity of this talking-listening-speaking ritual embedded her talk into more than just my memory. I began to realize that as a performer I could not breathe this woman's breaths, pause her sometimes excruciatingly long pauses (one was 11.4 seconds mid-sentence), and speak her carefully chosen words without bonding with her in a frighteningly intimate manner. Through working with the intricacies of her talk, this anonymous "someone," this "mystery woman" became a person, and part of that person merged with me. I found her words, her tones, her phrases and even her pauses popping up in my own "naturally occurring talk."[37]

We end this chapter with a quote by Barbara Myerhoff that beautifully sums up the values of engaging in the performance of ethnography:

> Cultural performances are reflective in the sense of showing ourselves to ourselves. They are also capable of being reflexive, arousing consciousness of ourselves as we see ourselves. As heroes in our own dramas, we are made self-aware, conscious of our consciousness. At once actor and audience, we may then come into the fullness of our human capability—and perhaps human desire—to watch ourselves and enjoy knowing that we know.[38]

Chapter seven focuses on the creation and staging of personal narratives which are, in a real sense, additional aspects of ethnographic research.

Summary

This chapter detailed the techniques involved in creating and staging ethnographic studies and everyday conversations.

Ethnography is a field study of a particular cultural group. One must first select a particular group to study; attain access and attempt to maintain an unbiased, open mind; and then determine the type of method to employ for data collection. The three primary means of data collection are: participant/observer, observation, and interview. In order to achieve emic (inside) knowledge of a cultural group, one should employ the participant/observer method of data collection supplemented with videotapes and, if necessary, interviews. Once the material is gathered, it must be studied and analyzed in order to discover the genre, topic, purpose or function, setting, key, participants, message form, message content, act sequence, rules for interaction, and the norms of interpretation of the event. The material is then edited, and transcribed into script form. The performance tries to reproduce the text of the event as well as the context, even though the [re]performance of the event will, by necessity, have a shift in context.

The performance of everyday conversation is an aspect of ethnographic study which attempts to monitor the way people use discourse in social life. The process of performing conversation involves selecting a project focus, taping the subjects, editing and transcribing the tapes, casting, rehearsing, performing, and evaluating the results. The performance of everyday conversation makes us aware of our own speech habits and makes us sensitive to the way others interact.

Notes

[1] Dwight Conquergood, "Performing As a Moral Act: Ethical Dimensions of the Ethnography of Performance," *Literature in Performance* 5.2 (April 1985), p. 1.

[2] Bryan K. Crow, "Conversational Performance and the Performance of Conversation," *The Drama Review* 119 (1988), pp. 23–24.

[3] Dwight Conquergood, "Between Experience and Meaning: Performance As a Paradigm for Meaningful Action," in *Renewal and Revision: The Future of Interpretation*, ed. by Ted Colson (Denton, TX: NB Omega Publications, 1986), p. 35.

[4] Victor Turner, *The Anthropology of Performance* (New York: PAJ Publications, 1986), p. 81.

[5] Kristin Langellier, "From Text to Social Context," *Literature in Performance* 6.1 (April 1986), p. 67.

[6] Turner, p. 152.

[7] Muriel Saville-Troike, *The Ethnography of Communication: An Introduction*, 2nd ed. (Oxford: Blackwell, 1989), p. 109.

[8] Carol Simpson Stern and Bruce Henderson, *Performance: Texts and Contexts* (New York: Longman, 1993), pp. 43, 51.

[9] Conquergood, "Performing As a Moral Act: Ethical Dimensions of the Ethnography of Performance," p. 4.

[10] Ibid., p. 6.

[11] Ibid., p. 6.

[12] Ibid., p. 7.

[13] Ibid., p. 8.

[14] Saville-Troike, p. 108.

[15] Ibid., pp. 121–122.

[16] Ibid., p. 121.

[17] Ibid., p. 123.

[18] Ibid., p. 126.

[19] Ibid., p. 125.

[20] Ibid., pp. 138–139.

[21] Ibid., pp. 136–138

[22] Elizabeth C. Fine, *The Folklore Text: From Performance to Print* (Bloomington: Indiana University Press, 1984), p. 94.

[23] Turner, p. 140.

[24] Ibid., p. 54.

[25] Ibid., p. 153.

[26] Crow, p. 27.

[27] Ibid., p. 29

[28] Nathan Stucky, "Unnatural Acts: Performing Natural Conversation," *Literature in Performance* 8.2 (November 1988), p. 33.

[29] Anita L. Rich, "The Performer's Process: Conversation Analysis and Performance As Method," unpublished article, Southern Illinois University, 1991, p. 8.

[30] Robert Hopper, "Conversational Dramatism: A Symposium," *Text and Performance Quarterly* 13.2 (April 1993), p. 182.

[31] Nathan Stucky, "Towards an Aesthetics of Natural Performance," *Text and Performance Quarterly* 13.2 (April 1993), p. 176.

[32] Deleasa M. Randall, "Staged Replication of Naturally Occurring Talk: A Performer's Perspective," *Text and Performance Quarterly* 13.2 (April 1993), p. 198.

[33] Stucky, p. 177.

[34] Nathan Stucky and Phillip Glenn, "Invoking the Empirical Muse: Conversation, Performance, and Pedagogy," *Text and Performance Quarterly* 13.2 (April 1993), p. 194.

[35] Phillip J. Glenn and Ronald J. Pelias, "Talking about *Talking Relationships*: Reporting Textual Understanding," paper presented at the Central States Communication Association Convention, Cleveland, OH, April 1992, p. 8.

[36] Joanne R. Gilbert, "Inspiration and Conversation: Breat(h)ing the Other," *Text and Performance Quarterly* 13.2 (April 1993), p. 186.

[37] Randall, p. 197.

[38] Barbara Myerhoff, "Life History among the Elderly: Performance, Visibility, and Remembering," in *Studies of the Human Life Course*, ed. by Kurt Beck (American Association for the Advancement of Science, 1980), p. 7.

Chapter Seven

Creating and Staging the Personal Narrative

> People in Native American families make everything into a story. . . .
> People just sit and the stories start coming, one after another.
> I suppose that when you grow up constantly hearing the stories rise,
> break, and fall, it gets into you somehow."
> —Louise Erdich, Native American

> The universe is made of stories, not of atoms.
> —Muriel Ruykeyser

Storytelling—sharing personal narratives—is an aspect of ethnography. Storytellers reveal and maintain their cultural identity by collecting and performing oral narratives. The sharing of stories, though not as commonly taught as readers theatre and chamber theatre, has been practiced for centuries. This chapter intends to focus attention on the performance of life stories—personal narratives—as a way of preserving and presenting our cultural heritage. As Susan Duffy writes:

> One wonders why relatively few programs in speech communication and
> performance studies have focused attention on the history and tech-
> niques of traditional folkloric storytelling beyond mentions . . . in
> introductory lectures in oral interpretation and performance of literature
> classes for the past several decades. We ignore the very soul of oral

traditions through our neglect of the history and the techniques of the oral transmission of cultural myths and legends.[1]

In the early days of humankind, one popular form of entertainment was performing and/or listening to the performance of oral epic songs. Homer, for example, our earliest bard, stood on a hillside and orally composed the *Iliad* and *Odyssey*. (Similarly, we have the French troubadours, jongleurs [composers and performers] and joglars [performers], rhapsodes, gleemen, as well as the Old English scops who performed throughout the countrysides.)[2] People who wanted to become bards would pay avid attention to Homer, noting and imitating his use of formulae and themes, and practice telling their own stories borrowing Homer's practices and techniques.

This oral tradition still goes on today. It may be a less popular form of entertainment in view of the proliferation of modern technology, but it is still profoundly moving when done well. Witness the persuasive appeal of Garrison Keillor and his stories about Lake Wobegone or Spalding Gray and his personal narratives such as *Sex and Death to the Age 14* and *Swimming to Cambodia*. Gray, actor, writer, and monologist, stresses the importance of keeping the personal story alive in an interview in *Dramatics* magazine:

> Personal storytelling is very important to me because we've become so media-ized that we begin to think that the stories the stars tell on Johnny Carson are more important than ours. And whenever I interview people, interview the audience on stage, and I draw their stories out, the audience begins to realize that it's a radical move. That everyone has interesting stories if they can learn how to shape them. If I am a preacher or a proselytizer at all, it's to say, "Get together with friends, tell stories, listen. Turn off the TV, put down the book, listen to a story." Because the more we are fragmented and the more people are moved around and are in motion and the bigger this country gets and the more media-ized it gets, tied together only through television, the more healing it is to tell personal stories about your day. It gives you a personal history, and it gives you a sense of existence and place.[3]

Personal narratives are the autobiographical stories you tell every day. Stories are heightened forms of discourse, and through them you are able to preserve your familial ties and your cultural heritage. You inform with your stories and you are formed by them. As you tell your personal stories, you give order and structure to your world as you make sense of the events in your life. Your personal narratives are ethnographic studies of who you are and who you might become. You have personal authorship and ownership of the stories you tell. (In fact, there are scholars today who view our lives as lived stories.)

Most personal narratives have the following characteristics:

- The events you recount are considered to be, for the most part, true;
- You are a character in the stories you tell;
- The events you recount have already taken place;
- The events in your story tend to reveal your personal values; and
- Though you may not know this consciously, your personal narratives spring from a common cultural bond you share with members of your audience.

A personal narrative or "auto-ethnography," then, is an intimate portrait or study of you. It is the sharing of a true incident involving real people. You reveal aspects of yourself through the stories you tell. We learn about your history, your family, your past, your beliefs, your traditions, and so on. When you present a personal narrative you indicate a willingness to share parts of yourself with others and these others see themselves in the stories you tell. As others listen to our stories, they recognize themselves—they sense a consubstantiality between themselves and you, a common bond.

Storytelling, then, is not a one-way street. It is not somebody telling something to somebody who just passively accepts what is said. Story-telling is actually an expression of intimacy between teller and audience—a way of connecting with others which casts you and your listener(s) as collaborators. You share your story, and the audience perceives this story through their own somatic and semantic involvement—their own intertextuality. Sandra Dolby-Stahl, who refers to personal narratives as "personal experience" stories, explains: "Performing a personal narrative is a gesture toward intimacy; it combines the animation of performance with the intimacy of esoteric references and personal life history."[4] As folklorist Richard Bauman explains, the **narrated event** (the actual story or text) is greatly affected by the **narrative event** (the context in which the story is retold).[5] The telling of your story, then, involves the **text,** which is often framed, altered, exaggerated or downplayed as a consequence of the **context**. This context includes the audience, locale, time, and circumstances surrounding the telling. We may tell the same "text" differently depending on the "context."

A personal narrative according to Kristin Langellier is "the province of a single speaker in an act of self-preservation"[6] and we might add self-presentation. Self-preservation and presentation are but two of the conscious (or unconscious) intentions you might have in sharing your personal stories. Indeed, sharing a story with others does inherently preserve your family traditions; personal values; religious, social, or cultural heritage—and keeps your past alive—as well as present a certain image of yourself. You may have many different reasons for wanting to share your stories with others. We share stories to be in the limelight for a moment thus gaining a sense of importance or perhaps of self-worth; to explain our past, background, society to others who although similar to us in some ways, have not had identical experiences; to establish our membership in a certain group; to seek the opinion of others in ascertaining the meaning or significance of an experience; to entertain; to invite others to see what we are like; or to persuade others to see a situation from a particular point of view, among others.[7]

So far, we have defined the personal narrative as a *solo* art form— somebody telling somebody else a story that is true and that has already happened. There are volumes written on the genres, analysis, performance styles, methodologies, and so forth of creating and performing solo personal narratives. What differentiates this discussion from those is that we are interested in finding out what happens when your personal stories are encoded into script form and then performed by a *group* of people who take on the roles of the "characters" you have created in your personal story.

Why participate in this kind of group performance? What is to be gained by a group presentation? In addition to the information that the scriptwriter learns about the process of transferring lived experience into script form, in addition to the sense of satisfaction and ownership one achieves in being able to write and direct one's own story, there is the knowledge gained from "reflexivity"—from being able to look at your life as performed from a more objective stance. As you watch your story, you learn more about yourself. As Victor Turner puts it, when people perform they "turn, bend, or reflect back upon themselves upon the relations, actions, symbols, meaning, codes, roles, statuses, social structures, ethical and legal rules, and other sociocultural components which make up their public 'selves.'"[8] Although you are not literally performing in your story, you gain this same reflexivity from writing your story and from observing it performed.

This group presentation of personal stories poses some questions: How exactly do you capture an oral, lived experience in a written, script form? How do you then take that fixed script form and turn it into a lived experience once again through an oral presentation? These questions are the focus of this chapter. The passages in italics you will find throughout this chapter are excerpts from the journals of students asked to compose and script personal narratives. You may find that you share many of their concerns and impressions.

> *Writing a personal narrative has been rewarding. Watching the project go from a seed of an idea to a full-grown production excited me. I have always loved to write and this was another opportunity to write with a new objective in mind. It intrigued me as I became aware of the alterations I had to make in my writing style to suggest others. This new awareness allowed me not only to examine my writing style, but also my personal well being.*

What we are proposing is that you (1) decide on a personal story that you would feel comfortable sharing with your class (the presumed audience), (2) write out this story trying to maintain as much as possible (or as much as desirable) the flavor of the original event, (3) adapt this story into a script with a narrator (which may or may not be you) and characters whose speech you report in the story, and (4) cast members of your class to play these roles and stage the story. We will examine each of these four steps.

EXPERIMENTS

The four activities that follow are useful to engage in to trigger memories which may suggest personal narrative topics.

1. *Memory of childhood games.* Working with a partner, in one minute name all of your favorite childhood games. Change partners and in one minute tell this partner specifically how to play one of the games and why this game is special to you.
2. *Memory of a special place or a special time.* Take two minutes and re-create in your mind a detailed picture of a special place or time from your past. Describe this time or place to a partner or to the group.
3. *Family history.* Think of something unique or memorable about your family. It might be a family tradition, a trip you remember taking, some episode that took place, or something about a particular family member. Be prepared to share this personal experience story with the group in one to three minutes.
4. *What's in a name?* Each person in a group tells the others any information or stories that he/she has about his/her last

name—how it came to be, what it means, where it came from, and so on. Interesting stories can be shared with the whole class.

Choosing a Personal Narrative to Share

Lately, I've been rummaging through memories to find the "right" personal narrative. I keep trying to think of something to share with my fellow classmates. I wonder what I could relate to them? What should I choose that will be interesting, but not too "touchy" a subject for my own personal comfort?

The first step in creating and staging your own personal stories is, of course, to select the story you wish to share. The assumption is that you are in a group performance class, and that this is an assignment in that class. The assumption is also that you have been in this class long enough to know your classmates well, and that as a consequence you feel comfortable sharing your story with them. In addition, some of the members of this class will be the performers in the script, and the others will be the audience for the script. Since the sharing of a personal narrative, as we have said, is a kind of intimacy, it is important that you believe your story will be accepted and appreciated by those in the audience. You have to feel comfortable sharing; you have to feel that the audience will appreciate your gift, accept it, and will return the favor when they stage their narratives.

I'm not sure what will interest the class. Then, I begin to wonder if that really matters. Perhaps if a time in my life "sticks" out to me, I'll be able to express myself more easily.

Some questions that immediately arise as this project is approached are: How do I find a story worth telling that won't bore everyone? How do I find a story that will be of interest to the class?

While it is probably normal to worry that your story might not be as interesting to your audience as it is to you, you might be surprised how interested the class really is. It is most likely true that if the story is of interest to you, it will appeal to others. Paul Hernani believes that we've been sitting huddled around campfires listening to stories for years, and that we have an inherent interest in listening to stories. Hernani writes, "Stories . . . help us to *escape boredom and indifference*—ours as well as that of other people" (Hernani's emphasis).[9] We all seek intimacy, and the telling and sharing of stories is one way to fulfill that need. As people share personal stories with us, we sense how much courage it took to self-disclose, and we invariably react positively to that.

The Genres of Personal Narratives

Each personal narrative has its own personality, much like the individual writers.

Personal narratives are as varied as the persons who tell them, but the events they recount have been classified by Patricia Sawin into three types or genres: "happy, humorous, or dismal, with the 'I' character being represented, correspondingly, as meritorious, foolish, or victimized."[10] Sawin goes on to explain:

> In other words, personal experience narrators often sacrifice the dignity of themselves as characters to gain other rhetorical advantages, especially in humorous accounts, and also in accounts of unpleasant experiences when a sympathetic reception is assured from those who have suffered similar misfortunes.[11]

You might find yourself gravitating toward the humorous story because even though you might make yourself seem foolish, that is a small sacrifice for the other rewards your story may receive, e.g., laughs, applause.

Writing about yourself is not that easy. There is such a fine line between "honesty" and "theatricality." What I mean is, do I write my past self the way I really think it was and run the risk of sounding too dramatic and heavy, or do I give it a comedic tone so that it is more enjoyable to watch?

Dolby-Stahl suggests that there are three genres, as well, but her genres include the story that features the "character" of the teller, the story that is "humorous," and the story that is meant to teach some "moral" lesson. She then itemizes the variety of themes that fit these genres:

> Without suggesting that this is an exhaustive list, I would list the following themes as those most common to the secular, single-episode personal narrative. Among those reflecting characterization of the teller are (1) honesty, integrity; (2) cleverness, wit; (3) bravery, heroism, fearlessness; (4) practicality, business acuity; (5) charm, seductiveness; (6) loyalty, patriotism; (7) generosity or affection; and (8) manliness or maturity. Humorous themes are generally classifiable as involving (1) embarrassing situations, (2) ironic situations, or (3) incongruent occurrences. Homiletic themes intended to elucidate moral lessons are reflected in stories based upon (1) terrifying situations, war-time experience; (2) horrifying situations, cruel events; (3) unjust situations; (4) poignant situations; or (5) practical problems in managing one's affairs.[12]

Once you select the genre for your personal narrative, you will have a built-in set of conditions that are culturally known and understood. Classical narrative genres familiar to all North American folklorists include the tall tale, stories of fishing and hunting, local anecdotes, stories about family gatherings and other social encounters.[13]

Composing Your Personal Narrative

Now it is time to write out your remembered story. Questions arise here: How do I capture my lived experience into story form? Should I include both narration and dialogue? How do I structure the story so that it has a beginning, middle, and end? How do I know what to include and what to leave out? What if my story is on-going and really does not have an ending? Does it have to be completely true? From what point of view should I tell the story? There are not clear-cut answers to all these concerns, but let us briefly address each one.

> *I began to understand that the personal narrative did not have to be written in formal language, but could be filled with the idiosyncrasies of everyday speech.*

> *I was confused as to how much narration to use and how much dialogue. I had trouble re-creating the dialogue—but the narrator had plenty to say!*

The question of narration versus dialogue is complicated, but it is basically related to whether you want the focus of your story on the narrator or on the characters you have re-created from your past. It might be useful at this point to review the material in chapter four where we discuss the rhythm of a story based on the relationship between **story time** (the time in which the events occurred) and **discourse time** (the time it takes to recount the story). A narrator's manipulation of time includes: **scene** (taking as much time to tell an event as it did to occur), **summary** (taking less time to tell an event than it did to occur), and **description** (taking more time to tell an event than it did to occur). Some people remember things in the form of a sequence of events and do not remember specific dialogue (called "reported speech" by folklorists)— lines that were spoken in the past. Although writing dialogue is very difficult, unlike fiction writers, you do not have to *create* the dialogue as much as *remember* it.

Words that I had said that night two years ago started to come back to me. Hearing them in my head I began to add the nuances I felt were necessary to bring the script to life.

Ask yourself what dominates in your remembrance of the events. If you remember your story as basically narrative driven, then you will probably have more narration than dialogue, and this is perfectly acceptable. If, however, you remember the voices of others, if what people said is what you hear as you replay the story in your mind and this is most significant, then the story you tell may have more dialogue than narration. Often the most important aspects of a story may be captured only by directly quoting those people who were involved. If these quoted words become the "object of interpretation, discussion, evaluation, rebuttal, support, further development and so on"[14] in your story as they do in a novel, their use is mandatory. Do not worry about trying to duplicate the exact words someone may have said in the past. Your object should be to try to capture the essence of what was said, trying to reproduce as much as possible the flavor of their speech, any pertinent regionalisms, and to allow the language to give us a sense of the characters' uniqueness. Look, for example, at the way Nick Foster's story "The Tow" captures the particular way a truck driver spoke to him in his personal narrative. Nick later admitted that these may not have been the driver's exact words, but that they reflected the way Nick remembered him:

Truck Driver: Well, ahm jist gonna stop bah the station and fill'er up. Oop, ah got a cawl. Well, it won't take us long now that I got ridda that extree weight. I once made it from Ft. Wayne to Anderson in sixty-five minutes. (*He works himself into a frantic laugh.*) Ah was runnin' eighty-five or ninety miles per hour the whole way! Huh huh huh!!!

Whereas in chapter six we were interested in linguistic accuracy, here we are more interested in the variety of ways stories are told and how audiences work with a teller to co-create these stories. We are not worried about comparing the real events with the narrated events. As Dolby-Stahl so aptly puts it, "The personal narrative always involves some manipulation of the truth of the experience."[15] We are interested in how the narrated events are molded, sculpted, or altered to fit the narrative event in which they are being retold. Remember, when a story is told, it emerges as much from the telling as from the living; it is constituted often, as we have said, by the context. Storytellers make on-the-spot alterations, elaborate on some sections, eliminate others. You are, of course, writing your story, not telling it, and your actors are bound by the lines you give them. But you are not bound to depict the story as you originally lived or heard it. Feel free to allow the audience, the potential actors, and the eventual context in which it will be shared to affect you as you write and script your personal story. It is, after all, your story; you are the author, and you are free to take liberties. Chances are no one but you will even know if liberties are taken.

Whether the story you tell has an obvious beginning, middle, and end depends on the type of story you tell. As Dolby-Stahl says, "With the . . . telling of the personal narrative the teller adapts the perceived experience to the demands of the genre and the specific situation."[16] Since we realize certain adaptations must be made in the story to meet the demands of the "telling"—the performance experience—consider how a beginning, middle, and end may be formulated to suit your particular story. Some personal narratives are of a recent past where no ending has yet occurred. In some cases, the story we tell is the story we are currently living. We sense or hope for a projected end, but we do not know at this time whether that projected end will become reality. As John Allison puts it, there are occasions when the end of the story is beyond the "temporal boundary of the narration."[17] In these kinds of stories you may give the audience the feeling that there is more to come that you have no way of relating at this time. Or you may want to fabricate or invent an ending, relating how you would like your story to end or what you think may happen. In the following personal narrative by Andy Catron, the relationship Andy has with Jessica is on-going, and although at this time Andy has a certain premonition about where the relationship is headed, he has no way of knowing whether what he suspects is what will happen. Consequently, Andy devised an ending that suggests a possible future between he and Jessica. Notice Andy's use of narration and "reported speech," and the clear structure his story demonstrates. (The story as script appears later in this chapter.)

A Personal Narrative
"Now I Know"
by Andy Catron

I was twenty-two years old, for God's sake. All I wanted to do was graduate from college and start my career in technical theatre. I was all set to take on the world. But we, as normal human beings, tend to overlook that one magical word: Love. I remember I was tapped on the back one day at work. "Andy," said this lovely voice from behind me. But I was extremely busy and couldn't be bothered. I had a light plot to do that was already late. So, I couldn't really take the time to talk to anyone. But when I did finally turn around to see where the voice came from, I was in awe of the beauty that was standing before me. I had seen her around several times while I was working, but neglected to say anything for fear of it sounding like a "come on." But now the ice was broken, and there she was.

"Hi," I said as sincerely as possible, but I'm sure I sounded like a fool.

"I had a dream about you last night," Jessica said with a slight tinge to her voice that I could have misconstrued as sexual.

"Oh, you did? May I ask what it was about?"

"No."

I always hated it when women did stuff like that. Well, I never got her to tell me about the dream, but I did manage to get her to go to dinner with me. That was the start of a wonderful relationship that lasted for months, until something came up that neither of us had ever anticipated.

"Andy, what are we going to do when you graduate in May?" Jessica asked.

You see, I was three years older than she was, and this was a subject that we either overlooked or just chose to ignore because of the consequences that were involved.

"Oh, my God," I thought to myself. I had to face this question now, and I really hadn't given it any thought. Oh, of course, I'd thought about it, just not with her in the picture, until now.

"I don't want you to leave," she told me with that quivering sound people get in their voices before they cry.

"I don't want to either, at least not to leave you. College I can do without."

I stopped for a second amongst all this graduation angst and thought about what had happened. My life was going to change because of this terrific woman. But did I really want it to? "Oh, God, what a mess."

"What?"

"Oh, nothing," I said, afraid she caught my little audible slip.

Our relationship gradually changed and every day there was the continuing discussion of our imminent future together or apart. It was another two months of quarreling and compromise before I realized that this woman who had become part of my life was so important to me that I couldn't stop seeing her because I was moving away soon.

"You know it's going to be very hard, don't you?" I asked her, hoping she was in agreement.

"Yes, I know."

"And we both have to try very hard to understand each other."

"Yes, I know."

"And we can't get frustrated every time something goes wrong."

> "Yes, I know."
> "And I love you."
> She paused briefly and with a smile that was in between tears and happiness, she said, "Yes, I know."
> We stared at each other for a second, I kissed her, and we spent a wonderful evening together. All the while thinking to myself, "Could she be the one?" . . . Yes, this may be the one.

Do not worry, then, that there may be no "pay off" at the end of your story. Remember that all stories do not have to end with a "punchline," and you need not try to make your story resemble a stand-up routine. (Some would say that writing this kind of comic personal narrative is the most difficult.)

As you already have seen, there are three obvious differences between a personal narrative and a literary story:

1. Your stories are based on experiences that are assumed to be true (even if the story is enhanced or altered in some way, even if you are not entirely reliable in your remembrance or telling of the events you recount). To function properly the teller and listener(s) of a personal narrative must understand that the story is to be accepted as true.

2. You will be an actual "character" in the events (thus your integrity and reputation are, in a sense, on the line—this is not something that happened to someone else, this is something that happened to you and you are responsible for the story and your participation in it). In addition, the other "characters" in the story are also real people, not fictitious creations.

3. As a result of 1 and 2 above, a third difference becomes obvious. You have really lived the experiences recounted in your personal narratives whereas narrators' stories are fictitious and were never really lived by anyone in the past.

Point of View

From doing my own personal narrative, I got a firsthand feel for point of view and for the relationships between and among characters.

The point of view of your story is an essential consideration. Review the five kinds of points of view we detailed in chapter four. Remember, you may be the narrator of your story, you might want to create an omniscient narrator, or you may want to have a member of your family, a friend, an associate, etc., narrate your story for you. Whomever you choose will greatly affect how the story is told and how it is perceived.

You are free to decide on the point of view from which to tell your story. If you want to focus primarily on your own behavior and reactions, perhaps choosing the first-person major character point of view is best. If you want to underplay your role in the story and focus on someone else's behavior and reactions, then you might want to opt for the first-person minor character point of view. If you want to elaborate on the story, providing information that you may not have been aware of or privy to at the time, you may want to choose the omniscient, all-knowing point of view. This point of view might involve your sharing information that you discovered retroactively. You have information now that you did not have then which might change the story. In the interim between living and telling the story, you may have debriefed the people who inhabit your story and you are thus able to fill in gaps or clarify indeterminacies. Your personal narrative, then, is frequently not just yours, but a compilation of the narratives of different persons. As we revisit our own stories to turn them into texts, we are able to see them from three different points of view: our own, the "characters" in the story, as well as the audience. Knowing who your audience will be makes it possible for you to anticipate responses which then may influence the way you present your story.

Structure

Before you attempt to provide your story with a particular structure, take some time to reread the material on story structure in chapters four and five of this text, as well as some favorite stories. Even though there are differences between literary stories and your personal stories, there are also many similarities which may serve as models for you. As you read literary stories, keep the issues of structure, narration versus dialogue, and point of view in mind. Look how some of your favorite writers open and close their stories. Are there openings that you could emulate? Do all stories have a sense of closure? How do stories from the first-person point of view differ from stories told from other points of view?

Robert Scholes describes a narrative as follows:

> A narration involves a selection of events for the telling. They must offer
> sufficient continuity of subject matter to make their chronological
> sequence significant, and they must be presented as having happened

already. When the telling provides this sequence with a certain kind of shape and a certain level of human interest we are in the presence not merely of narrative but of story. A story is a narrative with a certain very specific syntactic shape (beginning-middle-end or situation-transforma-tion-situation) and with a subject matter which allows for or encourages the projection of human values upon this material. Virtually all stories are about human beings or humanoid creatures. Those that are not invariably humanize their material through metaphor and metonymy.[18]

As Scholes suggests, stories need structure. We need to know what happened, why it happened, and in what order. As Scholes later writes, "Our need for chronological and causal connection defines and limits all of us—helps to make us what we are."[19]

The story as lived experience may not have had a simple chronology as many events can affect or happen to us simultaneously. Try to isolate, then, those events that contribute to this particular story. It might be useful to think of the sonata structure we discussed in chapter two or the "situation-transformation-situation" shape to which Scholes refers. The ABA' of the sonata form may be a good starting point for the writing of your story. A is the beginning of the story where the "who, what, where, when," and so on, is communicated and a situation is revealed. In B, you detail what happened in that situation. In A', you could relate how the situation ended, what you learned from the situation, how this situation changed or affected you, and so on. In Andy's story, for example, the A is his initial mind-set of believing that his career was more important than a personal life. The B is the development of the relationship between Andy and Jessica and his transformation. The A' is Andy's new mind-set that both career and personal life are important, and the projection of the script into a future, "Yes, this may be the one."

The structure of a personal narrative depends, of course, on the type of story you tell, but one basic structure is as follows:

1. *Set up.* This includes background information by way of orientation, and may include external conditions and factors that brought the participants into this particular place and time, and provided the means for what happened. The set up usually includes an element of suspense which piques the audience's interest.
2. *Climax.* The high point of the action.
3. *Conclusion.*

The story must, of course, include identification of the characters who are to appear in your story, a sense of the setting, and the time and place—the when and where of the story. This should be included in your set up.

"Time markers" are needed throughout so that we know when an event occurred and how much time occurred between events. We like to know how long ago these events first occurred and how different you are now from how you were then. (In my class, horrifying events from the past are recounted now with a humorous smirk or smile. Time has changed us.) Whereas in chamber theatre we focused on the virtual past and the virtual present, we now focus on the real/actual past and the real/actual present. As you write your story, consider how the conditions of presentation will affect the events you script. In other words, how will the narrative event (the performance of your story) affect the narrated events (the story itself)? The audience is usually composed of the members of your class—people you presumably know and trust and with whom you feel comfortable sharing what may be intimate details of your life.

There is a sense that most narrators of personal stories are unreliable in that they purposely withhold information to build suspense, and give us the punchline or payoff at the end. Every personal narrative—no matter what type—should contain some degree of conflict or tension. This is what gives the story its life and keeps the audience interested in discovering how this conflict will be resolved.

Although it may be simplest to write your personal story in chronological order, you may want to deviate from this structure. As you write your story, you may want to borrow from novel or film structures and incorporate devices like the "flashback" or the "flashforward." Seymour Chatman discussed possible structures employing the flashback and the flashforward. He writes:

> In realistic narratives, the time of the story is fixed, following the ordinary course of a life: a person is born, grows from childhood to maturity and old age, and then dies. But the discourse-time order may be completely different: it may start with the person's deathbed, then "flashback" to childhood; or it may start with childhood, "flashforward" to death, then end with adult life.[20]

In Carrie Schlatter's personal narrative, she includes within a past scene a flashback to a scene in the even more distant past. While attending the wedding of her best friend, Carrie, the narrator, rushes out of the room into the church restroom which then is transformed into a restroom she and her friend were in during their early school days. Here is that moment from Carrie's story, "She Smiled at Me." (Carrie's personal narrative script may be found in chapter eight.)

A Personal Narrative
from "She Smiled at Me"
by Carrie Schlatter

While getting dressed, I spoke to no one. The noise in the church encased me like a cocoon: the giggles . . . the laughter . . . the happiness destroyed me. I tore through the crowd and stumbled into the bathroom where I could be alone. When I looked in the mirror, I saw a twelve-year-old child standing next to her older, wiser, fifteen-year-old best friend, Bertha, who was saying, "You have to get your bangs as high as you can. That's the look now, really!!! Look, mine are at least three inches off my head." I never could get my straight, fine, brown hair to look as good as Bertha's thick, blonde tresses, and once again I felt inferior and ugly because of it. If only I could have a second, one moment to tell her how much she meant to me. But all of those people. Those people who hadn't known her as long as I had.

Scripting Your Personal Narrative

Really, the translation of my personal narrative into script form was not terribly hard. I had tried to become aware of the line divisions as I was writing the story.

It was easy to turn my story into a script because it was already there. I didn't have to work out characters and a plot line.

It was simple, mainly because as I was writing the story, I had ideas in mind for the script.

Start your script by giving your story a title. The title is for identification and discussion purposes, but it also may function as a key to understanding the story. Include, also, a *dramatis personae* that lists and describes each of the people who appear in your story—including you. This *dramatis personae* is provided so that someone else would be able to cast and direct your story from the information you provide.

One difference between the real event and my script is simply the number of people in the story. When the event happened, there were at least ten people in that barn. I didn't want to have the entire class crammed in the front of the classroom, so I started deleting people and combining people.

You may find that by necessity you will create fewer characters in your story than were in the real event. Minor characters may be played by one performer. This gives you a more workable number of people on stage, and helps you to concentrate on the main characters in your story. Include, also, where and when the scene takes place, and any set or furniture requirements. Include in your script any stage directions and, if not made clear by context, who is to be addressed on any given line.

The scripting of your personal narrative will require you to employ the same kind of adaptation techniques that you used when turning a literary story into a script. Consider how to divide the lines in your story so that the narrator's point of view is revealed. As with chamber theatre adaptations, it is probably best to start with the narrator—establishing time, place, and situation. Look at this opening from a personal narrative by Cassandra Strandin. Notice how she begins with the narrator addressing the audience, sharing vital information with it, and then brings out Cassie from the past and establishes a relationship between them. Notice, too, how Cassandra includes to whom lines are addressed as well as how lines are to be said. (The entire script is in chapter eight.)

**Personal Narrative Script
from "One Last Starry Night"
by Cassandra Strandin**

(*Narrator starts center stage, casually talking to the audience, as if someone has just asked about her parents.*)

Narrator (*to audience*): It's been two years since my dad died of gastric cancer. Still, the day he died is a vivid memory. This was a crucial and devastating time in which I felt trapped by my situation.

(*The Narrator brings on Cassie from her memory and places her center, next to the Narrator. Then, she delivers the next lines to the audience, sending Cassie to do the action described.*)

Narrator (*to audience, setting the scene, and trying to seem casual*): I went to school, knowing that my dad wouldn't make it through the day. (*Cassie crosses downstage as if leaving. The Narrator stops her before Cassie gets too far.*) Actually, I was called home at noon (*Narrator stops Cassie. She puts her arm around "herself."*)

Cassie (*to Narrator, sadly realizing, speaking quickly*): since my mother didn't think my dad would live through the next few hours.

(*Frightened, biting lower lip.*) I remember going down the hallway to my mother and dad's bedroom, hearing the most horribly raspy breathing.

Narrator (*to Cassie, in a soothing, understanding tone*): It's a noise that nobody can imagine unless they have heard it themselves. (*Narrator places Cassie in a chair by the "bed," then speaks to audience, almost overcome. She gets hold of herself before becoming overwhelmed.*) This breathing became the death music that crept into every minute that passed that endless day.

To Bifurcate or Not To Bifurcate

The telling of a personal narrative involves you as you were then and you as you are now. The reality of your knowing both how you were then and how time has changed you is a perfect rationale for the bifurcation (casting two performers to play one role) of the narrator (that is, if you choose to tell your story from the major character point of view as Cassandra did in her personal narrative). As Dolby-Stahl writes, "A storyteller gives us a glimpse of someone who *was* but is now changed, a self that shares some consistencies with the person we now see before us, but a self that *could not be known* to us save through a story such as this."[21] If there is a distinct difference between those two aspects of you, bifurcation can make this division clear. Here is Andy Catron's story in script form. Andy chose to bifurcate himself as narrator. Can you detect a difference between Andy telling the story and Andy in the past?

Personal Narrative Script
"Now I Know"
by Andy Catron

Dramatis Personae

Andy Present: He is a twenty-two-year-old man. He has brownish, blond hair, is six feet tall, and skinny. He is a man who is quick to anger, but is gentle deep down. He is a hard worker, but also enjoys having fun.

Andy Past: He is also a man in his early twenties. He is not unlike Andy Present except that his career is the most important thing in his life.

Jessica: She is a beautiful, young woman of remarkable charm. She is very mature for her age, and has a dazzling effect on men who know her. She is a very talented performer, and is also willing to do almost anything for her friends.

(*Andy Present enters and sees Andy Past sitting stage right working on a lighting instrument. He is very much into his work. Andy Past feels someone watching him and looks up at Andy Present. Past gives Present a slight smile, nods his head as if to say, "hello" and returns to his work. Andy Present chuckles to himself and shakes his head as he crosses center stage.*)

Present (*to the audience, jokingly*): I was twenty-two years old, for God's sake.

Past (*to Present, with intensity*): All I wanted to do was graduate from college and start my career in technical theatre.

(*Past goes back to work.*)

Present (*crosses to Past, mildly slaps him on the shoulder, then says to the audience, cynically*): I was all set to take on the world. But we,

Past (*to Present, irritated*): as normal human beings,

Present (*to audience*): tend to overlook that one magical word:

(*During this last line, Jessica enters, and stands behind Past. She looks at him and then says*)

Jessica (*to Past, who doesn't see her*): Love.

(*Jessica continues to look at Past wonderingly as Past continues his work.*)

Present (*to audience*): I remember I was tapped on the back one day at work.

(*Jessica taps Past on the shoulder.*)

Jessica (*to Past*): Andy?

(*Past looks ahead for a second, then goes back to his work.*)

Past (*to Present*): said this very lovely voice from behind me, but (*to Jessica, not looking at her*): I was extremely busy and couldn't be bothered. I had a light plot to do, and it was already late. So, I really couldn't take the time to talk with anyone.

(*Present goes to Past and physically turns him to look at Jessica.*)

Present (*to audience*): But when I did finally turn around to see where the voice came from,

Past (*looking at Jessica*): I was in awe of the beauty that was standing before me. (*Turns to address Present*): I had seen her around several times while I was working.

Jessica (*to Present, accusingly*): but neglected to say anything.

(*Present shrugs his shoulders as if to say, "I'm sorry."*)

Past (*to Jessica*): for fear of it sounding like a "come on."

(*Jessica chuckles.*)

Present (*to Past*): But now the ice was broken. (*He turns and says to audience*): And there she was.

Past (*to Jessica, not knowing what else to say. After a little hesitation.*) Hi.

Present (*to audience*): I said as sincerely as possible.

Past (*To Present*): But I'm sure I sounded like a fool.

(*Present looks at Past and shakes his head "no."*)

Jessica (*to Past*): I had a dream about you last night.

Present (*to the audience*): Jessica said with a slight tinge to her voice,

Past (*to Present, suspiciously*): that I could have misconstrued as sexual.

(*Present indicates to Past to turn around and talk to Jessica.*)

Past (*to Jessica*): Oh, you did? May I ask what it was about?

Jessica (*to Past*): No. (*She smiles.*)

Past (*to Present, who shakes his head in frustration*): I always hated it when women did stuff like that.

Present (*to audience*): Well, I never got her to tell me about the dream.

Past (*to Present*): But I did manage to get her to (*to Jessica*) go to dinner with me.

(*Jessica nods "yes." Past ushers Jessica to table upstage left, they sit and are having a great time talking at dinner. Present follows them and stands behind them.*)

Present (*to audience*): That was the start of a wonderful relationship that lasted for months, (*Past and Jessica move their chairs closer together*) until something came up that neither of us had ever anticipated.

Jessica (*to Past*): Andy, what are we going to do when you graduate in May?

Present (*to audience*): You see, I was three years older than she was,

Past (*to Present*): and this was a subject that we either overlooked,

Present (*to Past*) or just chose to ignore because of the consequences that were involved.

Past (*to self*): Oh, my God,

Present (*to the audience*): I thought to myself.

Past (*to Present*): I had to face this question now, and I really hadn't given it any thought.

Present (*to audience*): Oh, of course, I'd thought about it, just not with her in the picture.

Past (*to Jessica*): Until now.

Jessica (*to Past*): I don't want you to leave,

Present (*to audience*): she told me with that quivering sound people get in their voices before they cry.

Past (*to Jessica*): I don't want to either at least not to leave you. College I can do without.

Present (*to audience, pause*): I stopped for a second amongst all this graduation angst and thought about what had happened.

Past (*to Present, contemplating the consequences of this statement*): My life was going to change because of this terrific woman,

Present (*to audience, knowing the right answer*): but did I really want it to?

Present (*to audience*) and **Past** (*to self*): Oh God, what a mess.

Jessica (*to Past*): What?

Past (*to Jessica*): Oh, nothing,

Present (*to audience*): I said, afraid she caught my little audible slip.

(*Past and Jessica get up and take a walk hand in hand in front of Present.*)

Present (*to audience*): Our relationship gradually changed, and every day there was the continuing discussion of our imminent future.

Jessica (*to Past*): Together?

Past (*to Present*): Or apart?

(*Present shakes his head "no."*)

Present (*to audience*): It was another two months of

Past and **Jessica** (*to each other*): quarreling and compromise

Present (*to audience*): before I realized that this woman who had become part of my life was so important to me that

Past (*to Present*): I couldn't stop seeing her because I was moving away soon. (*Turning to Jessica*): You know it's going to be very hard, don't you?

Present (*to audience*): I asked her, hoping she was in agreement.

Jessica (*to Past*): Yes, I know.

Past (*to Jessica*): And we both have to try very hard to understand each other.

Jessica (*to Past*): Yes, I know.

Past (*to Jessica*): And we can't get frustrated every time something goes wrong.

Jessica (*to Past*): Yes, I know.

Past (*to Jessica*): And I love you.

Present (*to audience*): She paused briefly and with a smile that was in between tears and happiness, she said,

Jessica (*to Past, with the utmost sincerity*): Yes, I know.

Past (*to Jessica*): We stared at each other for a second, and

Present (*to the audience, with a smile*): I kissed her,

(*Past gently kisses Jessica.*)

Past (*to Jessica*): and we spent a wonderful evening together.

(*Past and Jessica walk out together slowly, hand in hand.*)

Present (*to audience*): All the while thinking to myself,

Past (*turns around and says to Present*): Could she be the one?

(*Present nods his head "yes."*)

Past (*to Jessica, smiling*): Yes, this may be the one.

If the "consistencies" between the "you that was" and the "you that is" outweigh the differences; if your story is of a recent past and time has not measurably changed you, then bifurcation is not necessary. Look at the opening of Nick Foster's script, "The Tow" in which he has not bifurcated because the events were recent and Nick detected no changes in himself from past to present. In the script, Nick incorporated the technique of "freeze action" to stop the progression of the scene as the Narrator spoke to the audience rather than to the characters in the scene.

Personal Narrative Script
from "The Tow"
by Nick Foster

Dramatis Personae

Narrator: He is twenty-one, and casually dressed. He and his room-mate have just set out to go to Indianapolis, Indiana. His father is out of town, and he is using his father's Audi 5000 with turbo. They are just leaving Muncie, Indiana when something goes wrong.

Brian: He is twenty-three, and is casually dressed as well.

Truck Driver: He is the epitome of all scum! He looks just like those truck drivers in the movies. He is very dirty, and extremely unedu-cated! He talks with an accent, of sorts, and is very free with what he says!

Narrator (*to the audience*): It was Saturday, February 12, 1995. I remember the day quite well. (*He gets in the car with his friend, Brian*) We were on our way to Indianapolis, when it happened.

Brian: (*to self*): A strange ding!

Narrator: (*to audience*): Ding!

Brian: (*to Narrator*): Ding!

Narrator: (*to audience*): Ding (*to Brian*) What WAS that sound? (*to audience*) Then I knew. The car was telling me something. It was overheating! So I . . .

Brian: (*to Narrator, interrupting*) . . . We added some antifreeze . . .

Narrator: (*to audience*): but it was useless. This would require much more than antifreeze. My only hope was to . . .

Brian: (*to Narrator*): get to a gas station. Maybe they can fix it.

Narrator: (*to audience*): So we did . . .

Brian: (*to Narrator*): But they couldn't . . .

Narrator: (*to audience*): . . . so we waited. (*pause*) It seemed a helpless situation. (*Revelation!*) Then, I remembered . . . I had my AAA gold card!!! So, I pulled out my cellular phone and called for a tow truck.

Casting and Staging Your Personal Narrative

My personal narrative ended up revealing a different side of my personality than my classmates have ever seen.

Why should we preserve our personal, intimate life stories in a public forum? What is to be gained from a group performance of an intimate story? As Dolby-Stahl has made clear, "The power of performance enhances any storytelling, but especially one that offers to share some aspect of the teller's inner life."[22] Dolby-Stahl, and most of the other scholars we have cited, are talking about solo performance, but what we have in mind is group performance where the teller is both in the story and out of the story. Both telling the story and showing the story. Both subjective and objective. The teller is the subjective "I" even though someone else may be playing this "I," and the teller is also the "eye" that sees and objectively tries to direct a production which features his or her own life experience.

As I wrote my script, I felt like I was writing about someone else. I had objectified the experience that much. This made it easier for me to cast and direct it.

In this way, you record your heritage in script form, and then try to make sense of it, to objectify it for an audience. Now your script becomes an event! As we pointed out earlier, seeing your script performed forces a kind of reflexivity that allows you to see your story as an object somehow separate from you, which helps you to study and learn from it. In addition, you learn something from those people taking on the roles you have created. You hear your script, and this listening may reveal information you were not consciously aware of. In general, as folklorists make clear, narratives are constructed from multiperson talk. This group format allows your narratives to be reenacted by "multipersons."

Casting poses interesting problems and responsibilities, just as it did when we discussed staging ethnographic studies. What are the ethical dilemmas we face when we cast performers to play real people as opposed to fictitious creations? Is this a liberating feeling or does it produce added anxiety and stress? How do we portray a friend or classmate? How do the performers in your production keep from going over the line into mockery or parody? How do we best represent the members of our family, friends, or relatives with performers? What do we owe to the original participants when we stage our stories? The best solution to these issues is to emulate Anna Deavere Smith, whose acclaimed one-woman shows demonstrate her ability to "take on" a variety of different "real" people whose stories she collected. Smith's first play, *Fires in the Mirror: Crown Heights and Other Identities* was a performance of various people Smith had interviewed who were connected with the 1991 riots in Crown Heights. Her second work was *Twilight: Los Angeles 1992* which chronicled the views of many involved in the recent L.A. riots. Smith revealed in an episode of "Sixty Minutes" that she does not *impersonate* the various people she presents in her one-woman shows as much as she tries to give her *impression* of them. This is similar to what the narrator in prose fiction does. He or she gives us impressions of the people who inhabit the story. When asked to play real people, performers should take their cues from the script creator and try to give impressions of the people as characterized in the story. This process is, of course, aided by the director/scriptwriter's input. It is recommended, however, that before the personal narratives are cast, there be an open class discussion of the idiosyncrasies, behavioral mannerisms, habits, quirks, etc. of each member of the class. Just as caricaturists tend to exaggerate one element of a person's physical appearance (e.g., Richard Nixon's nose, Jay Leno's chin, etc.), and impressionists like Phil Hartman, Dana Carvey, and Rich Little comment on rather than give exact replications of those they imitate, actors portraying their friends and peers may tend to rely on exaggeration of personal habits rather than considering a more realistic portrayal. This could cause misunderstandings and hard feelings. If a discussion is held first, not only does everyone get a self-evaluation, but the potential for anxiety and tension is lessened. If an atmosphere of sharing and mutual understanding has been established, chances are everyone will be more comfortable engaging in this kind of "acting" exercise.

> As far as someone to play me, I asked someone that had known me for several years. She knew my speech patterns, gestures I would use, and some of my best facial expressions.

There is not much difference in the staging of a personal narrative script and the staging principles detailed in chapter five of this text. In general, the narrator usually begins the tale center stage and then moves in accordance with his or her point of view (though this is but one convention and certainly does not have to be rigidly adhered to). The narrator attempts to establish a relationship both with the "characters" in the story and with the audience. The "characters" react to each other as they reacted to each other when the story occurred. You may use your memories of this experience to help with characterization and basic blocking of your story.

I felt as though I needed to place all the action in one place, adding to the intense suffocation that I experienced the day my father passed away.

Begin by deciding what the set will look like. Often you will need to condense the various locales in the past events to accommodate theatrical staging. Decide what furniture you will need and where it will be placed. Determine where exits and entrances will be, and write this information in your script. Analyze your interpretation of character intent and motivation and let that be the impetus to move characters in relation to each other and to the furniture you are using. Remember, the narrator must have a relationship both with the audience and with the other characters on stage. If you bifurcate, how will you establish the kind of relationship between those two sides of you? In general, during moments of summary, the narrator would move some distance from the scene. During moments of scene when dialogue predominates, the narrator may be close enough to observe reliably what was done and said. During moments of description, the narrator should be very close to the object, person, or event being described.

Some directors find it frustrating to direct their personal narratives because they cannot make the performers react in the same way that the people in the lived event reacted.

It was hard not to give line readings—telling the actors exactly how to say a line as I remembered it. I didn't want to offend them.

I felt frustrated because it was hard to accept that the actors wouldn't do it exactly like I had remembered.

It was hard to take myself out of the scene and try to look objectively at it. I didn't want to be pushy or to squelch the actors' creativity.

It was difficult to direct because frustration set in. I could remember numerous details from that specific day, but there was no way to have the actors perform each movement. Also, I faced the challenge of line interpretation. Again, I recalled nuances that would have been impossible to communicate.

These frustrations are real. The solution is complicated but harkens back to the idea of collaboration. If you think of your cast as helping you re-create the story—adding to the story their own personalities and impressions—you will be less frustrated. The "truth" of your personal narrative may already have been sacrificed by theatrical conventions; expect that the cast members will bring their own truths to the script.

I was curious to see what their interpretations of what I wrote would be. They were different but valid.

It was difficult to get the actors to be exactly as I remember the characters. The actors seemed to take on some new characteristics that weren't like the original characters. Then, I relaxed, and decided that these changes were interesting, and seemed to work well.

Audience Response

We spoke earlier about the concern many beginning storytellers have that their story won't be of interest to the audience. The reality is that the stories you tell have embedded universal themes and formulae which you may or may not be conscious of. Although Andy and Cassie's stories were unique and personal to them, both stories dealt with universal, culturally-understood themes: love and death. We are a product of a particular culture, and you will be pleasantly surprised to see members of the audience nodding in agreement as universal truths that you may have thought were isolated personal acts are revealed. Dolby-Stahl expresses this well:

> An individual listener/interpreter responds to a narrative performance from the perspective of personal reality, and that personal reality is grounded in a multifaceted social base . . . . Especially in the personal narrative, the embedded folklore is perceived by the listener as a thick web of shared traditions connecting the teller's personal reality and personal sense of history to those of the listener. Identifying these traditions is the listener's first step in responding to the narrative. Though the listener may be unaware of this process of identifying folklore, the listener may well *experience* a redundancy of meaning, a feeling that these same embedded items or processes have meant something personally before now.[23]

As a result of the audience feeling that your story may have "meant something personally before now," they (as well as you) are encouraged to reexamine their life experiences which then may trigger material for additional personal narratives.

I found this assignment to be very rewarding on a personal level. Although at first I had been wary to tackle the story of my father's death, I'm pleased that I did. After two years of dealing with the loss of my father, I felt ready to put my feelings on paper. That day has played itself over and over in minute detail for two years, and I finally found the courage to put words to the pain that I experience when I think of that day. Although I am sure that day will continue to haunt me, at least I realize how far I have come in the very lengthy grieving process. Also, I feel good that I shared my love for my father with my classmates. It is important to me that people know just how significant my father has been in my life. Now, with this short narrative, a few more people will understand. I have come away with a feeling of accomplishment. This has been the most rewarding assignment for me because I was allowed free reign of my creative abilities—a most needed outlet.

The last chapter of this text includes a number of different scripts. There are readers theatre compilation scripts, chamber theatre scripts, an ethnographic study script, and a conversation analysis. These scripts are included to give you an idea of the variety and types of scripts that may be created and staged employing the experimental theatre techniques outlined in this text.

Summary

This chapter focused on creating and staging personal narratives— true stories from your past. The process involves selecting a story that you are willing to share, writing down that story keeping in mind structure and point of view, encoding the story into script form, and casting and staging the story in class.

Notes

[1] Susan Duffy, in a review of "The World of Storytelling: A Practical Guide to the Origins, Development and Applications of Storytelling" by Anne Pellowski, *Text and Performance Quarterly* 12.2 (1992), pp. 189–191.

[2] For a detailed account of the composition and performance of oral epic songs see Albert B. Lord, *The Singer of Tales* (New York: Atheneum, 1968).

[3] Jeffrey Goldman, "Dancing with the Audience: A Conversation with Spalding Gray, Actor, Writer, Monologist, and Connoisseur of Neuroses," *Dramatics* 63 (November 1991), pp. 24–29.

[4] Sandra Dolby-Stahl, *Literary Folkloristics and the Personal Narrative* (Bloomington: Indiana University Press, 1989), p. 43.

[5] Richard Bauman, *Story, Performance, and Event: Contextual Studies of Oral Narrative* (Cambridge: Cambridge University Press, 1986), p. 6.

[6] Kristin M. Langellier, "Personal Narratives: Perspectives on Theory and Research," *Text and Performance Quarterly* 9.4 (1989), pp. 243–276.

[7] See Patricia E. Sawin, "'Right here is a good Christian lady': Reported Speech in Personal Narratives," *Text and Performance Quarterly* 12.3 (1992), p. 194.

[8] Victor Turner, *The Anthropology of Performance* (New York: PAJ Publications, 1986), p. 24.

[9] Paul Hernani, "On the How, What, and Why of Narrative," in *On Narrative*, ed. by W.J.T. Mitchell (Chicago: University of Chicago Press, 1981), p. 199.

[10] Sawin, pp. 194–195.

[11] Sawin, p. 195.

[12] Dolby-Stahl, p. 28

[13] See Bauman, p. 6. Bauman acknowledges that he is showing a male gender bias in his catalogue of narrative genres. Rosan A. Jordan and Susan J. Kalcik, eds. of *Women's Folklore, Women's Culture* (Philadelphia: University of Pennsylvania Press, 1985), p. ix, write, ". . . genres and performance contexts that are especially characteristic of men have most interested folklorists as worthy of study, while folklore that flourishes within the private domain of women has been underrated and ignored." They claim that genres often associated with women, such as "personal experience narratives, popular beliefs, and various kinds of humor have often been dismissed as 'minor genres' or, less formally, 'old wives' tales' or 'just gossip.'"

[14] Mikhail M. Bakhtin, *The Dialogic Imagination*, transl. Caryl Emerson and Michael Holquist (Austin: University of Texas Press, 1981), p. 337.

[15] Dolby-Stahl, p. 18.

[16] Ibid.

[17] John M. Allison, Jr., "Narrative and Time: A Phenomenological Reconsideration," *Text and Performance Quarterly* 14.2 (April 1994), pp. 108–125.

[18] Robert Scholes, "Afterthoughts on Narrative: Language, Narrative, and Anti-Narrative," in *On Narrative*, ed. by W. J. T. Mitchell (Chicago: University of Chicago Press, 1981), p. 206.

[19] Scholes, p. 207.

[20] Seymour Chatman, "What Novels Can Do That Films Can't (and Vice Versa)" in *On Narrative*, ed. by W. J. T. Mitchell (Chicago: University of Chicago Press, 1981), p. 118.

[21] Dolby-Stahl, p. 22.

[22] Dolby-Stahl, p. 43.

[23] Dolby-Stahl, pp. 118–119.

Chapter Eight

How It Was Done: Sample Scripts

In this chapter you will find a variety of different kinds of scripts: chamber theatre adaptations, readers theatre compilations, personal narratives, ethnographic studies, and a script of naturally occurring conversation. These scripts were selected because they are excellent examples of the creative potential inherent in this kind of theatre. Some of these scripts defy conventional classification as their genres blur, consequently they fit into more than one category. The "Fabulous 40s" script, for example, is both a compilation script and a series of oral histories and personal narratives. "Growing Pains" is a compilation script inspired by naturally occurring talk recorded from prevention workshops. The script of an Alcoholics Anonymous meeting combines conversation analysis with ethnography.

These scripts are provided as examples of the various experimental theatre types discussed in this text, and they may be used for classroom instruction. Should you decide to stage these scripts for the public, you must first acquire the rights to do so. This usually involves seeking permission from both the original author(s) as well as from the script-writer.

Chamber Theatre Adaptation
"The Last Rung on the Ladder" from *Night Shift*
by Stephen King
Adapted by Joshua Coomer

(This script has a double bifurcation; both the narrator [Larry] and his sister [Katrina] are seen as children and years later when they are adults. The audience is a therapy group the older Larry is attending to help him deal with the loss of his sister. The story is an account of an incident in the past between Larry and "Kitty" as children, that relates to a similar, fatal, incident later in life.)

Dramatis Personae

Narrator (N): Larry in the present. He is in his mid- to late-thirties, and is divorced. A well-to-do lawyer. However, he is a lonely man; he does not have any close friends.

Larry (L): Larry in the past. He is a ten-year-old boy. He loves his sister with a wonderful innocence only children possess; it is wonderful because, at the time, the child really doesn't realize the depth of the love.

Katrina (KA): Katrina in the present. She is Larry's younger sister who he calls "Kitty." She is in her early- to mid-thirties. She did not do so well with her life; generally, she is a depressed person.

Katrina (K): Katrina in the past; called "Kitty." She is an eight-year-old at the time of the "barn thing." A trusting, bright-eyed girl who adores her older brother.

Setting: A semi-circle of chairs is set up downstage center. A ladder is down center in the empty space. Directly upstage of the ladder is Kitty's bed. A door is slightly stage right of the bed.

(Narrator—Larry Present—is talking to a therapy group. He is comfortable with the group of people; he has been sharing with this group for several months. The story he is about to tell, however, makes him very uncomfortable, particularly because Katrina's letter just arrived yesterday. He is at first fidgety, but as the story slowly unfolds, he becomes almost trance-like [not at all monotone or comatose, but rather baffled and amazed by it all]. He is holding the letter, much

like a child holds his/her favorite blanket. The love he feels for his sister is the driving force which makes it possible for him to speak.)

Note: *The audience is seated in a semi-circle, facing the stage area. This leaves enough room for the action to be played within the semi-circle. The Narrator is seated on the far stageleft side of this semi-circle.*

N (*to audience, slowly, nervously, guiltily*): I got Katrina's letter yesterday. I read what was in it and the next thing I knew I was standing in the living room with the phone in my hand, getting ready to call Dad. I put the phone down with something like horror. He was an old man, and he'd had two heart attacks. Was I going to call him and tell him about Katrina's letter? To do that might very well have killed him. So I didn't call. There was only a single sentence below the . . .

KA (*only her voice is heard*): "Dear Larry:"

(*N hears her voice as she says this.*)

N (*to self*): But a sentence can mean enough.

(*L and K enter, giggling and having fun. He whispers in her ear, "Let's jump," she nods in agreement, and they walk stage right towards "ladder." Freeze. N watches all this with amusement.*)

N (*to audience*): I was two years older than Katrina, whom everyone called Kitty. It's her I want to tell you about. (*Pause.*) It happened . . . the barn thing . . . (*L and K unfreeze, look up at beam with anticipation*) . . . one Saturday in November. There was a ladder nailed to a crossbeam high up in the third loft, a ladder that went straight down to the main floor. We were . . .

L and **K** (*together, to each other, mocking their mother's concerned, stern voice*): forbidden to climb on it because it was old and shaky! (*giggles*)

N (*to audience*): If you climbed up that rickety ladder . . .

L (*to K and self*): There were exactly forty-three rungs, Kitty and I had counted them!

N (*to audience*): . . . you ended up on a beam that was seventy feet above the floor. And then if you edged out along the beam about twelve feet, you stood over the haymow.

K (*to L and self*): and then you could jump!

N (*to audience*):   It was a forbidden sport, all right. And it was a dangerous sport, too. (*Pause.*) But the temptation was just too great.

(*L and K stand facing audience at foot of "ladder," looking at each other.*)

N (*to audience*):   We stood at the foot of the ladder, looking at each other.

(*N watches L and K, fondly remembering their innocence.*)

L (*to K*):   Dare you.

K (*to L*):   Dares go first.

L (*to K*):   Girls go before boys.

K (*to L*):   Not if it's dangerous.

N (*to audience*):   Everybody knew she was the second-biggest tomboy in Hemingford.

L (*to K, and partly to himself*):   Okay. Here I go. (*L mimes climbing all forty-three rungs. This is done while N speaks next lines.*)

N (*watching this, but speaking to audience*):   I was ten that year, about ninety pounds. Kitty was eight and twenty pounds lighter. The ladder had always held us before, so we thought it would always hold us again, which is a philosophy that gets men and nations in trouble time after time.

(*L has made it to the top. He struggles for balance. This next little bit of dialogue is a ritual between them.*)

L (*to K, waving*):   Hi, down there!

K (*to L, waving*):   Hi, up there!

L (*to self, and to anyone or anything that might want to listen to this proclamation of freedom and youth*):   I jumped! (*L steps off beam and freezes for a moment.*)

N (*to audience*):   And gravity took hold. (*Watches as L unfreezes and imitates a long, fast fall. This is not "slow motion," so it should be a tight, breathless two seconds where L doesn't really move. Then he hits the "hay." L can make his own sound effect—whoosh!—or something similar. As soon as he lands, K starts up the ladder—forty-three rungs, quickly.*)

N (*to audience, but watching the action*):   As I crawled out of the hay, I saw that Kitty was halfway up the ladder. (*K is up and is inching her way over on the beam.*) Then she was on the beam, high above me.

K (*to L, waving*): Hi, down there!

L (*to K, waving*): Hi, up there!

N (*to audience*): She edged along the beam, graceful as always. (*K does this as he says it. When in place, K steps off the beam into the swan dive position—arms swept behind her, back arched—and freezes.*)

L (*to self, and again, to the world, completely delighted*): And then she swanned!

N (*to audience, with goose-bumps up and down his body*): Talk about things you can't forget. For a moment she seemed to hang in the air. She was Kitty, my sister, her arms swept behind her and her back arched, and how I loved her for that beat of time! (*She unfreezes, falls, lands, gets out of hay, and brushes herself off, absolutely happy.*) The game seemed to go on forever.

L (*to K, parental tone in his voice*): We finally agreed on one more turn each. (*K nods in agreement. L starts up the ladder again.*)

N (*to audience*): Going up first . . .

L (*to self, with a little fear beginning to creep into his voice*): I felt the ladder moving beneath me . . . and I could hear . . .

N (*to audience and himself*): Very faintly, the whining rasp of old nails loosening up in the wood.

N and **L** (*N to audience, L to self, very frightened*): And for the first time I was really,

N (*to audience*): actively

N and **L** (*N to audience, L to self*): scared.

N (*to audience, really reliving that fright*): I hurried out over the hay and dropped off. (*L does this as N speaks. As soon as L lands, K is heading back up the ladder.*) The fun of the game was gone. I came out to the middle of the barn to see Kitty hurrying up the ladder.

L (*to K, very alarmed*): Hey, come down! It's not safe!

K (*to L, still on ladder, not at all alarmed*): It'll hold me! I'm lighter than you!

N (*to audience, but watching K*): That was when the ladder let go. The rung she was standing on gave way, and then both sides of the ladder split. (*K mimes this by jerking her body to suggest the ladder breaking. Both of her arms are straight above her, and her legs are kicking wildly—this can be suggested by simply moving* *the knees back and forth, maybe the feet if it doesn't look too awkward.)*

K (*to L, screaming in panic*): Larry! Larry! Help me!

N (*to audience*): I knew what had to be done. She was better than sixty feet above me, her legs kicking wildly at the blank air.

L (*to K, trying to sound calm, but absolutely terrified*): Kitty! Just hold still! Hold still! (*K stops kicking immediately.*)

N (*to audience, but watching K*): She obeyed me instantly.

(*L starts to transfer hay from the big pile, making a new pile under the broken ladder. He goes back and forth, many times. He is completely scared and the adrenaline is pumping. He can transfer for about twenty seconds.*)

K (*to L, scared*): Larry, I can't hold on much longer!

L (*to K, again trying to remain calm*): Kitty, you've got to! You've got to hold on! (*He continues to transfer hay, going as fast as he can.*)

K (*to L*): Larry! The rung! It's letting go! (*K starts to kick again in blind panic.*)

L (*to K, screaming*): No! Stop that! Just let go, Kitty! (*K stops kicking.*)

N (*to audience*): She let go and dropped the second I told her to.

(*K mimes the fall. It has no joy in it this time. When she lands, it is a nasty, hard hit. K will have to collapse to the floor as quickly as possible. She can utter a grunt as the wind is knocked from her lungs. She lays perfectly still. It is unclear at this point, to L that is, whether she is alive.*)

L (*to K, almost crying with fear*): Kitty? Kitty?

K (*to L, quietly, eyes still closed, hard to breathe*): Larry? Am I alive?

(*L hugs her. He cannot be any happier than he is at this moment.*)

L (*to K, still hugging*): You're alive, you're alive.

(*L helps her to her feet. They limp over to stage right, turn around, come back in the house door, which is directly upstage of where the ladder was, and she mimes getting into her bed.*)

N (*to audience*): She had broken her left ankle. (*Small smile.*) After Dad got through with me, I ate standing up for a week. (*Pause.*) I went in to see her before bedtime. (*N just watches as L stands looking at K, she looks back at him. Several seconds pass. N speaks to audience, but watches K and L*): She looked at me so long and so lovingly that I was uncomfortable.

K (*to L, matter-of-factly*): Hay. You put down hay.

L (*to K*): 'Course I did. What else would I do?

K (*to L*): I didn't know what you were doing. I was too scared to look.

L (*to K, incredulously*): You didn't know? Didn't know what I was doing? (*K shakes her head "no."*) And when I told you to let go you . . . you just did it? (*K nods her head "yes."*) Kitty, how could you do that?

K (*to L, shrugging, lovingly*): I knew you must have been doing something to fix it. You're my big brother. I knew you'd take care of me. (*L and K freeze.*)

N (*to audience*): When the cast came off, that was the end of the barn incident. It was the end, but somehow not the end. Somehow it never ended until nine days ago, when Kitty jumped from the top story of an insurance building in Los Angeles. The headline read:

CALL GIRL SWAN-DIVES TO HER DEATH.

(*L and K exit. As they leave, KA enters from behind N and moves to center. She is terribly depressed. Nothing in life appears worthwhile to her.*)

N (*to audience, but so quiet that it is almost to himself*): We grew apart and lost touch. I moved and kept thinking that I've got to write Kitty and tell her that, but I never did. (*Pause. He somewhat regains his composure.*) The letter was postmarked two weeks before she died. It would have gotten to me a long time before, if not for the forwarding addresses. She must have gotten tired of waiting.

(*N starts to read the letter, silently, just mouthing the words. KA looks at N while she speaks the letter aloud. He hears her but doesn't see her.*)

KA (*to N*): Dear Larry, I've been thinking about it a lot lately . . . and what I've decided is that it would have been better for me if that last rung had broken before you could put the hay down. Your, Kitty.

(*KA just keeps looking at N as he speaks this last speech. No emotion can be detected from her stare. N puts the letter in his pocket.*)

N (*to audience*): Yes, I guess she must have gotten tired of waiting. I'd rather believe that than think of her deciding I must have forgotten. I wouldn't want her to think that, because that one sentence was maybe the only thing that would have brought me on the run. (*Pause.*) I think of her as I start to drift off to sleep . . .

(*KA takes the frozen swan pose K had assumed earlier. She has a radiant smile. She looks truly happy, like she was at eight years old.*)

N (*off in space, as if trying to communicate with KA*): She was the one who always knew the hay would be there.

The End

Personal Narrative
"One Last Starry Night"
by Cassandra Strandin

(*This script was prepared by Cassandra as an assignment in an advanced oral interpretation/performance studies class. It is a personal narrative which details the events that occurred the day her father died of cancer. The main character is bifurcated to indicate the difference between the way Cassandra feels about the event now, and the way Cassie felt about the event then.*)

Dramatis Personae

Narrator (N): Cassandra Strandin, age 20. Although she is more objective now than she was in the past, there are times when she has to pull herself away from the situation. The story is Cassie's memory. She is the director of the scene. The father referred to is not there. He is someone who causes too much pain to re-create.

Cassie (C): Cassie Strandin in the past, age 18. Her life has radically changed. She's always been quiet, but now she's putting on a false face for her friends and family.

Mother (M): She's in her middle 40s, and is very worn out by the impending death of her husband. At this point, Cassie and her mother are starting to distance themselves from one another.

Blythe (B): Blythe is Cassie's sister. She is 15 and wrapped up in the home situation with her father's death. Cassie and Blythe have a closer relationship with one another than they do with their mother.

Setting: The Narrator is talking to her fellow classmates.

(*Narrator starts center stage, casually talking to the audience, as if someone has just asked about her parents.*)

N (*to audience*): It's been two years since my dad died of gastric cancer. Still, the day he died is a vivid memory. This was a crucial and devastating time in which I felt trapped by my situation.

(*N brings on C from her memory and places her center; N stands at C's side. Then, N brings on B and M, placing them as a tableau around the "dad's" bed. C does the action which N describes in next lines.*)

N (*to audience, setting the scene, trying to seem casual with hands at waist*): I went to school, knowing that my dad wouldn't make it through the day. (*C crosses downstage as if leaving. N stops her before C gets too far.*) Actually, I was called home at noon. (*N stops C. She puts her arm around "herself."*)

C (*to N, sadly realizing, speaking quickly*): Since my mother didn't think my dad would live through the next few hours. (*frightened, biting lower lip*) I remember going down the hallway to my mother and dad's bedroom, hearing the most horribly raspy breathing.

N (*to C, in a soothing, understanding tone*): It's a noise that nobody can imagine unless they've heard it themselves. (*N places C in a chair by the "bed," and speaks to audience, almost overcome. She is, however, able to control herself before becoming overwhelmed.*) This breathing became the death music that crept into every minute that passed in that endless day.

C (*to N, in a dazed voice*): I stayed by my dad's bedside with my sister, Blythe, and my mother,

N (*to audience, becoming pained. The characters from the memory do the actions described in low tones*): singing his favorite hymns, reading Shakespeare; and telling him how much we loved him—

N, C, M (*as if taking a moment for personal reflection*): even though he remained unconscious. (*N ushers C out and the others stay focused on the scene.*)

N (*to audience, trying to break the tension*): Finally, I walked outside, taking a break from the suffocating environment. (*N takes C with her.*) It was a cold January night . . . (*N grabs jacket for C who is oblivious to the cold*) . . . with a clear, starry sky.

C (*to N, scared, but trying to act resolved*): As I looked up, I had this feeling that gripped my stomach: Dad was going to die that night.

N (*to audience, explaining the pain*): All at once, memories flooded my mind.

C (*to N, sad and angry*): I could see myself nestled in my dad's big bear hug. (*C squeezes herself.*) I could hear his booming laughter and see his warm smile. He had been so full of life.

N (*to C trying to soothe*): I tried to comfort myself with the idea that my dad would be like a star, always present and watching over me. (*As if remembering what happened next—to audience with lump in throat*) Quickly, I went back inside to sit with my mother and sister in my parent's room. (*N takes jacket and puts C in a chair.*)

M (*to B, exhausted*): Blythe, why don't you go to bed. We'll wake you up if something happens.

N (*to audience, remembering kindness*): She knew we were all exhausted from the stressful year that had led to this last tragic day.

B (*to M and C, looking for reassurance*): Are you sure I should?

C (*to B in a motherly tone*): Yes, I'm sure. You need your rest, too. You don't need to get sick. Good night.

N (*to audience, sadly knowing; B goes off*): She went down the hall to her bedroom, while my mother and I stayed with dad. My mother,

M (*to C, as she settles herself for rest. Later she does what N describes*): tired from weeks without rest . . .

C (*to "dad," quietly, underneath N's next lines*): Please, Daddy, wake up. We still need you. Poor, sweet Daddy.

N (*to audience, quietly, as if not to wake her mother*): finally fell asleep, holding my dad's bony hand. I sat on his other side, reading plays and talking to him. (*C does as N describes.*)

C (*to Dad who is not there. She is emotionally hurting*): Daddy, I love you.

N (*to audience, almost getting caught up in her explanation*): I had not called him "daddy" in years.

C (*cutting off N and addressing her passionately*): but it was my desperate attempt to bring him back from the world into which he was slipping. I just kept hoping he would open his eyes one last time and say,

N and **C** (*to "dad"*): I love you, too, little one. Goodbye.

N (*to audience, trying to be matter-of-fact*): Soon after, he died with a last rattling breath. I sat there in shock not wanting to believe he'd died.

C (*to N, frantically, as she does the action*): I shook my mother awake. (to M, with equal fervor) Mother, Dad isn't with us anymore.

M (*to C, in a panic*): Get your sister!

N (*to audience, as she moves C down the hall and helps C get B*): I went down the hall in a fog, woke my sister, and then we all stood around his bed for the last time. (*The three of them face the bed with backs to audience, but then after a 2 count, C turns to N*)

C (*to N, angrily*): I didn't feel like a family with Dad gone. I felt so alone.

N (*to audience, as she ushers C to the window in a motherly way, and the other two move offstage left as N gestures.*): Next, I waited at the window for the necessary officials to take the body away to be cremated. (*Watching C in wonder, but addressing audience*): I didn't even glance at the stars for comfort. (*Turns back on scene, takes center stage, reflects in a knowing, melancholy manner*): No, for many months to come, there could be no star-filled nights.

The End

Compilation Script
"World War II from the Homefront: Those Fabulous 40s"
compiled by Donald E. Heady and members of
The Third Age Theatre in Muncie, Indiana

(*This is one of several scripts composed and performed by members of The Third Age Theatre—a group for performers over the age of 55. The group was formulated by Donald E. Heady, and is now under the direction of Franklin Gray. The diverse group performs all over the Indiana area, and has also appeared at the Senior Theatre Festival on the campus of the University of Nevada-Las Vegas. They have now developed four different compilation scripts. This particular script relates the true personal reminiscences, memories, oral histories, narratives, and letters of the cast surrounding the bombing of Pearl Harbor and our entrance into World War II. Interspersed throughout the script are songs and commercials from the "fabulous 1940s." For permission to use all or part of this script, contact Franklin Gray, Department of Theatre and Dance Performance, Ball State University, Muncie, Indiana 47306.*)

(*This script involves fifteen performers, coded as 1, 2, etc.*)

(*In blackout, Chorus sings "Sentimental Journey." When lights come up, follow spot catches 7 and 8 ballroom dancing. Right before end of song, it is abruptly cut off and the radio announcement of bombing of Pearl Harbor comes on. [On Tape: "We interrupt this program . . ."—include here parts of Roosevelt's "Day of Infamy" Speech].*)

(*Lights up on 1 and 2, sitting in chairs around a radio, as though in a living room.*)

1: I can remember the very chair I was sitting in, in the living room. We had company that day. It was after church and we had had dinner and company came out to visit us in the afternoon. We heard it on the radio, it was about 1:00, I think, that we heard that Pearl Harbor had been bombed. Of course, my husband was the father of two children so there wasn't the threat of his having to go to war unless it lasted and lasted.

2: I remember very well. I was in the living room, and I was listening to some kind of song and the news came on. My husband was out in front doing something. He couldn't have been cutting the grass because it was December 7th. And I said, "The Japanese have bombed Pearl harbor." He said, "That's nonsense! That's the best fortified place we have in the world." And, of course, he was dead wrong.

(*3 sings Pepsodent Commercial.*)

15: My sister and I had gone skating at Gibson's Arena. We weren't there very long when we saw our Dad. He called us over and said the Japanese had bombed Pearl Harbor. We knew all about Pearl because my uncle was stationed there in the Navy. A month later, my dad received word that his brother had been killed in the bombing.

(*Group sings Pepsi-Cola Commercial.*)

(*Lights cross fade to 3, 4, and 5 sitting in chairs around another radio.*)

3: In those days on Sunday afternoons, the young people from the church would get together and have parties, or go for rides or something. On that particular Sunday, a group of us kids were sitting in one of the kid's cars in front of our house. We were just sitting there listening to music when they broke in and announced that Pearl Harbor had been bombed.

4: I remember that day. I was in the kitchen trying out a new recipe on the family. My mother said I could dirty more pots and pans fixing one dish than she did making a whole meal. The announcement came on the radio. My mother went to the back door and called out to my father, who was out fixing the cistern, "We're in for it now. The Japanese have just bombed Pearl Harbor."

5: It was a typical Sunday at our house. Everyone was kinda lazy. Of course, when we heard the news we were stunned, as I think everybody was. But we thought that our country was certainly prepared for such a thing, and it certainly would only last for, maybe, 90 days. It would just be a breeze.

(*6 sings Campbell soup commercial.*)

7: I had just graduated from Armament Cadet School at Lowery Field in Denver, Colorado. I was in a room in the Albany Hotel after having spent the evening carousing at the Cadet Club in the same hotel. Of course, it was earlier in Colorado than here and I think I was just getting up and I had the radio on in the room. All of a sudden came the announcement: "All armed personnel return to your home bases immediately." Well, I was supposed to have a 30-day leave, and I never did get it.

(*8 sings Chiquita Banana Commercial.*) (*Lights cross fade to 6 standing center stage.*)

6: I don't remember any particular event. I was pretty young. I think my parents very gradually let me know what was going on, but I think they kinda guarded me from it.

(*9, 10, 11 sing Wildroot Cream Oil Commercial.*)

8: You know, I was a pretty self-centered teenager. It was about 10 days until my 15th birthday. And I don't remember too much except, you know, a feeling of a Sunday afternoon at home, a warm comfortable farm house. My brother had enlisted in the Army Air Force prior to that, long prior, and was going to be stationed in South America. I can't remember exactly where he was at the time. But, our immediate concern was for my brother. I'm confidant that I was protected, sheltered.

9: My friend, Joanna, and I were downtown at the Mandarin Inn, eating lunch. We hadn't seen each other for a little while. We were talking about the fact that both of us had gotten engaged since we had last seen each other. As we were sitting there eating, we heard on the radio that the Japanese had bombed Pearl Harbor. I looked over and Joanna had tears rolling down her cheeks from her big brown eyes. Her fiancé was in military service. She said, "It's going to be a long war." She got married on December 30, 1941, and I was married January 1, 1942. Our weddings were hurried because time suddenly became so precious that we didn't dare waste it.

(*5 sings Aunt Jemima Pancake Commercial.*)

11: I was a 16-year-old high school senior and it was a sunny afternoon in Missouri, warm enough that Dad was outside working on the leaves or something in the yard. I was lying across the bed upstairs and had the radio on while I was reading an assignment or something. And it came on. I went to the window and said, "Dad, Dad, the Japanese have bombed Pearl Harbor." And he said, "Oh, Betty it's just another one of those crazy things like the War with the Worlds."

(*12 and 13 sing "Let's Remember Pearl Harbor."*)

12: We now return you to our regular programming.

13: *(with Southern accent)*: Now, let's give a great big National Barndance welcome to a little girl who is sure to be a star. Here she is our own cousin Minnie Pearl.

(*Applause from group. 14 does a two-minute Minnie Pearl monologue.*)

(*13 sings "I'll Be Home for Christmas."*)

2: These letters were written to Amy Norrell while she was an army nurse stationed in Belgium. They were written by her mother, a widowed farm woman who lived in Bluffton, Indiana.

> Christmas Eve, 1944
> 9:00 P.M.
>
> Dear Girl:
>
> Wonder where this Christmas Eve finds you and just what you are doing tonight and tomorrow. Your letters are coming in so slow, I'm wondering if you have been moved again. Last letter, received last Monday, written December 7, that is really slow. Have your gifts found you? I feel you and Warren are having less Christmas than any year you've been away. It isn't a very happy one for anyone, I'm afraid. The news from the front has been so sickening this last week. It means so many of the boys will not get home. Uncle Charles is so worried about Richard and I'm afraid Dean is back in the thick of it too, for he went into Germany through Belgium the first time. I've not seen Margaret all week, it has been so bad and cold, I wonder how much news she gets. They haven't an electric radio, so it doesn't run as steadily as ours.
>
> This is Christmas Eve. The house is clean and straightened up. Gifts are around the little tree. I wish Jackie and Margie were here, they will come tomorrow. Jackie will have so many things he won't know which way to turn. Nina and Carroll were here today. Carroll had received your card about the subscription to LIFE, and was so pleased about it. I also received a card like that Friday, and was so surprised and pleased, too. Thanks so much, you never should have done it though, after what you sent.
>
> Well, I'll get my stove, I guess, Ha! At least the Ration Board <u>said</u> I could. Next thing is to find one. Somehow and some way I must have burned the first one they sent and I was frightened they'd not issue a second, but the permit came Saturday and is up in the big cupboard now. Ha! I will surely appreciate one if we can get it, for the old stove doesn't look very good. The oven is almost past baking in. The pieces on the top are rusting out until two of them have several holes, so I knew it was time for a change. Came very near buying Mrs. Mangs' last fall. Had better close for tonight, may add more tomorrow. Good night, honey, and may yours be a Christmas with much happiness wherever you may be.
> Your mother.

(*1 plays "Praise the Lord and Pass the Ammunition" until 6 is in place.*)

6: Our entry into the war had a great impact on those of us at home. It was the first time many women worked outside the home. Some drove trucks . . . (*She goes over and puts a hat on 1 who mimes driving a truck.*)

1: Because two of my husband's, Carl's, brothers went to war and the dairy had to continue, the daughters-in-law delivered milk. I happened to drive the wholesale truck. A big truck that delivered to grocery stores. The store where the pizza place is in the village used to be Vershire's grocery store. That was the last grocery store to make deliveries. That was one of my stops. I drove the truck and figured the bill and this tall handsome—he was really good looking—fellow from Arkansas would carry the milk in and the empties out. He and his family came up here with what they could bring in their car. And my mother-in-law put them up in one of the vacant houses. They would go to bed when it got dark—because they didn't have lights—and get up at daylight. I was pregnant with Melanie and about the time we would hit Vershire's, I was sick to my stomach. And he would say, "If you'd get up earlier, you would feel better." And I thought to myself, "You wait a few months and you'll see why I am sick to my stomach at 8 o'clock in the morning." Vershire said I was the best milkman he ever had. (*She picks up bottles in metal case and begins rattling them.*)

(*Group sings "Milkman Keep Those Bottles Quiet."*)

6: For the first time, many women went to work in defense factories where they were introduced to the "snood," (*She gives snoods to women involved.*) and some wore slacks for the first time. These women weren't always welcomed by their male co-workers.

(*Men [7, 12, 13] ad lib comments like: "Hey, Blondie, what do you think you're doing?" and "Hey, Blondie, don't get your blonde tresses all dirty sleeping on that bench!" and "Hey, Blondie, what's that dripping on your head?"*)

3 (*gets up and crosses over to 5 and begins to work*): Those crazy men sure like to tease me. I can't even catch a little nap at break time.

5: Why do they tease you about being a blonde? I'm blonde and it doesn't bother me.

3: When I first started working here, the foreman asked me what I wanted to be called, and I told him, "anything but Blondie." So now they tease me about it.

5: You seem to be getting stacked up there.

3: Take a look behind you and you'll see why. If she doesn't stop flirting and get on with her work, I'm gonna do something drastic. We're never going to make our quota this way, and I need the extra money.

5: Yes, and I was hoping we'd get an E flag to fly out front. I see you're still getting stacked up.

3: Yes, and I'm getting tired of it. We're never going to make our quota. Watch this. (*She burns the flirt [6], who jumps in the air and goes off followed by 7 who thinks he did something.*) Now, maybe we can get some work done!

5: Blondie, you're something else!

6: In many defense plants, workers were paid bonuses for extra output. If a plant was consistent in going over quota, a large flag was flown over the plant. It had a big E for excellence and efficiency. When that flag flew over your workplace, you had a lot of pride because it meant you were doing your part for the war effort! For some women, the war meant following your husband to another part of the country and often finding interesting work. (*Hands 9 a steno pad and pencil.*)

9: Wives were on the move, like I was. War work was important, and employees were hired when available, often on a temporary basis. I obtained the most interesting job I had ever had: Secretary to Dr. Bostwick Ketchum, a marine microbiologist from Harvard at the Woods Hole Oceanographic Institute. Many government projects were in progress at that fascinating facility. One group took daily boat trips to Martha's Vineyard and we could hear sounds of loud explosions, like bombs going off. But all projects were hush-hush—secret. No one discussed the work. Our project was for the Navy. I can now tell that our goal was to discover the best possible paint formula with a copper content which would leach out poison after it was applied to ship bottoms. This would cause barnacles to drop off, and ships could move through the water much more easily. Without some treatment, barnacle build-up could add thousands of pounds to a ship, slowing its progress at an amazing rate. Treated plates were tested, checked, weighed, and examined periodically. I would meet with several scientists with my shorthand notebook and take dictation, go transcribe, have them read back their words, mark and delete and revise and add facts—and I would retype. No computers—no self-correcting typewriters—no tape recorders. The end result was a report to the U.S. Government about the size of a big Sears catalog. We WEIGHED that final report, and it weighed more than seven pounds. I still wonder if anyone ever read that report.

(*12 sings "I'll Get By."*)

2:   Tuesday Morning
9:45 A.M.

The day after Christmas. The little tree looks so bare, I'd like to take it down. A pile of wrappings over here by the stove. The table still sitting with a few messed up dishes on it. So, it looks as if your mother should be busy. Is it ever cold today. Monday A.M. it rained for a while then turned to snow and really snowed hard all day. Was so bad that Mike and family and Margaret and the girls left about 4:00 instead of staying late as usual. About 6:00 it stopped snowing and turned cold. It was 6 degrees this morning by our thermometer, the coldest morning we've had. Hope it doesn't start blowing or we'll really have drifts.

Thanks so much for the lovely perfume, you should never have gotten that for me, after all the other gifts of money and the subscription. Margaret loved hers too and the bottle was beautiful.

I could chatter all morning, but I must get busy. The roads aren't so bad that the mail may get here nearly on time.

Hope I get letters from you and Warren today. Wonder where he spent Christmas. Be some time before I know about either of you.

So much love,
Mother

Did your gifts find you before Christmas?

(*1 plays "Atchison, Topeka, and Sante Fe" until group puts chairs in two lines facing stage right. High voices in upstage chairs, and lower voices in downstage chairs. Group sings "Chattanooga Choo Choo." 7 and 8 dance and pantomime ending of song.*)

4: When I was 17, my dad arranged for all of us to take a trip to California. And somewhere outside Chicago, they connected a great number of cars that were a troop train to our train, I don't know. Those guys were just ready to party from dawn to dusk. And of course when they came by our compartment, they said, "Oh, you've gotta come back with us to the club car." And, of course, I was too young to go to the club car, so they just stayed right there in our coach. All of these guys. And they were singing all these songs and getting me to sing along with them. And my father was getting more and more nervous as the time went on, but I thought it was wonderful! All these young, handsome servicemen.

(*10 plays and 15 taps to "In the Mood." After first section, 6 and 14, 8 and 7 dance "Lindy" in background.*)

9: I remember this cute little sailor that wanted to give me lots of attention. And I thought, I shouldn't let him flirt with me. And I turned my head the other way. And I thought since then, why didn't I make him a little bit happy?

5 (*while 13 plays man with blanket*): When my husband came back from overseas, he was sent to Camp Butner, North Carolina for redistribution. So I very quickly got myself together and got myself a train ticket and headed for Camp Butner. Fortunately, I got a train that had air conditioning in it. And, as usual, the trains were very crowded. And everybody either brought their lunch or could go to the dining car, but that was very expensive. So the day went on. The gentleman I sat with was older and he said he was from Bluefield and he was in the grocery business. We exchanged stories and as the evening came on, they came around and asked if we wanted a pillow. It cost 5 cents. You could recline your chair. He had a blanket with him and he kept wanting to cover me up. And I did not want him to cover me up. Every time I'd kinda get settled and I'd doze off, first thing I know, he wanted to put his blanket over me. Finally, the train stopped and somebody got off and I very quickly moved to the other seat. When we got to his stop, he wanted me to get off the train and visit him and his wife. And he really wanted to keep me warm.

(*10 plays and sings "Caldonia."*)

9: My husband, "Putt," finally got orders to ship out for the European theatre. I was seven months pregnant. So when he left, I packed to return to Indiana. My mother told me—since NO ONE but service personnel could get a plane—that if, as I traveled, I felt the least bit tired, to see the conductor, get off at the nearest hospital, and demand a bed to rest in for the night. Sure enough, standing on the jolting train—aisles were full of sleeping servicemen on their way home, all seats were full, even standing room was at a premium—I had to get off the train in Maysville, Kentucky and I called Mom from a hospital. "I'm a little tired. I'll continue home tomorrow." She answered, "I'm so glad you were wise enough to stop." And as soon as she hung up the phone, their farm work was dropped, and everyone helped get her to Maysville, Kentucky that same day. My son, two months premature, was born at 10 A.M. the next morning. What would I do with a BOY? I didn't know anything about boys. He wore pink baby clothes.

(*1 plays "I'll Be Home For Christmas" as bridge.*)

2:   January 5, 1945
          Friday Night, 9:00 P.M.

Dear Girl:

Well, your mother feels "sorta" like I'd mothered a couple of "swans." Do you feel like one? Ha! I know that is a poor way to put it, but when I'm about my work here in the <u>very</u> plain home and down at the barn with the animals and think that two of my very own children are so far away in places we use to never even <u>dream</u> of seeing, <u>you</u>, a nurse, doing work I used to want to do badly. Warren flying those big planes. It just seems it can't be <u>us</u>. Only one terrible thing about it—the reason for my children and millions of other sons and daughters being in foreign places. You must have been in Paris long enough to see quite a lot of the more famous sights of the city.

News coming in, so bad again, seventh army driven back <u>15 miles</u>. I wonder if you girls knew how badly it was going against the Allies when you were being moved at Christmas time. Received your Christmas letter today, and was so glad you have better surroundings, but you are about close enough to the front. I know the closer the hospitals, the more boys can be saved. How many girls from your old unit are with you, you've mentioned two?

Dorothy called tonight so excited she could hardly talk. A write-up in the Bluffton paper about Warren, <u>direct from "over there</u>," and <u>you</u> were mentioned, too. Evidently, he is going out on missions already. I think I'll call Mrs. Morton tomorrow and have her clip it out and I'll send it to you.

Dorothy has found a stove which is to come out soon as road conditions improve. Can hardly wait. So many things on my single-track mind anymore.

Margaret, Jackie and Betty were here last night. Margaret and Jackie came in the afternoon to iron, Betty came from school. So nice to have them. Margaret is feeling pretty worried, but I know any letters will be very slow coming from the front now. She received his (Dean's) "purple heart" this week. Margaret got out her skates this A.M. tried to skate on the road, but it was too rough.

I nearly forgot to tell you—my single-track mind—your big box of dishes and perfume arrived <u>yesterday</u>. Postmarked Nov. 16, got home Jan. 4th.

All perfume in good shape, but two small dishes broken. Not the little square ashtrays, but the small oval ones, a larger oval one <u>cracked</u>. The double affair <u>with the handle</u> was not broken at all and you'd have thought it would have been. I believe the girls can just wait until they come to get their boxes. I'd feel so badly if they should be broken now.

Why do I have to be so busy? We are getting so much to read LIFE and THE POST come every week. Can't begin to read the latter, but read LIFE cover to cover then sent it on to Margaret and the girls, they give them to <u>their</u> neighbors, so your one gift makes a lot of people happy.

I must write Warren now, finally heard from him this week, it was written Christmas Eve. He was working on a letter from you. They were finally getting some mail.

Good-night, honey,
Mother

(*11 sings "We'll Meet Again."*)

(*2 and 7 come forward*)

7: After VE day, I was on a Dutch Steamer heading back home before I was to be shipped to the Pacific front. I had a two-year-old son that I had never seen. Then, the announcement came over the radio that Hiroshima had been bombed, and the war was over.

2: A similar thing happened to my brother-in-law. He was aboard a troop ship out of Europe. They thought they would head right to the Southern Pacific. About an hour out to sea, the captain's voice came over the loud speaker saying: "Now hear this! The destination of this ship is the United States of America."

(*Group cheers as 1 plays a bit of "America the Beautiful." 6 comes forward to sing "I'll be Seeing You." She repeats the last part of song with whole group joining in.*)

The End

Ethnographic Study Script
"Alcoholics Anonymous"
written by Ken Dingledine, Laura Jansen,
Audrey Snyder, and Michelle Hensley

(*This script was the final project in an Ethnography class. This group spent eight weeks attending, recording, and studying open meetings of members of Alcoholics Anonymous. This script is the result of their merger of a particular "cultural group" with theatrical conventions.*)

Setting: Church basement. Chairs, tables. At the front of the room is a table with coffee, candy, cards that announce A.A. meeting times, and pamphlets. On the walls are posters titled "The 12 Steps" and "The 12 Traditions." Chairs are arranged in a circle.

(*We see Pam, who is arranging pamphlets, getting coffee ready. Observers enter. Arch enters. Greetings/small-talk are exchanged. Jane and Mike enter. More greetings, etc. It is obvious that Pam, Jane, Mike, and Arch are familiar with each other. Shannon enters tentatively. She stands somewhat apart from the others. Pam approaches her.*)

Pam: Hi, I'm Pam. Can I get you some coffee?

Shannon: No, thanks.

(*Pam calls meeting to order.*)

Pam: It's a little after eight; let's get started. (*The group sits.*) Hello, everybody and welcome to the regular Tuesday night meeting of the Enjoying Sobriety Group. This is a nonsmoking, open discussion meeting. My name is Pam and I'm an alcoholic.

Group: Hi, Pam.

Pam: I'd like to begin with a moment of silence followed by the Serenity Prayer.

(*There is a moment of silence; those in the circle sit with heads bowed.*)

Pam: God grant me the serenity

All join Pam: To accept the things I cannot change;
       The courage to change the things I can;
       And the wisdom to know the difference.

Pam: Now, I'd like to read the non-A.A. announcements. The Serenity Club, as some of you may know, recently burned down. The meetings normally held there will now be held at 1610 S. Macedonia. Does anyone have any non-A.A. announcements?

Arch: Yeah, this coffee tastes like shit, Pam; who made it? (*Laughter*)

Pam: Arch, you drink the same coffee every week; you'll probably have five more cups! (*More laughter.*) I'd like to start the meeting out with the A.A. preamble; I've asked Jane to read it for us.

Jane: Hello, I'm Jane and I'm a grateful recovering alcoholic.

All: Hi, Jane.

Jane (*reading from meeting times card*): Alcoholics Anonymous is a fellowship of men and women who share their experience, strength, and hope with each other that they may solve their common problem and help others to recover from alcoholism. The only requirement for membership is a desire to stop drinking. There are no dues or fees for A.A. membership; we are self-supporting through our own contributions. A.A. is not allied with any sect, denomination, politics, organization or institution; does not wish to engage in any controversy; neither endorses nor opposes any cause. Our primary purpose is to stay sober and help other alcoholics to achieve sobriety.

All: Thank you, Jane.

Pam: Arch, would you like to read the twelve steps for us, please?

Arch (*opens the book* Alcoholics Anonymous *also known as THE BIG BOOK and recites*): 1. We admitted we were powerless over alcohol—that our lives had become unmanageable. 2. Came to believe that a Power greater than ourselves could restore us to sanity. 3. Made a decision to turn our will and our lives over to the care of God *as we understood Him.* 4. Made a searching and fearless moral inventory of ourselves. 5. Admitted to God, to ourselves, and to another human being the exact nature of our wrongs. 6. Were entirely ready to have God remove all these defects of character. 7. Humbly asked Him to remove our shortcomings. 8. Made a list of all persons we had harmed, and became willing to make amends to them all. 9. Made direct amends to such people wherever possible, except when to do so would injure them or others. 10. Continued to take personal inventory and when we were wrong promptly admitted it. 11. Sought through prayer and meditation to improve our conscious contact with God, *as we understood Him,* praying only for knowledge of His will for us and the power to carry that out. 12. Having had a spiritual awakening as the result of these steps, we tried to carry this message to alcoholics, and to practice these principles in all our affairs.

All: Thanks, Arch.

Pam: Okay, Marlene, would you read the 12 Traditions?

Marlene (*reading from THE BIG BOOK*): 1. Our common welfare should come first; personal recovery depends upon A.A. unity. 2. For our group purpose, there is but one ultimate authority—a loving God as He may express Himself in our group conscience. Our leaders are but trusted servants; they do not govern. 3. The only requirement for A.A. membership is a desire to stop drinking. 4. Each group should be autonomous except in matters affecting other groups or A.A. as a whole. 5. Each group has but one primary purpose—to carry its message to the alcoholic who still suffers. 6. An A.A. group ought never endorse, finance or lend the A.A. name to any related facility or outside enterprise, lest problems of money, property and prestige divert us from our primary purpose. 7. Every A.A. group ought to be fully self-supporting, declining outside contributions. 8. Alcoholics Anonymous should remain forever nonprofessional, but our service centers may employ special workers. 9. A.A., as such, ought never be organized; but we may create service boards or committees directly responsible to those they serve. 10. Alcoholics Anonymous has no opinion on outside issues; hence the A.A. name ought never be drawn into public controversy. 11. Our public relations policy is based on attraction rather than promotion; we need always maintain personal anonymity at the level of press, radio, and films. 12. Anonymity is the spiritual foundation of all our traditions, ever reminding us to place principles before personalities.

All: Thanks, Marlene.

Pam: Since we're self-supporting, the collection will now be passed.

(*A cup is passed around the circle. Marlene, Pam, Arch, and Jane contribute.*)

Pam: Now, we'll distribute tokens. Beginner's Token—24 hours?

(*Shannon rises, walks to Pam and receives token; Pam hugs her. The group applauds.*)

Pam: 30 days? (*Silence.*) 60 days? (*Silence.*) 90 days?

(*Marlene rises to receive token and hug from Pam; the group applauds.*)

Pam: 6 months? (*Silence.*) 9 months? (*Silence.*) One year?

(*Jane rises for token and hug. Big applause from group.*)

Pam: Any year thereafter? (*Silence.*)

(*Shannon, Marlene, and Jane pass their tokens around the circle.*)

Pam: Now, I'd like to open the floor for people who have had a problem with alcohol (*Silence.*) . . . or does anyone have a topic they'd like to throw out, have some feedback on? (*More silence.*) Okay, my name is Pam, and I'm an alcoholic.

All: Hi, Pam!

Pam: If someone had told me ten years ago that I'd enjoy being sober, I'd have told them they were full of shit. (*Laughter.*) Being sober ain't bad at all. If I can do it, so can you. I was really surprised that I enjoyed being sober. So why the hell do we have to come to these damn meetings, anyway? Well, the program works for these reasons—you want sobriety badly enough and once you have it, you want to share it. And if you take a poll in this room, 90% of us didn't make it on the first try. (*Reaction from Arch.*) I made a lot of errors, had so much hatred for myself, but now I am it and I know it. Take care of number one. When I was on the sauce, I wasn't a Catholic, I wasn't an American, I wasn't a woman, I was just a drunk . . . loveless and unloving, respectful of no one and nothing, least of all myself. If you're not sober, there's three places you can end up—an institution, prison, or dead, and when you're dead, you're just a dead alcoholic—so you may as well be sober. Don't drink—a day at a time. Go to meetings. You don't quit, you just stop. It never gets any easier.

All: Thanks, Pam!

Arch: I'm Arch and I'm a recovering alcoholic and drug addict.

Group: Hi, Arch!

Arch (*sarcastically, turning to Pam next to him*): Alcohol is an addiction, isn't it? (*Laugh.*) Well, I tried a lot of changes . . . I changed bars, I changed friends, I changed judges, jails, bail bondsmen, I changed from beer to whiskey. (*Laugh.*) But, never in my life at a bar was I asked to come back. I was committing chronic suicide. I was putting a liquid bullet into my brain every night. Then, I came to these damn meetings to save my ass. And then I found out it was attached to my soul. (*Laugh.*) I used to sit in here, thinking them people are corn balls, idiots, jerks, all these corny sayings like "I love you" and saying this to a man. I was taught a man never cries . . . once I did that, that's the best thing that ever happened to me . . . it's the first step. You've got to have stubbornness or tenacity in sticking with the program. Lot of pain with family . . . it's the key to long-term success. Everything's not going to be a bowl of cherries, though. I consider myself a very spiritual person, not a Christian, but I . . . I realize people have different higher powers . . . I kind of like that . . .What works for me might not work for everybody else. I may drink tomorrow, but with God's help, I'll stay sober today. If I go to bed sober at night, it's a real successful day. I can get up in the morning without shaking, grateful that I can think straight. I won't get drunk tonight, because I'm here. I'm just glad to be alive . . . that's the bottom line.

Shannon: Hi, my name's Shannon and I'm an alcoholic.

All: Hi, Shannon.

Jane: Hi, I'm Jane and I'm a grateful recovering alcoholic.

All: Hi, Jane!

Jane: I come to these meetings to be honest, to trust, and to have friends. A.A. can work whether or not you're completely down and out. I had a good job and family, I wasn't a binger, my life wasn't unmanageable, I just episodically abused liquor. I can guarantee that one way not to endear yourself to your mother-in-law is to get drunk publicly in a small community. (*Laughter. Mike, her husband, nods.*) I was spiritually and morally bankrupt. I neglected my family—decided just to "get along," ignoring my higher power. Then A.A. taught me a new way of life, changed the way I look at people. Someone will get up and tell their story. Then five or six people will get up and tell their stories. And you realize their stories are your story. Most important, I think, is spirituality. It's not really religion but a spirituality. Don't jump into actions or reactions without a higher power. God, my God, is very patient. Thank goodness for that. And day by day, one day at a time, I've stayed away from that first drink. I love myself. That's something I could never say. (*Reaction of disbelief from an observer.*) If we could do it alone we wouldn't be in these rooms.

Mike: You've got to understand that all these people would be dead if it weren't for each other.

All: Thanks, Jane and Mike.

Don: I heard a lot of honesty and humility, and that will keep you sober. That's all for tonight's meeting. Thanks everyone for coming. Let's finish with the Lord's Prayer.

(*All stand and hold hands in circle and recite.*)

All: Our Father, who art in heaven

Hallowed be thy name

Thy kingdom come, Thy will be done

On earth as it is in heaven

Give us this day our daily bread

And forgive us our trespasses

As we forgive those who trespass against us

And lead us not into temptation but deliver us from evil

For thine is the kingdom and the power and the glory forever.

Amen.

(*All look up and add, with clasped hands punctuating the words.*)

All: Keep comin' back. It works!

(*The meeting is over. General good-byes follow and the people file out.*)

The End

Readers Theatre Compiled Script
"Growing Pains" by Marjorie Duehmig
inspired by naturally occurring talk recorded
from prevention workshops

(This compiled script has been designed to require no spectacle; no set, costumes, or props. The performers, through the use of movement, set the stage for the audience. It can be performed, therefore, in various spaces and can travel easily. The script has been used for prevention workshops and has been enthusiastically received. It is especially helpful to note that when this script is produced, a talk-back session may be incorporated where the actors and audience can discuss issues important to teenagers: stereotyping, peer pressure, teenage sexuality, and so on. In the original production, each performer wore a pair of jeans, tennis shoes, and a brightly-colored shirt. Sheila and Stanley wore red, Rebecca and Robert wore green, George and Jennifer wore blue, and Terrence and Tina wore yellow.)

Dramatis Personae

Sheila: The Popular . . . She is a cheerleader, majorette, and a swing choir member. She's perky, and a lot of people's special friend. Sheila is a little air-headed and silly. She's the kind of girl who would go into seclusion for a week if she got a pimple.

Jennifer: The Angst-Ridden . . . She is Sheila's best friend. They have been best friends since 4th grade. Sheila likes to hang around Jennifer because it makes her look better. Jennifer has a bad complexion and feels that she is overweight (though she's not). She is not nearly as popular as Sheila and gets her feelings hurt often.

Tina: The Actress Wannabe . . . She is a bit odd, but whenever Sheila is out on a date and Jennifer is alone (which is often), Tina is good friends with Jennifer. She has the hardest time defining herself. She likes the strange and unusual.

Rebecca: The Snob . . . She has everything; rich parents, a 4.0 GPA, president of every club. She is, however, the least liked of the group. There are many things to envy about her—as she constantly reminds everyone. She is very lonely, but masks it with an ego that no one can deal with.

Stanley: The Big Man on Campus . . . He is the captain of nearly every team in the school. He is the epitome of high school machismo. He dates Sheila, who is the most popular girl in the school and that's what everyone expects.

George: The Stanley Wannabe . . . Friends since childhood, George has always emulated everything Stanley is and does up until high school, when he didn't make any of the teams. Jennifer likes him because he is Stanley's best friend and her best friend dates Stanley. Visions of double dating dance in Jennifer's head.

Terrence: The Shy . . . He has had a crush on Tina ever since he saw her in the high school play. He is a friend of George's; they met in auto mechanics class. He is an underachiever, and gets a lot of grief because of his parents' too-high standards for him.

Robert: The Intelligent Nerd . . . Probably the most stereotyped character. He is everything a nerd should be: smart, wears eye-glasses, has a pocket protector, and is socially inept. He has a crush on Rebecca. He thinks she is smart and that they may have something in common. The reason the boys allow him to hang with them is that he's always good for a laugh.

(Girls set up a pantomime tableau of a slumber party on the floor at the front of the stage. The boys enter and sit in a row pointing in front of them. The cast freezes in this position and Robert enters and crosses center.)

Robert: Uncertainty: A noun meaning having doubts or an inability to form an opinion. *(Robert turns back to audience, Jennifer mimes combing Tina's hair. Sheila mimes painting fingernails, Rebecca mimes reading a magazine.)*

Jennifer: Oh, Tina, I have to tell you what happened last night! Sheila stayed over last night and, well, I was telling her about George . . . and how I . . . well, ya know . . . like him . . . and . . .

Tina: George . . . OHHH, sounds like someone's got a crush!

Sheila: Jenny and George sitting in a tree . . .

Tina & **Sheila**: K-I-S-S-I-N-G . . .

Jennifer: Hey, cut it out . . . I'm serious, I really like him.

Tina & **Sheila**: First comes love . . .

Jennifer: Oh, you guys are so junior high.

Tina & **Sheila**: Then comes marriage . . .

Jennifer: Please, just stop it!

Tina & **Sheila** (*very loud*):   Then comes George pushing a baby carriage. (*All laugh.*)

Tina: O.K., you guys, what happened, give!

Jennifer: Well, I told Sheila since she dates Stanley, his best friend, I thought maybe she could help me out.

Rebecca (*to audience*): And visions of double dates danced in her head.

Jennifer: So she decided to call him. Well, O.K. so, I kinda sorta asked her to call him . . . well, O.K. so anyway, we called him, well, Sheila did most of it . . . and then she made this really sexy voice by holding her nose and said . . .

Sheila: Hello, George, remember me? This is Marley.

Rebecca: Honestly, Sheila, I thought you were above that kind of thing.

Jennifer: And then she started laughing so hard that she couldn't talk, so I grabbed the phone and slammed it down.

Tina: You're just lucky he didn't know who it was.

Jennifer (*thinking*): Oh, God . . . He might have had the call traced and found out.

Sheila: They only do that on television.

Jennifer: What if he finds out it was me . . . he might never like me. Oh, I could just die!

(*Girls freeze, except Rebecca who stands.*)

Rebecca (*condescendingly*): Immature: An adjective meaning undeveloped, raw, without experience.

(*Rebecca walks across stage on her line, then freezes, looking disgustedly at the boys. The boys who are in a tableau of a movie theatre unfreeze and point at the screen, poking each other. Robert turns around and mimes being loaded down with concession stand goodies. He joins the other boys.*)

Robert (*he mimes handing out the popcorn and candy*): Here, guys, anybody want some popcorn or Ju Ju Beans?

Stanley: Shut up, nerd breath, and sit down. This is the best part of the movie and you better not make me miss it.

Robert: How many times have you guys seen this film?

George: Six.

Terrence: Is this the sex part?

Stanley: Shut up, I'm warning you.

Robert (*gulp*): You mean that girl is going to take off her clothes?

George: SHHHH! I don't want to miss any of the good stuff.

Robert: I've never seen anything so . . .

George: Beautiful in all my life.

Robert: Hey, guys, I don't know about this. It seems somewhat degrading to women.

George: It's only degrading if you think it is.

Robert: But what if that was your sister up there? And the only job she could get was—

Stanley: I told you politely, I'm not going to tell you again. Stop it with the mouth. This is my favorite part, so shut up! Here it comes . . . (*now mimicking the movie they are watching*) it's love, I know it's love. Take me Walter, take me!

Terrence (*to Robert*): What are they talking about?

Robert: All I know is this ice cream bar is starting to melt.

Stanley: I can see right now that you two have got a lot to learn about what is cool.

(*Guys freeze as they are. Jennifer unfreezes and takes center stage.*)

Jennifer: Insecure: An adjective meaning having fears, filled with anxiety, self-doubts.

(*Cast breaks freeze when Robert snaps his fingers and goes to the back of the audience space. The cast forms an acting class tableau.*)

Tina: On the first day of my drama class, the teacher, Mr. Ignatowski, makes us go up in front of the class and act stuff out. He doesn't even tell us what our motivation is or anything! All he does is stand in the back of the auditorium and yell . . .

Robert (*pretending to be Mr. Ignatowski*): All right people, once more with feeling . . . you are trees, big maple trees in the cool evening breeze. All right, now, emote people, emote!

Tina: And all these lunkheads did what they were told. Sheila really got into it and began moving, and said:

Sheila: I'm not a maple, I'm a weeping willow and I'm so so sad. (*Sheila strikes a dramatic pose.*)

Robert: Excellantamundo! We have some fine talent here. Come on the rest of you. Go with your emotions. I can feel that some of you are just not giving over to the feeling. Emote, my darlings, emote!

Terrence (*trying to impress Tina*): My leaves are turning colors. (*Poses.*)

Robert: Yes, yes, yes, my little act-rons! Oh, I feel just like Henry Higgins!

Tina: And all of a sudden Mr. Ignatowski notices me standing there not doing anything, and he gets really red in the face and asks me:

Robert: All right, Miss Bernhardt, what are we going for?

Tina: And I said, "I feel very stupid, and I am never going to have to be a tree." Then he said that if I didn't stop acting like a prima donna, he would never cast me in any of his plays ever again.

Robert: And I really mean it, missy!

Tina: I know Meryl Streep did not start out playing a tree. It's all I've ever wanted to be! What am I going to do now? (*Pause*) Do they take girls in the French Foreign Legion?

(*Cast stands in a lineup and salutes.*)

George (*like an army officer*): Attention! Forward march, hep, two, three, four, hep two, three, four.

(*The cast marches and moves to a large triangle shape configuration with their backs to the audience.*)

George: About face.

(*The cast turns toward the audience.*)

George: At ease. (*He now goes back to being himself.*)

(*Each cast member mimes gazing into a mirror, except for those reading definitions who speak to the audience.*)

Stanley (*he believes he is perfect!*): Imperfection: A noun meaning to be marred by scars, blemishes, or defects.

George: She probably won't ever go out with me again. I'm such a dumb jerk. I tried to be so cool. I did everything Stanley told me to do, then she didn't even let me kiss her good night. Maybe she thinks I smell bad or that I'm ugly. I just know she thinks I'm a jerk. Maybe I should have paid her way into the dance or borrowed my brother's Brut cologne or told her how pretty she looked. Maybe I shouldn't listen to Stanley. But he always has a girlfriend. God, why am I such a dumb jerk?

Tina & **Terrence** (*looking at each other, shyly on the line, then turning away from audience*): Uncertainty.

Robert & **Rebecca** (*looking at each other, condescendingly on line, then turning away from audience*): Immaturity.

George & **Jennifer** (*looking at the ground shyly on the line, then turning away from audience*): Insecurity.

Sheila & **Stanley** (*looking at each other confidently on the line, then turning away from audience*): Imperfections?????????

Terrence (*facing audience*): Dad wants me to be a football player. Mom wants me to be a doctor. I don't even know who I am yet.

Tina (*facing audience*): Who am I?

George (*facing audience*): I am, who?

Rebecca (*facing audience*): I, who am!

All (*facing audience*): Who am I?

(*During this segment, the cast stays in their places talking to themselves and the audience.*)

Robert: Self: A noun meaning being distinct and unique. The "ego," the "I."

Stanley (*singing confidently*): I gotta be me. I gotta be me.

Terrence: My own song to sing?

George: Yeah, but what if you only sing in the key of Z?

Sheila (*cheering confidently*): M-E, M-E . . . ME, ME, ME, ME, ME . . . ME!

Tina: How can I be my own cheerleader . . .?

Jennifer: If I never learned how to shake my own pom poms?

Stanley: Everyone is talented in their own way!

Robert: Running into my locker is called talent?

Sheila: Everyone has their own special place!

Jennifer: What if mine is inside the locker?

Stanley: I just gotta be me.

Sheila: ME, ME, ME,ME, ME (*big flourish*) Yeah!

Stanley (*crossing stage right*): I am totally way cool!

Sheila (*crossing stage left*): I'm O.K., and I guess you're O.K, too.

George (*crossing to Stanley*): I wanna be cool.

Jennifer (*crossing to Sheila*): I wanna fit in!

Terrence (*crossing to Stanley*): I gotta be cool.

Tina (*crossing to Sheila*): I gotta fit in.

Rebecca (*not wanting to admit it, crossing to Sheila*): I have to fit in?

Robert (*crossing to Stanley*): I have . . . gotta be cool?

(*Guys stand in a line like a pseudo-fifties singing group.*)

Stanley: A one, a two, a one, two, three, four

(*They all begin to snap fingers, Robert is off the beat. Meanwhile, the girls focus on the guys, very impressed by their showing off. Sheila steals close to the boys during the chant to get a better look.*)

Guys (*chanting*): We wanna be cool. Ah, Yeah, way cool

We're gonna be cool. Ah, Yeah, way cool

We are already cool. Ah, Yeah, way cool

We're JOOOOOOEEEE COOOOOOOLLLLLLLL!

Sheila (*returning to the girls, giggling*): Wow, is Stanley cool. He's got a stereo in his Malibu!

Jennifer (*to Sheila*): I gotta fit in.

Tina: I gotta fit in!

Rebecca: I have . . . gotta fit in!

(*Sheila and the girls begin to do cheerleading cheers, none is as successful as Sheila.*)

Sheila: Ready? O.K. Two bits, four bits, six bits, a dollar . . . All for our group stand up and holler!

Girls: Yeah! Yeah! Yeah!

Sheila: Ready? Ok. Group. Group. Group.

All: Group. Group. Group.

Sheila: Cheerleaders!!!

All: Group. Group. Group.

(*During the cheer, the cast forms a pyramid, guys on the bottom, Tina on top. Sheila stands to one side and leads them in the cheer.*)

Stanley: Football team!

All: Group. Group. Group.

George: Letterman's Club!

All: Group. Group. Group.

Jennifer: Student Council!

All: Group. Group. Group.

Terrence: FFA!

All: Group. Group. Group.

Tina: Drama Club!

All: Group. Group. Group.

Robert: Chess Club!

All: Group. Group. Group.

Rebecca: Yearbook staff!

All: Group. Group. GGGGRRRROOOOUUUUPPPP!

(*The pyramid falls and the cast laughs and has fun with the predicament they're in. Sheila looks envious of them. Stanley grabs her arm and she falls playfully into the pile of bodies on stage. They are laughing wildly. When Tina stands they become silent.*)

Tina: Sometimes I feel like I'm the only one in the entire universe who feels the way I do. I'm scared because Jennifer only likes me when Sheila's not around. I'm afraid I'll never have a best friend.

Terrence (*goes to Tina, takes her hand and leads her back to the group on this line*) Acceptance: A noun meaning being included.

Rebecca (*obviously making fun of Jennifer*): My, that dress looks lovely on you!

Jennifer: This isn't a dress I'm pitching a tent.

Stanley (*mimes seeing a dog, not talking to Jennifer*): Hey, who let that dog inside the classroom?

Jennifer: It isn't a dog, it's just me.

Sheila (*goes to Jennifer, hugs her*): Inferiority complex, that's you all over.

Jennifer: I thought it was a Friday the 13th movie.

Robert: Inferior: An adjective meaning feeling lower in quality than others, feeling less than normal.

(*The cast freezes as they are, except Sheila who comes downstage to speak directly to the audience. The actors treat the audience members as though they are their personal confidants.*)

Sheila: This has been the absolute worst day of my life. Stanley forgot to pick me up, so I had to walk to school today—in heels! I know that he's mad about the other night. His parents were gone and we were at his house, and he wanted to . . . and I couldn't. My sister had a baby when she was 17, and she had to get married. Now, she's twenty and divorced. I want to go to college. I'm just afraid that maybe something would happen to me. . . us. Oh, I know all about birth control. My mom told me and she said she would go with me to the doctor, but I was too embarrassed. Maybe I should have gone. What if he goes out with someone else because I said no? Maybe I'll have to say yes to keep him.

(*Cast now acts as Sheila's unconscious, ugly fear. They all unfreeze and move into a circle around her, mocking her.*)

All: Say yes, lose your pride, say no, lose your guy
Say yes, lose your pride, say no, lose your guy
Say yes, lose your pride, say no, lose your guy.

(*Sheila shrinks to her knees, burying her face in her hands. They all freeze except Stanley who moves across stage in his over-confident walk. He speaks openly to the audience.*)

Stanley: I'm captain of the football team, I play center on the basketball team, I wrestle, and am the pitcher on the baseball team. All of my life is dedicated to practice. Trouble is coach says I may not get any sports scholarships because I haven't decided which sport I want to go into. He says that you have to pick one and develop the muscle groups for it, but I have this plan. I've decided that I'll go into football. This guy from another school knows where I can get some steroids. So, this guy and I are going to work together. By next season, I'll be ready for those scouts. I am a little scared, but I don't think steroids are as bad as everyone claims.

(*Now the cast becomes his biggest fear of ridicule. They mime having big muscles and speak as though they were very stupid. They circle him, and get down on their knees as if to praise their God of jockdom.*)

All: Duh . . . dumb jock
Duh . . . dumb jock
Duh . . . dumb jock
Duh . . . dumb jock

(*Stanley puts his head down in shame. The cast freezes in this position as George gets up and speaks to the audience.*)

George: Why does everyone think there's something wrong with you if you cry? This is what happened yesterday in social science, we had to watch this movie called "Peege," about a lady with Alzheimer's disease. There were all these scenes that showed her when she was younger, with her and her grandson, I couldn't help it, I cried. It was so sad. My grandma died last year, and it reminded me of her. Now none of the guys will leave me alone about it.

(*The cast takes on his fear of ridicule and mime having wings. They circle him.*)

All: Mama's-Boy. Mama's-Boy. Mama's-Boy.

(*George folds his arms across his chest, and the cast freezes in this position, except for Jennifer who gets up and speaks openly to the audience.*)

Jennifer: I wish I was like Sheila. She always has a date. I always spend Friday and Saturday nights babysitting. The money's good, but I usually end up eating the extra income. Now, I'm so fat that I can't stand it. Sometimes it makes me throw up. The guidance counselor at school thinks I should go to a doctor because she thinks that I'm bulimic. I can't tell anyone; I'm so ashamed.

(*The cast circles her zombie-like, with arms outstretched, whispering her fears.*)

All: You are obese. You are obese. You are obese.

(*They freeze, except Rebecca who comes forward and speaks. She starts out as her snob self, but as the speech progresses, we see her very vulnerable and lonely—her true self.*)

Rebecca: I have no flaws, absolutely none. I have a 4.0 grade point average. I'm listed in *Who's Who Among High School Students*. I'm the yearbook editor, president of the foreign language club, my parents are very, very, very wealthy. What I can't understand is . . . why no one ever asks me out. I went to the homecoming dance alone because no one asked me. I had to go because I was head of the committee. No one asked me to dance. I smiled and acted like I was having a wonderful time, and it's so terribly hard to try and not let it show that one is so desperately lonely.

(*The cast puts their index fingers on their noses and prance around her in a circle, using a very stuck up tone of voice.*)

All: They're laughing at you
   They're laughing at you
   They're laughing at you

(*They freeze, except for Robert.*)

Robert: Do you know what my favorite thing in the world is? Keats! I think his poetry is marvelous. I like to spend my free time reading Keats, and doing algebraic equations. I guess you could say I'm academic, but really, I'd like to spend some time doing other things—like playing baseball. I was really good. My mom made me stop because she thought I'd get hurt. I'd like to read comic books, but dad says I'll never get anywhere wasting my time with them. I have some rare ones that are worth a lot of money, but he doesn't know that. I wish I could tell him, but I can't.

(*The cast surrounds him using a very parental tone, pointing fingers at him.*)

All: Don't waste your time
Don't waste your time
Don't waste your time

(*They freeze; except for Terrence.*)

Terrence: My dad keeps bugging me to try out for the football team. My mom keeps interfering with my class schedule. She thinks I should be a doctor. The only thing that I'm really good at is auto mechanics. But my parents don't hear me when I tell them. Last weekend, we had this fight. My dad got mad and punched the wall, and my mom started to cry. I left the house, I had to get out of there. I saw these guys I know at school and we all went out. They had some beer. I got drunk for the first time. I didn't like the way it tasted, but I felt a lot better.

(*The cast circles him, leering.*)

All: Would you jump off a bridge if your friends asked you to?
Would you jump off a bridge if your friends asked you to?

(*The cast freezes; except for Tina.*)

Tina: Every time I go to that awful biology class, the teacher calls on me and expects me to know the answer. Just because my brother, Tom, went off to college to become a marine biologist. He was her star pupil. Next week, when we have to dissect a frog, I'm going to be absent.

(*The cast circles Tina, arms outstretched menacingly.*)

All: Shadow. Shadow. Shadow.

(*During the next sequence, the cast makes a giant circle. They take on menacing tones. They each repeat their line five times, saying it faster and faster until the lines are nearly on top of each other. The lines should be softer, then louder, building with intensity until together they say the final line and freeze in angry, menacing poses.*)

Sheila: They're all gonna laugh at you!

Stanley: Get off your high horse, Mr. Smartypants!

Rebecca: If brains were a disease, you'd live forever!

Robert: If you'd just apply yourself!

Jennifer: You're as graceful as a cow on crutches!

George: Nobody likes you, everybody hates you, just go eat some worms!

Terrence: Can't you do anything right?

Tina: Why can't you be like everybody else, you're so odd!

All: You're so odd!

(*They freeze in their poses and hold them for a moment, then the cast lets out a big sigh together, breaking the freeze. The girls walk to the back of the stage area and turn away from the audience. The men form a line at the front of the stage as they say their lines.*)

Terrence: Who am I?

George: Am I who?

Robert: I, who am.

Stanley: I'm real cool!

Guys: We are so cool, too cool. Joe cool.

Robert: O.K., so I'm not cool. What is cool going to get me? No Nobel prize, that's for sure!

(*Sheila walks up to Robert, taps him on the shoulder and waves, he turns away from her blushing.*)

Sheila: We're in that awkward stage . . . somewhere between the toyroom and the bedroom.

Tina: And alone.

(*Cast finds a space on the stage where they are alone for the next section.*)

Terrence: Alone: An adjective meaning solitary; by oneself.

Jennifer: I am so unhappy. Last night, I stayed in my room and cried the whole night. I guess this is what love really is—always hoping, hoping and never getting. . . oh, George, don't you know how I feel? If I could just talk to you, that's all just talk. Well, maybe not all—I have to find a way to reach you. I have to, but how?

(*Rebecca moves to her position in the triangle position, directing her next line to Jennifer.*)

Rebecca: And they say it's just puppy love.

Jennifer: I have to find a way to reach you. I have to, but how?

Sheila: Love: A noun meaning a strong bond formed by an emotional attraction.

(On the next few lines, cast members take their places in the triangle position.)

Jennifer: What is love?

Terrence: Love is what?

George: Love, what is?

Terrence *(to Tina)*: If I told you I loved you, what would you do? I'd gladly say it if only I knew.

Robert *(to Rebecca)*: You never ever look at me . . .
But I love you, I do.
I never thought I'd feel this way . . .
If you only knew.
I keep on reading Keats each day,
And hoping every night,
That you would turn my way one day
And call me "Mr. Right."

George: I'd ask Sheila out . . .
But she's in love with Stanley.
Tina's sweet, but I doubt . . .
That she thinks I'm very manly.
Rebecca dislikes me a lot.
She can be so unkind.

(to Jennifer): Hey, you . . . yes you,

(he sits down by Jennifer) Would you like to be mine?

Tina *(to Terrence)*: If I told you I loved you, what would you do? That's one thing I wish I knew.

Rebecca: If I could be in love,
But all these boys are silly.
They are all so very young,
even Joe and Hank and Billy.
But they never think of me.
Well, that's their first mistake.
I know I'd be the very best date
a boy could ever make.

Jennifer *(to George)*: I know you're only here with me because I'm the only one left. Oh, George, don't you think you could like me a little bit for who I am?

(Stanley crosses to Sheila and kisses her.)

Sheila: Stanley kissed me when it was freezing.

(*Robert kisses Rebecca, awkwardly.*)

Rebecca: Robert kissed me in the hall.

(*Terrence crosses in front of Tina and only looks at her.*)

Tina: But Terrence only looked at me, and never kissed at all.

(*Sheila runs upstage away from Stanley.*)

Stanley: Sheila's kiss was lost in jest.

(*Rebecca slaps Robert and walks off in a huff to Sheila.*)

Robert: Rebecca's lost in play.

(*Tina watches Terrence, then turns to audience dreamily, says line and joins the other girls.*)

Tina: But the look in his eyes haunts me night and day.

(*Tina drops to her knees and the rest of the girls join her forming a line on their knees, hands together as if saying a bedtime prayer. Guys are standing behind the girls in a line facing away from the audience.*)

Girls: Heavenly father full of grace, bless my boyfriend's handsome face. Bless his hair that never curls, and keep him safe from other girls. Bless his hands so big and strong. And keep them, Lord, where they belong. I love him, Lord, but please don't tell, if Dad found out he'd give me . . . He's got faults and you know why. But bless him, Lord, 'cause he's my guy.

(*Girls immediately pose like they are again at the slumber party, while boys form a telephone booth with Stanley inside.*)

Sheila: I think something is wrong between Stanley and me. Three nights have passed and he hasn't called. I waited for him after school in the usual place, and he hardly spoke to me.

Rebecca: He's just like all the rest.

Sheila: He keeps forgetting to pick me up after school, and then he acts like I cut his heart out when I complain. Last week, I took him out to eat, you'd think he'd remember that!

Tina: He "lets" you do something for him?

Sheila: I don't care about the dinner, I just miss him. I wish he'd talk to me. I'd do anything if he'd just talk to me.

Jennifer: You're ready to die for him.

Sheila: I think I'll die without him.

(*Guys form a phone booth around Stanley.*)

Guys: BRRRRRIIIIIIIINNNNNNNNGGGGGGG

Stanley: Hi, UMMMMMMM, it's me . . . look . . .

Sheila (*miming talking into a phone; to the girls*): It's him!!!!

Stanley: Look . . . could I come over?

Sheila: I guess so.

(*Stanley enters the scene, the other girls giggle and push Sheila toward him.*)

Stanley: Could we go somewhere private?

Sheila: OK.

(*They walk downstage away from others. The rest of the cast goes to the back of the acting space and turn their backs to the audience.*)

Sheila: What did you want to talk about?

Stanley: Well, I wanted to say that I was sorry about the other night. I guess I got carried away. It's just that you're so beautiful—you get me so crazy.

Sheila: That's O.K.

Stanley: The real reason I asked you to come over the other night was because I decided I wanted to give you something.

Sheila: What?

Stanley: I'm not too good at this, so . . . here . . .

(*Stanley mimes giving Sheila his class ring.*)

Sheila: Oh, Stanley, your class ring?

Stanley: Will you go steady with me?

Sheila: Oh, yes, Stanley, this is just what I wanted. I love you.

Stanley: I do you, too.

Sheila: Isn't it funny, I thought that you were never going to talk to me again, and here you are giving me your ring to wear.

Stanley: Aren't you going to give me a kiss?

(*Sheila gives him a quick kiss on the cheek. He grabs her and begins to kiss her more passionately. She struggles and becomes angry, finally breaking away. She throws the class ring to the ground.*)

Sheila: Stanley, I thought you really meant what you said, I thought you loved me. But you only want the other thing.

(*All freeze except for Stanley.*)

Stanley: Temptation: A noun meaning to provoke or cause to do something or behave in a certain way.

(*Cast stands and moves into couples on each line.*)

Sheila (*confused*): Is sex love?

George (*very confused*): Sex is love?

Jennifer (*very, very confused*): Love is sex?

Stanley (*to Sheila, who turns away from him*): If we don't go through with it I'll get sick. (*They freeze.*)

Rebecca (*to Robert, who turns away embarrassed*): Come on, I'm not going to get pregnant, I have protection.

Robert: Wouldn't you rather conjugate some verbs? (*They freeze.*)

Terrence (*to himself, almost under his breath*): If I don't get it tonight, I'll never get it, the big I-T!

Tina (*overhearing Terrence, moves downstage away from others, to herself*): I'm not sure I'm ready for that! (*They freeze.*)

Sheila (*changing her mind, to Stanley*): Well, maybe . . . just a little ways . . . just this once, but if I don't like it, you have to stop. (*They freeze.*)

Jennifer: Compromise: Noun meaning a mutual concession, a middle course of action.

George: I do like you for who you are.

Jennifer: Do you mean that?

George: Yes.

Jennifer: I hope nobody paid you to go out with me.

George: What do I have to do to convince you, I like you. Yes, I knew that you had a crush on me. Yes, I knew, but when I found out that you liked me, I decided to check up on you.

Jennifer: You did?

George: Yes, and guess what I found out?

Jennifer: What?

George: That I do like you . . . you.

Jennifer: Why?

George: Because . . . because you look at me as though I'm somebody important, because you care about your friends. I saw you with the kids you babysit for, and they like you. I like you because you are a good person.

Jennifer: George, I like you, too. You are somebody important to me.

(*He puts his arm around her, and she puts her head on his shoulder. They freeze.*)

Rebecca: Respect: A verb meaning deserving of high regard or a noun meaning earning high esteem.

Robert: Or to refrain from interfering with.

Rebecca: Robert, what are you reading?

Robert: Uhh, some college catalogues. I've been accepted to these three schools, and I'm trying to decide which one to actually attend.

Rebecca: I know what you mean. I have the same problem.

Robert: You . . . have a problem?

Rebecca: Yes, it seems hard to believe, doesn't it. Let's see where you're going . . .

(*She mimes taking books from him, which then "drop."*)

Robert: I'll get them.

Rebecca: No, let me . . . hmmm, Columbia, hey, I've been accepted there, too. Yale, Harvard . . . and what's this? Spiderman?

Robert (*ashamed*): Please, just give it to me.

Rebecca: Can I see it, please? I used to love comic books. I have a whole collection of Wonder Woman.

Robert (*impressed*): You do?

Rebecca: Yes, if you'd like we could go to my house, and I'll show them to you.

Robert: I'd like that very much.

Rebecca: I never knew anybody could have the same passion as I.

Robert: I thought you'd think I was stupid for having that.

(*He shyly takes her hand, and they turn their backs to audience, and then freeze.*)

Tina: Knowledge: A noun meaning learning through study and actual experience.

(*The cast begins to hum the graduation march, they form two lines, girls shortest to tallest in back in one line, and guys shortest to tallest in the other.*)

Robert: Commencement: A noun meaning the first step in a long journey; or a graduation ceremony.

Boys: Should I get a job?

Girls: Should I go to college?

(*Rebecca goes far upstage as if giving the graduation speech. The rest of the cast looks very bored, yawning, and fanning themselves.*)

Rebecca: My fellow classmates, we have finally shed our youth and now march head long into our lives. In the time we began, blah, blah, blah, blah, blah, blah, blah, blah . . . etc.

(*She notices that no one is listening and quickly finishes her speech.*)

Rebecca: And in conclusion, here's hoping the members of our class realize that we all can make a difference!

(*Rebecca leads them in changing the tassel to the other side. They all cheer! They hug and break into couples for their final speeches, miming talking to each other until it is time for them to say their lines.*)

Rebecca: Valedictorian, what a life!

Robert: Rebecca, would you sign my yearbook?

Rebecca: Certainly, to my own personal Spiderman, who does whatever a spider can. Love, Rebecca. Robert, my parents gave me a new car for graduation, would you like to go for a ride?

Robert (*with gained confidence*): Sure, uh, who wouldn't want a ride from their own personal Wonder Woman?

Sheila (*to Stanley*): I'm so glad we're still friends.

Stanley: Yeah, me too.

Sheila: I'd like you to come to my graduation party . . . even though we're not dating anymore. I'd still like us to be friends.

Stanley: Sure, I'll come. I'd like to be friends.

Sheila: Good, I've always wanted you to meet my sister.

(*She takes his arm, and they cross the stage.*)

George: Jennifer, I've been meaning to tell you something.

Jennifer (*panic-stricken*): What did I do?

George: This isn't about you . . . it's about me.

Jennifer: What's wrong?

George: I've enlisted in the army, and I want to know if you'll write to me. I figure I can make enough money that I can send you a plane ticket to visit me once I find out where I'll be stationed. Will you do that for me? Will you write to me?

Jennifer: Of course, I'll write to you. Maybe by the time you find out where you'll be stationed, I'll have earned my own money and you won't have to send me a ticket. My aunt just got me a job selling cosmetics, I can make a lot in commissions if I work hard, and I would, if it meant getting to see you again.

George: Look, my mom and dad are over there. Come on, I want them to meet you.

(*They hold hands and walk across the stage; when they pass Tina, she breaks away from Terrence.*)

Tina: Oh, please, don't do this to me!!!

Terrence: Why?

Tina: Don't tell me this now. Don't tell me that you love me just when I've been accepted into the Acting Academy. I thought you said you just wanted to be "good friends"?

Terrence: I guess I never knew how I really felt . . . until today.

Tina: It's just the excitement of graduating and all.

Terrence: I know, I know . . . (*he pauses*) . . . but I really do love you.

Tina (*softly*): I know . . . (*There is a pause.*)

Terrence (*trying to fill the pause, awkwardly*): A very nice ceremony
. . .

Tina: Yes, it was.

Terrence: I guess this is good-bye?

Tina: Good luck. (*She begins to walk away, but stops on Terrence's line.*)

Terrence: Marry me?

(*She pauses, then turns to the audience.*)

Tina: What do I do now?

Jennifer: Decision: A noun meaning the act of concluding, making a determination.

Terrence: Marry me?

Tina: Be a housewife?

George: Go into the military?

Jennifer: Be an Avon lady?

Robert: Yale . . . or Harvard?

Sheila: Pledge a sorority?

Stanley: Pro ball?

Rebecca: Magna Cum Laude!

All: Where do we go from here?

Robert: Future: A noun meaning a period of time that is impending, unknown to us now.

The End

Chamber Theatre Adaptation
"the letting down of the hair" by Anne Sexton
Adapted by Judy E. Yordon

(*This is a poetic prose piece by Anne Sexton. It is a contemporary retelling of the Rapunzel fable with a confessional twist. In this adaptation, the central character has been divided into four voices— four women dressed in white. The only set pieces are four stools which the actresses move as needed.*)

Dramatis Personae

(*NOTE: All four actresses are part of the same person.*)

1: The pessimistic/realistic self, suicidal, who realizes the role in society women have been forced to assume and struggles with it.

2: The optimistic/idealistic self who tries to make the best of her situation.

3: The "Ruth" character—the symbol of hope unfulfilled.

4: The parental/familial/societal voice.

Scene One: Attracting Thousands

All: I live in a stone room.

1: Far from the luxury of draperies and transistors, far from the movie theaters and coffeehouses, far from the men in their business suits, far from the children playing with the Lincoln Logs.

2: I have only the daily newspapers

3: and letters from Ruth.

All: To tell the truth. I am a recluse. I'm as hesitant as Emily Dickinson. Like a novice I'm all dressed in white. A recluse yes.

2: Yet each day I attract thousands.

Scene Two: The Stone Room

All: As I said, a stone room five stories high.

1: Like the stones of Chile. Like the craggy rocks of Gloucester, that desperate seacoast. Like a lion in a zoo.

2: (*to 1*): I adjust to my environment.

1: I came up here long ago.

2: I didn't hide because I was ugly. I wasn't made of wolfsbane. I wasn't made of kidneys.

All: I was made tall and of yellow hair.

2: I'd had a normal life: men and lipstick, daiquiris and sunburns. My skin was the color of a teacup, fair but fragile. And hair, yellow-yellow hair.

All: Brush. Brush.

1: A stone room as still and clean as a razor blade. All the time of the child in me this room was my secret. Oh, Mr. Man-in-the-Moon, where was your radar? Memory? Memory, here is your knife. A room to crawl into and hide. Better than the laundry chute. Better than the broom closet. A room unused except by birds.

2: Yes, as a child I would enter through a closet, standing tiptoe on a chair, up through the trapdoor into the forbidden—

1: the dead maybe live up here, groaning every hour as they keep watch from the lookout window.

4: Mother can't find me, little yellow ball. Father, you could find me if you would only look, but father is too sleepy to look. Else he'd come flying, come flying. Brother, old sneak mouth, can't find my hide-and-seek. You'll never see.

All: A stone room five stories up, the shape of a merry-go-round, and eleven feet in circumference.

1: A room like the inside of a churchbell

2: a chalice

3: a cave

4: a perch

1: queer bird that I am.

3: A hidden place like the inside of a seed pod.

All: Brush. Brush.

      Scene Three: The Death of Everyone Except Myself

4: Here is my mother. On my eighteenth birthday she said to me, (*to 1*) "Why hair to the floor? Why? Every time you brush it you make me feel I'm coming out of anesthesia."

All: But I couldn't cut it. I was faithful to my hair.

4: My father was indifferent. As he walked the rooms of our house, he acted as if he were reading the *Wall Street Journal* on the window pane. "It's as normal," he would say, "as coffee for breakfast. Long hair. Short hair. Who cares?"

All: It wasn't normal at all. It was special.

4: My brother, the younger, ever the teaser. "What do you want to be taken for, Lady Godiva?" My brother, the younger, ever the adorer. "Please be mine," like an old-fashioned valentine, and then he printed it out on yellow paper: "Your hair is the color of the moon."

All: And Ruth.

3: "Hey, dust mop!" as my hair caught on the legs of the antique tables. "Hey, Spanish moss," as her half-blind adored greyhound ran after it like a string toy. Ruth, the boy child making jokes. Ruth the joker. Ruth the girl child of two suicide attempts. Ruth the desperate and Ruth the wise who told the world, "As the Arab said: 'Enlarge the place of thy tent.'"

All: Brush. Brush.

4: One night my hair got in the pea soup that mother was stirring. She shouted, "The sight of you! The sight of you makes me wish I were dead!"

1: The next day she got her wish.

4: She and my father out driving during a Sunday ice storm, on their way to a cocktail-brunch of caviar and Bloody Marys, skidded in the gray Lincoln and hit a telephone pole. They died instantly. Their necks snapped. My father's cigarette was still burning in his hand when the police arrived. They were buried side by side, heads loose, two broken dolls. Where was the blessedness? Where were the deep roots that grew me? "You'd better cut your hair," my brother said after the funeral.

1: As if I could bring them back with a pair of scissors. After that I came up to my stone room for good.

4: But my brother didn't desert me. Little brother, now a man of sorrow, now a man in a pain hood.

1: Yet I couldn't help him.

2: (*to 1, accusingly*): I could only help myself.

All: I lived in a stupor of hair.

4: Brother pushed trays of food up through the trapdoor daily. I have not seen him face to face since. However, he occasionally sends notes. On the first anniversary of my parents' death the note read: You killed them. <u>You killed them. Moon girl, a black curse on you.</u>

1: But that was a long time ago. Yesterday a note to my middle age.

4: (*a different voice, societal*): <u>Come down, come down, you yellow-haired martyr.</u>

Scene Four: Ruth

2: But most of the time it's just the newspaper carefully refolded and the mail.

1: Envelopes addressed to

All: The Lady of the Hair.

1: And so forth.

4: Letters from the people.

3: And once in a while an aerogram from Ruth with its Japanese stamp. Ruth is my only contact with the past. Ruth my little Zen girl with her short cropped hair. Ruth, the American girl with lovers, one after the other, long after she was married. Ruth. She changed like a seascape, ever changing, ever embracing. No matter what it was she was faithful to it. She was as obedient to each obsession as an old man washing his feet. She was large with her awareness; she was pregnant with her instincts. She had enlarged the place of her tent. Here in America she found the answer. "The puzzle to me is solved," she said with a new grace. And then her banker husband, First National Bank, V.P., was sent to Tokyo. Tokyo, the city in the world with just one English-speaking psychiatrist. Or so she said. Her husband was in therapy four times a week. To be a banker was to have half a mouth. Or so she said.

All: Brush. Brush.

Scene Five: The Letting Down of the Hair

All: Here in my room I have my hair to care for.

2: In the soapstone sink I wash from nine to eleven forty-five in the morning.

1: Washerwoman, washerwoman, you make yourself dizzy.

2: Washing this hair is a dance, a dance to be done at dawn. There is so much hair, so much sucked-up honey, that I must wash it in sections.

1: It is cumbersome and arduous

2: and yet it is my work in life.

1: Then, as the clock tower chimes twelve noon, I carry it back and forth, over to the window, section by section, and hang it out the window to slap down the five stories onto the ground. I let it out to dry.

2: I let it out to give it a life of its own.

1: At first it hangs there like a rope, it hangs there like old yellow cereal that no one will eat.

2: Then, if there is a hopeful wind, the breeze takes it; hair by hair, yellow by yellow.

4: Over the years the people have gathered to watch it fall down and dry out. They call out, just as the clock strikes twelve: LADY! LADY! LET DOWN YOUR HAIR!

2: I am becoming a tourist attraction

1: and there is nothing I can do about it. The Gray Line bus arrives daily with a taped recording of facts—usually false—about what I do and who I am. And then there is the college crowd, who seem to have adopted me, and one obese woman who comes each day and beats out with a stick at the children who reach for the hair and want to tug it.

4: The people have become very devoted or very disgusted.

2: They often write to me.

1: I don't answer them, of course, for my hair cannot speak and it is the hair they write to. Fifty letters came just last week in response to a TV crew that came out on Monday to film the letting down of the hair.

2: Here is a sampling of last week's letters:

> Concord, N. H
> Dear Lady of the Hair,
>
> Your hair is haunting and moving. I love it. I couldn't see your face on our eighteen-inch screen but I could see your hair. I could see your lovely old Victorian house. But the psychologist on the show this morning said perhaps that for you death was the key. He said that your long hair is a symptom of a phobic fear of death. Don't you know that we go on to a larger life? Don't you know that there IS no such thing as death! There is only change.
> Dying is a glorious experience for the one it happens to and even for those left behind for a while, it is glorious if we have true understanding.
>
> Yours sincerely,
> Bernice Engle

1:     Acton, Mass.
      Dear Crazy-Hair,

      Please help to make the world saner not crazier—it's bad enough as it
      is. God bless you and help you—you need help.

      Unsigned

3:     New York, N.Y.
      Dear Matchmaker,

      We met at your hair up there in mass. Joel came out from Harvard
      every week of his senior year. Now we are living together in New York.
      Last week he wrote a poem to your hair but he won't send it. I wish I
      could write. I'm quite illiterate and have no idea how I passed third
      grade. Sometimes I think that Joel loves me. Sometimes I think he
      loves you. I wish I were you. I wish I were my doctors or my OT's or my
      teachers or my doctors' wives or you. Do you know when I was, I
      guess, around six I looked at my Siamese cat and said out loud, "I wish
      I was you, you're so beautiful and you don't have to wear any clothes."
      Peace.

      Suzy Pearlmuter

4:     Dear Lady,

           Jesus, how <u>do</u> you do it?
      ten times, enough times for the entire universe and that same feel of

           Wham! Right in

      the old solar plexus refuses to give up

           You are <u>so</u> beautiful
           and I want some of that
      beautifulness

           and I wanted it since a year ago when I first found you. After last
      Saturday in Boston and seeing you again I wanted it 'specially badly.
      And today I want it even more.
           Lady

           can you spare
           a dime of yourself

                          for
                          Mary Jane?

Scene Six: Letters from Ruth

3: Today's mail brought a letter from Ruth, a letter and a crucifix. It is a letter about Christ and the awful mystery. It is a letter about the sickness unto death. I have found Christ, she writes, hours on my knees in mental prayer. (The greyhound puppy, of course. I could hear her saying, My dog is Christian, too.) All my life I have lived in shadow. P.S., she added, I've even discovered what your hair means. It is a parable for the life of a poet.

All: Ruth has Christ, and I, I have only my hair. Am I like a poet? I mean to ask her about that.

Scene Seven: The Sickness Unto Death

2: My hair is almost washed.

4: The people are waiting down below and calling out for me. Just as I am carrying it over, my brother opens the trapdoor and speaks. Speaks for the first time in all these years. "It's bad news," he says quietly. I stand very still, tangled in the midst of the hair. "Ruth's cousin just called. She's dead. She killed herself. First she hung the dog. And then she hung herself."

All: I am silent, and then I say,

1: "Thank you for telling me,"

4: And he closes down the trapdoor.

1 and **3**: The sickness unto death,

3: Ruth dead. Ruth gone. The dog hung up like a piece of meat in a butcher shop. Ruth hung up like a thief.

2: This change.

1: This awful change. And I with the letter she wrote just five days ago. (*2,3,4 begin clock sound*) And the crucifix from her puppy's mouth. The clock strikes twelve and I just stand here. It's too late now. I wanted to ask Ruth what my life meant. Ask her about my tent. Ask her about the parable. Now there is no one to ask. There are the people down below calling up

2, 3, 4: LADY! LADY! LET DOWN YOUR HAIR!

1: but I could hardly ask them.

The End

Conversation Analysis Script
Transcribed by Laura Jansen and Melissa Jones

(This script of naturally occurring conversation was prepared by two students in an advanced oral interpretation/performance studies class. The girls video recorded two strangers for approximately one hour in an attempt to find a section where the two subjects seemed most unaware of the camera. The conversation was then transcribed into this script.)

L: Linnea

K: Krista

L: *(legs forward, left slightly bent; hands in lap, pen on bed)*: His

ex-girlfriend was at his house. (.) *(tugs on right sock)* She's *(picks*

up pen) all jealous and stuff ↓

K: *(puts hands down on bag, looks at L)*: OHO:: Ö *(picks up bag*

handles, looks down)

L: (.) And so she saw that I was in the car and (.) *(K picks up bag and*

puts it on floor) and I'm like you don't have a girlfriend do you *(pick*

up pictures and set them down right) and he's like (.) no I don't but

she just gets jealous and ya know so I *(K reaches over to pick up*

orange juice and raises up to mouth, lifts right leg) just cannot be

mean to her and I'm like you can't live your life because she's all *(L*

holds pen in left hand and taps on knuckles of right hand. K brings

glass down slightly.) jealous (.) ⌈so⌉

K: Sounds (*L stops hitting pen on knuckles of right hand*) like a real

good guy there Linnea AHA =

L: (*twists pen in hands*): = I know and so today I go (*K resumes*

drinking juice, left hand in lap) so how'd it go or whatever and he's

like oh (.) (*K stops drinking*) fine and (*K puts glass down, holds*

with both hands) then just after he's like well would you like to go

out with me again and I'm like sure (*K looks at L, smooths her skirt*

with right hand, holds glass in left)

K (*right hand holds glass*): Warning warning warning

L: (.) I'm sure

K: AHAHA

L: You can't let (*rolls her eyes*) go of yer girlfriend

K: (*left leg comes up and drinks with glass in right hand, left hand*

on knee): How old is he

L (*K stops drinking and holds glass at stomach*): (.) Twenty (.) he

flies (.) and stuff

K: Is he in school?

L: Next semester he will be (.) An you know he's

Do you know

K: Is he from town..... Is he a Towny =

L: = Yes Lafayette

K: Oh God (*K drinks again*)

L: I know (.) Um do you know what his major is it used

to be (.) aviation (*K places glass right*) but you know what (*smiles*)

it is now

K (*smiles*): (.) Liberal Arts (.) (*K turns back to L and rolls eyes, left

hand on left knee, clasps right hand on left hand*)

L: (.) Supervision (.) he's gonna be a supervisor

K: (.) It's 'cause he (*pulls up left sock with right hand*) probably

flunked out of aviation=

L: = No he couldn't afford it (.) (*L flexes and points left foot*) he

wanted to do it but since his parents made so much money (*stops

flexing and pointing*) he couldn't get financial aid and (*bobs her

head from side to side on the "dahs"*) dah dah dah dah but I don't

see why he couldn't take off a year

K (*stops playing with sock, hands clasped together*): So why

doesn't he work a semester go to school a semester

L: I know

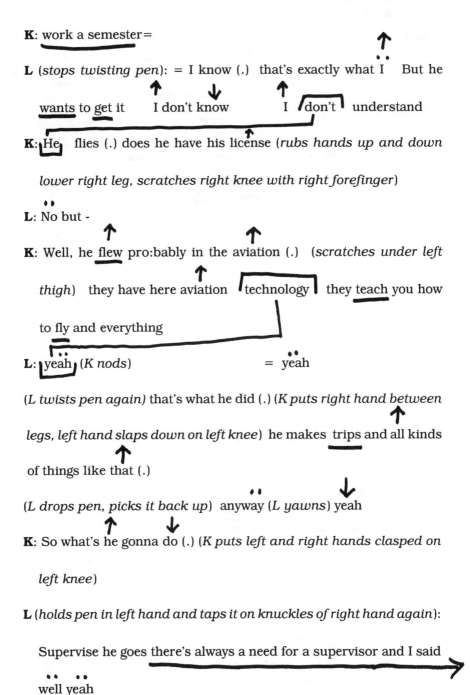

K: work a semester=

L (*stops twisting pen*): = I know (.) that's exactly what I   But he wants to get it   I don't know   I don't understand

K: He flies (.) does he have his license (*rubs hands up and down lower right leg, scratches right knee with right forefinger*)

L: No but -

K: Well, he flew pro:bably in the aviation (.) (*scratches under left thigh*) they have here aviation technology they teach you how to fly and everything

L: yeah (*K nods*)   = yeah

(*L twists pen again*) that's what he did (.) (*K puts right hand between legs, left hand slaps down on left knee*) he makes trips and all kinds of things like that (.)

(*L drops pen, picks it back up*) anyway (*L yawns*) yeah

K: So what's he gonna do (.) (*K puts left and right hands clasped on left knee*)

L (*holds pen in left hand and taps it on knuckles of right hand again*): Supervise he goes there's always a need for a supervisor and I said well yeah

K: He's gonna supervise (*shakes a little and rocks left leg back and forth slightly*) Ryan's Steakhouses for the ⌐rest⌐ of his life   AHA

L (*taps pen on knuckles again*): He┐ goes (*K looks down, releases left leg*) I'm sure that's what I mean I'm sure that's (*stops tapping pen on knuckles*) where he'll end up (.) and I don't know that kinda stuff scares me

K (*picks lint off her clothes, looks down*): Linne:a (*laughs*) that's fine =

L (*crosses left leg over right at ankles, twists pen in hand*): = It does

K: I mean just look at ⌐Jeff⌐

L (*flexes toes*) : ⌐Because┐I don' —

K: What does Jeff   do   nothing (.)

L: Yes but Jeff makes a lot of money an —

K: He doesn't even he makes a lot of money doing nothing

L: (.) he does fun stuff though he knows a lot about a lot of things (*K straightens right leg*)

K: (.) He makes ⌐about⌐ —   (..)   thirty (*laughs*)

L: ⌐he┘ does he could make so much mon —

K: five thousand a year (.) that's it (*6 second pause*)(. . . .)

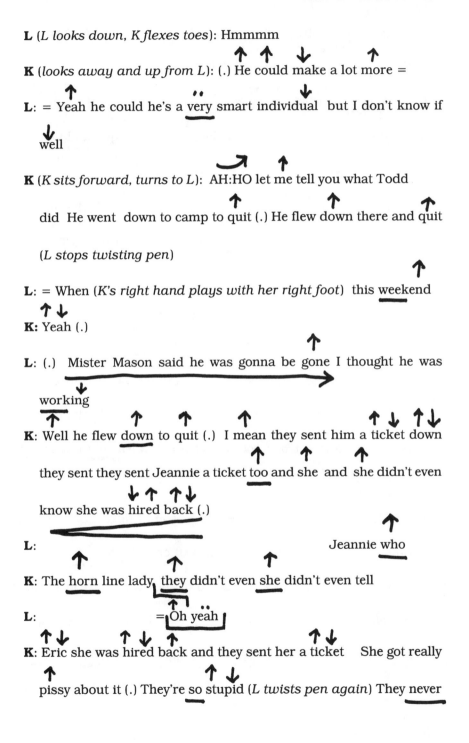

L (*L looks down, K flexes toes*): Hmmmm

K (*looks away and up from L*): (.) He could make a lot more =

L: = Yeah he could he's a very smart individual but I don't know if
well

K (*K sits forward, turns to L*): AH:HO let me tell you what Todd
did He went down to camp to quit (.) He flew down there and quit

(*L stops twisting pen*)

L: = When (*K's right hand plays with her right foot*) this weekend

K: Yeah (.)

L: (.) Mister Mason said he was gonna be gone I thought he was
working

K: Well he flew down to quit (.) I mean they sent him a ticket down
they sent they sent Jeannie a ticket too and she and she didn't even
know she was hired back (.)

L: Jeannie who

K: The horn line lady, they didn't even she didn't even tell

L: = Oh yeah

K: Eric she was hired back and they sent her a ticket   She got really
pissy about it (.) They're so stupid (*L twists pen again*) They never

tell 'em (.) anything (.) I'm surprised   Jeff (*K puts right hand on*

right knee) didn't get a ticket (*laughs*)

L: okay so what happened

K: Ha Ha = And up anyway (.) So he flew down to quit and he told

L: = I'm sure (.) probably (.) so what happened

K: 'em he resigned and Mason lost it and kind of had a nervous

breakdown and he was like (.) No you can't quit (.) and Ta Todd was

like (.) I'm not going 'a teach drill You already have somebody else

writing the drill (.) (*K looks at L*) And so Mason's like (.) Well name

your price you know how much is it gonna take

K: And so Todd leaves and he calls Jeff and um (.) he calls Jeff and

asks Jeff how much he thinks he should (*L smiles*) ask for (.) Jeff

goes (.) (*K leans forward, rocks,   looks out*) Not a dime under thirty

thousand AH And

K (*scratches right knee*): So he told Mason (*K flexes and wriggles

right foot*) that and um Mason eh bout crapped his pants And oh

it's just funny (.) (*K looks at L*) So I think he's gonna give in Because

he called Jeff back and he's like (.) Man I just can't pass up the

money. Cause (*K scratches side of upper thigh.*) Phantom Regi-

ment wants him to write their drill but they can't pay that and that's all he does he doesn't have any other job (*K raises right arm straight up above head*)

L: Oh he doesn't

K: uh uh (*K goes back to scratching up and down right thigh, and flexes foot*)

L (*stops twisting pen, and hits knuckle again*): (.) Plus you get like (.) food and all that kinda stuff when you're away with a (.) a drum corps

K: Yeah but (.) well you (.) he would rather work with another corp where he would be more respected and treated nice He's just got wailed on last year ripped (.) (*L stops hitting knuckle with pen*) ripped to shreds I think

L (*looks down*): yeah, that's why

K (*looks at L*): Mason should write the drill AHA

L: = I'm sure is he gonna be our (.) (*starts hitting knuckle again*) um (.) visual coordinator

K: Visual coordinator, AHA

L: Probably give himself a raise

K: Probably pay (.) He'll probably pay himself Lenny's

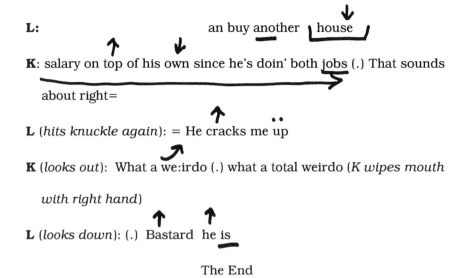

L: an buy another | house |

K: salary on top of his own since he's doin' both jobs (.) That sounds

about right=

L (*hits knuckle again*): = He cracks me up

K (*looks out*): What a we:irdo (.) what a total weirdo (*K wipes mouth*

with right hand)

L (*looks down*): (.) Bastard he is

The End

Chamber Theatre Adaptation
"The Open Window" by H. H. Munro (Saki)
Adapted by Judy E. Yordon

Dramatis Personae

Narrator (N): He assumes the responsibilities of a "butler," acting deferential, hanging up coats, straightening up, etc. He remains close enough to Framton to pick up his thoughts, but he knows much more than he is willing to share.

Vera (V): Mrs. Sappleton's self-possessed, fifteen-year-old niece, who creates "romance" at short notice.

Framton Nuttel (F): A very nervous young man who has migrated to this rural retreat to undergo a nerve cure.

Mrs. Sappleton (S): The lady of the house Framton comes to visit. She seems, at first, to be delusional.

Four minor characters: Framton's sister (1) and Mrs. Sappleton's husband (2) and two young brothers (3 and 4) who have been out hunting.

(*Stage is empty except for Narrator who is straightening the furniture. Framton knocks on door at right. Narrator answers door, helps Framton remove his hat and coat, and hangs them up. He asks Framton his name, receives Framton's letters of introduction, and seats him in chair stage right, and crosses left. Framton seems nervous and uneasy.*)

N: Mrs. Sappleton, there is a Mr. Framton Nuttel here to see you. (*Vera enters, Narrator hands her letters of introduction which she hastily scans and returns to Narrator. Narrator stands above Framton to his right after Vera crosses and sits on sofa stage left.*)

V: My aunt will be down presently, Mr. Nuttel; in the meantime you must try and put up with me.

N (*to audience*): Framton Nuttel endeavoured to say the correct something

F (*to N*): which should duly flatter the niece of the moment

N (*to F*): without unduly discounting the aunt that was to come. (*He steps down to talk to audience.*) Privately he doubted more than ever whether these formal visits on a succession of total strangers would do much towards helping the nerve cure which he was supposed to be undergoing. (*F's sister, who has been hiding behind Framton's chair, appears and stands above F and to his right.*)

1: I know how it will be

N: His sister had said when he was preparing to migrate to this rural retreat;

1: You will bury yourself down there and not speak to a living soul, and your nerves will be worse than ever from moping. I shall give you letters (*she drops letters on Framton, which N picks up and puts in his pocket*) of introduction to all the people I know there. Some of them, as far as I can remember, were quite nice. (*1 exits off right.*)

F (*to no one in particular*): Framton wondered whether Mrs. Sappleton

N (*to audience*): the lady to whom he was presenting one of the letters of introduction

F: came into the nice division.

V: Do you know many of the people round here? (*to the audience*) asked the niece, when she judged that they had had sufficient silent communion.

F: Hardly a soul. My sister was staying here, at the rectory, you know some four years ago, and she gave me letters of introduction to some of the people here. (*N hands F one of the letters of introduction which F hands to V.*)

V: Then you know practically nothing about my aunt? (*V does not look at the letter, takes it, and hands it to N.*)

F: Only her name and address. (*F looks at N, confused.*)

N (*to audience*): He was wondering whether Mrs. Sappleton was in the married or widowed state.

F (*to N*): An undefinable something about the room seemed to suggest masculine habitation.

V: Her great tragedy happened just three years ago, that would be since your sister's time.

F: Her tragedy?

N (*to audience*): Somehow in this restful country spot tragedies seemed out of place.

V: You may wonder why we keep that window wide open on an October afternoon. (*She points downstage center at an imaginary "open window."*)

F: It is quite warm for the time of the year, but has that window got something to do with the tragedy?

V: Out through that window, three years ago to a day, her husband and her two young brothers went off for the day's shooting. They never came back. In crossing the moor to their favourite snipe-shooting ground they were all three engulfed in a treacherous piece of bog. It had been that dreadful wet summer, you know, and places that were safe in other years gave way suddenly without warning. Their bodies were never recovered. That was the dreadful part of it. (*V now loses her self-possessed note and becomes falteringly human.*) Poor aunt always thinks that they will come back some day, they and the little brown spaniel that was lost with them, and walk in at that window just as they used to do. That is why the window is kept open every evening till it is quite dusk. Poor dear aunt, she has often told me how they went out, her husband with his white waterproof coat over his arm, and Ronnie, her youngest brother, singing, "Bertie, why do you bound?" as he always did to tease her, because she said it got on her nerves. Do you know, sometimes on still quiet evenings like this, I almost get a creepy feeling that they will all walk in through that window—(*She breaks off with a shudder. F is aghast.*)

N: It was a relief to Framton when the aunt bustled into the room (*S rushes in talking a mile a minute and making apologies as the N talks to audience*) with a whirl of apologies for being late in making her appearance.

S: I hope Vera has been amusing you?

F: She has been very interesting.

S: I hope you don't mind the open window, my husband and brothers will be home directly from shooting, and they always come in this way. They've been out for snipe in the marshes today, so they'll make a fine mess over my poor carpets. So like you menfolk, isn't it? (*F attempts to answer, but cannot. S continues talking about the "scarcity of birds" and the "prospects for duck in the winter" as the N speaks to the audience.*)

N: She rattled on cheerfully about the shooting and the scarcity of birds, and the prospects for duck in the winter.

F (*to N, horrified*): To Framton it was all purely horrible. (*F tries several topics of conversation, the weather, his health, etc., while the N speaks to audience.*)

N: He made a desperate but only partially successful effort to turn the talk on to a less ghastly topic; he was conscious that his hostess was giving him only a fragment of her attention, and her eyes were constantly straying past him to the open window and the lawn beyond.

F (*to N*): It was certainly an unfortunate coincidence that he should have paid his visit on this tragic anniversary. (*F turns to S and raises his voice to gain her attention in an attempt to once more change the subject.*) The doctors agree in ordering me complete rest, and absence of mental excitement, and avoidance of anything in the nature of violent physical exercise.

N (*to audience, with patient indulgence*): Framton laboured under the tolerably widespread delusion that total strangers and chance acquaintances are hungry for the least detail of one's ailments and infirmities, their cause and cure.

F: On the matter of diet they are not so much in agreement.

S: No? (*She says this in a voice which only replaced a yawn at the last moment. We hear 4 say "Bertie, why do you bound," and we see three figures slowly coming out of the audience toward the "open window."*)

N: Then Mrs. Sappleton suddenly brightened into alert attention—but not to what Framton was saying.

S: Here they are at last! Just in time for tea, and don't they look as if they were muddy up to the eyes!

N: Framton shivered slightly and turned towards the niece with a look intended to convey sympathetic comprehension.

F (*looking at V*): The child was staring out through the open window with dazed horror in her eyes.

N: In a chill shock of nameless fear Framton swung around in his seat and looked in the same direction. (*F crosses downstage to look out the "open window."*) In the deepening twilight three figures were walking across the lawn towards the window;

F: they all carried guns under their arms,

N: and one of them was additionally burdened with a white coat hung over his shoulders.

F: A tired brown spaniel kept close at their heels.

N: Noiselessly they neared the house, and then a hoarse young voice chanted out of the dusk:

4: I said, "Bertie, why do you bound?" (*F runs to where N has hung up his hat and coat, gathers them up, and the N helps F make a quick exit out the front door right.*)

F: Framton grabbed wildly at his hat and coat;

N (*coming downstage to look out the "open window" at F*): the hall-door, the gravel-drive, and the front gate were dimly noted stages in his headlong retreat. A cyclist coming along the road had to run into the hedge to avoid imminent collision.

(*2, 3, 4 enter through the "open window."*)

2: Here we are, my dear, fairly muddy, but most of it's dry. (*2 addresses N*) Who was that who bolted out as we came up? (*and before N can answer while N is removing the men's soiled jackets*)

S: A most extraordinary man, a Mr. Nuttel, could only talk about his illnesses, and dashed off without a word of good-bye or apology when you arrived. One would think he had seen a ghost. (*V and N exchange quick, knowing glances.*)

V: I expect it was the spaniel. (*She speaks very calmly.*) He told me he had a horror of dogs. He was once hunted into a cemetery somewhere on the banks of the Ganges by a pack of pariah dogs, and had to spend the night in a newly dug grave with the creatures snarling and grinning and foaming just above him. Enough to make anyone lose their nerve.

N (*to audience, with a smile*): Romance at short notice was her speciality.

The End

Collage Compiled Script
"We the People"
by Melissa Van Meter

(*This script is compiled from various history books, "America, the Beautiful," lines from the preamble to the Constitution, and "The Pledge of Allegiance." It teaches the formulation and basic tenets of the Constitution, and is intended for upper elementary or high school students.*)

Dramatis Personae

Mr. Do Right: the Narrator, a delegate to the Constitutional Convention (*Washington's equal*)

America: A very beautiful country in distress (*a woman*)

Villain: Against the Constitution (*Shay's equal*)

Townspeople: Their basic purpose is to support Do Right and convince the Villain (*Shay*) that the Constitution is for the good of the people. There are three of them: Voice 1, 2, and 3.

Voices 1, 2, and **3**: Outspoken citizens in favor of the Constitution

Setting: The main street of Philadelphia

Time: 1787

(*As the show begins, the chorus is lined up vertically from upstage to downstage. Do Right is center stage. The Villain is behind the chorus. America is behind them all, hidden.*)

Do Right: In 1787, Americans were bursting with energy. They were busy building bridges, digging canals, and inventing wonderful things. The main invention was the nation. Now most nations do not have to be invented. They are there already. They have always been there. No one had to make . . .

Voice 1 (*suggesting a French dialect*): France . . .

Voice 2 (*suggesting an English dialect*): England . . .

Voice 3 (*suggesting a Danish dialect*): Denmark . . .

Do Right: You might say that history made them.

America: They don't have any fathers or any birthday. (*America steps through the line of countries to the center of the three voices, they greet the new country.*)

Do Right: Our fathers brought forth on this continent a new nation (*approaching America*) . . . A new nation. We brought it forth, almost invented it.

America: What had been thirteen colonies became thirteen states.

Do Right: And what had been thirteen states became . . .

All: The United States of . . .

America: America! (*Everyone looks at America in amazement.*)

All: We have won our independence from England. (*During the next line, the chorus members talk amongst themselves.*)

Do Right (*noticing what is happening*): There were thirteen states but they were not acting as if they were the United States. Instead, they were acting like separate little countries.

America (*upset about this*): Now each had its own interests.

Group 1: Each state made its own money.

Group 2: Each state made its own laws.

Group 3: Each had its own way of taxing.

America: The Country was in trouble. (*Villain captures America, Townspeople are worried.*)

Villain: All over Europe, the people think that the "United States will fall apart." (*Laughs as if to assure us that this is precisely what he wants to happen.*)

America (*as a plea*): By working together, the states had won their freedom. If they did not stay together now . . . (*stops because she can't bear to think of the result.*)

Villain: Shay's Rebellion in Massachusetts badly frightened many Americans. (*Goes around townspeople scaring them.*) They were afraid that riots and revolts that I had caused would happen in other states. (*Thinks, but doesn't think it is possible.*) Unless the United States gets a better government, and builds a stronger Union, it will fail. (*Wicked laugh*)

(*Townspeople consider what has been said, Voice 1 says the following and the others begin to chant the same thing.*)

Voice 1: Reform the state government and our troubles will go!

Chant: Reform the state government. . . . (*becoming stronger and then softer under Do Right's next line. Chant ends abruptly at the end of his line.*)

Do Right (*to audience*): Members of the Congress, the time has come to act!

Villain: The common people <u>were</u> afraid that the country would fall apart.

Voice 1 (*very excited, spreading the news*): Men from each state came together to what is known as . . .

Voice 2 (*joining in*): . . . the Grand Convention

Voice 3 (*joining in*): . . . in Pennsylvania.

America: They had ideas about the kind of government that was needed to build a great, free America.

Do Right: We, the delegates, will meet together every week day, even Saturdays.

(*Townspeople cheer and begin chant again.*)

Voice 1, 2, 3: Reform the state government (*continues under the next line.*)

Do Right: On September 17, 1787 it was completed. . .

All (*with their own attitudes*): The Constitution of . . .

America: America! The delegates came together to save their country. Peace had come to the common people when the Constitution was signed.

(*Do Right proudly hands the townspeople the rest of the script on parchment paper. The Villain is becoming flustered because he is beginning to realize that the states are unionizing.*)

All (*excited*): Sing the Constitution Song. We the people of the United States in order to form a more perfect Union . . .

Voice 1: establish justice . . .

Voice 2: insure domestic tranquility . . .

Voice 3: provide for the common defense . . .

Voice 1: promote the general welfare . . .

Voice 2: and

Voice 3: secure the Blessings of Liberty . . .

All: to ourselves and our posterity, do ordain and establish this Constitution for the United States of America.

Villain: Doesn't mean a thing! After all, how could it?

Do Right: It gives the power to the people.

Voice 2: We have been given more freedom than any other Nation has ever had.

All: We the People . . .

Villain (*interrupts*): What right had they to say, "We the People?" Who authorized them to speak the language of, "We the People," instead of, "We the States?"

Voice 2: States are free to make their own laws as long as they don't go against federal laws. To stand as one nation and grow we must have some common bond—the Constitution is this bond.

Do Right: Articles were created to define the rights and privileges of the states and the central government.

(*One person begins, and each adds on, building to the end. As each adds on, they assume a pose of feet together, looking straight out, right hand over heart.*)

America: The United States of America . . .

Do Right: For which it stands . . .

Voice 1:   One Nation . . .

Voice 2:   Under God . . .

Voice 3:   Indivisible . . .

All: With liberty . . . and justice . . .

Villain (*doubting*): for all? I'm beginning to understand, but still I'm afraid that your property may be taken by this American government, setting what taxes they want to set.

Voice 3: They stated that Congress can levy taxes for defense and general welfare.

Voice 2: Then to keep Congress from having too much power, they said that no bill will become law until the President signs it.

Villain: Your President may easily become king, then what will become of you and your rights?!?

Do Right: He shall have power by and with the consent of the governed—all of us.

Voice 2: To prevent the President from having too much power, the Constitution states that he will do some things only with the advice of the Senate.

All: We the People . . .

Voice 1: have the power to take his presidency away if necessary. But proudly we shall respect his guidance.

America: The United States is different.

Do Right: Remember, this Constitution implies that all Americans are free and equal.

America (*she tells what she has to offer*): Blest with victory and peace, may the heaven rescued land praise the power that hath made and preserved us a nation over the land of the free and the home of the brave.

Villain: Thus, I consent, sir, to this Constitution because I am not sure that it is not the best. (*To America*): America (*to audience, as prayer*): God mend thy every flaw.

(*Constitution song is started by America, and one by one the others join in.*)

The End

Personal Narrative
"She Smiled at Me"
by Carrie Schlatter

(*This is a script prepared by a student in an advanced oral interpretation/performance studies class. It is a personal narrative that tells of Carrie's reaction to the impending marriage of her best friend, Bertha. In this script, Carrie choose not to bifurcate herself. One performer, therefore, plays Carrie in the present and Carrie in the past.*)

Dramatis Personae

Carrie Present (N): She is 19 years old and looks back on this event with a combination of love and fondness. She is reliable in that the things she says are true, but she is also slightly unreliable because some of her feelings are slightly overly emotional. She has a sense of total control over everything in her story; in fact, at times she stops the action totally, only to resume it when she sees fit. Everything she reveals to us, she reveals for a reason. She is a brunette.

Bertha (B): She is 20 years old, and a little nervous, anxious, and excited. She is about 5'6", and must have long blonde hair. She wears a veil to suggest that she is a bride.

Female and Male Chorus (F1, F2, M1, M2): They are in their 20s, and they assume several different roles throughout the show.

Setting: The stage is empty at first. As soon as N begins to speak, F1, F2, M1, and M2 enter and begin setting the stage. On stage right there is a frame suggesting a full length mirror and two chairs. Center stage includes three wide steps leading to a large platform. The audience is separated in half, making a center aisle.

N (*enters from back of house, looks around the "church," stands center stage and addresses the audience. She sounds very matter-of-fact, and yet fond of these memories.*): The girl who had been my best friend since I was two years old, the girl who had taught me to put on Maybelline mascara and say,

B (*entering and joining N*): No shit, Sherlock,

N (*laughs, still to audience, same manner as before*): the girl I was with when I smoked my first Marlboro, the girl I fought over

B (*arguing as a ten-year-old does*): Barbies and attention,

N (*noting B and going on to audience*): the girl I cried with over parents and boys, was now a woman.

B (*to herself and N, frightened*): And she was getting married!

N (*to audience*): I'd always known I would be in her wedding, but it still seemed strange. We weren't ten- and thirteen-year-olds dreaming of the lavish weddings we'd have when we were grown—we were seventeen and twenty—and it was real. (*B, F1, F2, M1, and M2 go to designated Church area stage right. F1, F2, M1 and M2 are members of the bridal party. They fuss with their clothing, help B put on her veil, take pictures, etc. Basically, they are bustling about laughing and talking. We hear "smile" as one takes pictures, "You look beautiful" as another fusses with the veil, etc.*)

N (*she is the past Carrie and is very nervous. She speaks to herself as she checks her watch.*): I arrived at the church an hour before the ceremony began. (*to audience*) In a way, the thought of Bertha being married made me feel I might lose a little bit of myself. (*Glancing at B, freezes B, F1, F2, M1, M2.*) Even though I didn't see her every day (*looks longingly at B*) like we had as childhood neighbors, she remained a guiding force in my life. (*to self*) The part of me I was losing was the little bit of the child still left in me. It was the part of me that remembered tea parties with lemonade,

B (*unfreezing, joining N*): that liked making bird's nests out of freshly mowed grass,

N: the part of me that longed for the days when our biggest dilemma was trying to convince our mothers we were old enough to ride our bikes to the creek alone. (*Her head has been down and she now lifts it.*) But those days were gone.

B (*making her way back to F1, F2, M1, M2*): Life as we had known it was gone.

N (*walks right and action resumes, people talking, growing increasingly louder*): While getting dressed I spoke to no one. (*The noise is terribly loud, the same ad libs as before, a lot of laughter and sporadic words.*) The noise in the room encased me like a cocoon. (*she pulls herself down left*) The giggles . . . the laughter . . . the happiness destroyed me. I tore through the crowd and stumbled into the bathroom where I could be alone. (*She regards herself a moment in the "mirror" that faces the audience, softly touching her face. Once she begins to speak, B comes down to join her.*)

When I looked in the mirror I saw a twelve-year-old child standing next to her older, wiser, fifteen-year-old best friend who was saying,

B (*playing with N's hair and sounding every bit of fifteen*): You have to get your bangs as high as you can. That's the look now, really!!! Look, mine are at least three inches off my head. (*She bounces back to the wedding party undergoing a transformation from fifteen to twenty during the brief walk. She freezes.*)

N (*turning her back to them*): I never could get my straight, fine brown hair to look as good as Bertha's thick, blonde tresses, and once again I felt inferior and ugly because of it. (*glancing back to party*) If only I could have a second, one moment to tell her how much she meant to me. (*N turns around and the action resumes. She takes a step toward them.*) But all of those people. (*Her anger is growing, and she takes a few steps towards them. With each step they grow louder.*) Those people who hadn't known her as long as I had. Those people who did not care as much as I did—(*Narrator reaches a peak of anger on this line, she speaks loudly as does the wedding party.*) were not allowing me to talk. (*She dismisses them to the back of the church, and speaks softly to audience.*) I couldn't say (*softly to B*), I love you. (*Wedding music begins, N watches.*)

F1 (*she is at the back of the room, shoving N and F2 [as bridesmaids] towards the front*): Walk slowly, girls. SLOWLY.

N: Muffy, the church's wedding coordinator, hissed. With her dyed blonde hair and her designer suits

F1 (*proudly to all*): she knew she possessed the world and everything in it.

(*N is now in place as bridesmaid. M1 is groom, and M2 is best man.*)

F1: The two flower girls, please. (*F1 stands at the front of the "aisle."*)

N (*to audience*): We were in place. David, the organist, changed the music because the bride . . . (*The music changes to traditional wedding march. All turn to look at Bertha as she walks to the front; to self*) I had never seen anything as exquisite as Bertha. (*to audience, trying desperately to describe her so they may see it*) Her dress caught the dim lights, making sparkling jewels to match her eyes.

B (*to N, sounding very frightened*): As she stood in place, letting go of her father's arm

N: Our eyes met. Hers lingering in mine, saying

B: Here we are old friend. Thank you so much for being here. (*She looks at M1 and they say "I do," then all freeze.*)

N: At that moment, I started to cry. (*She is aware that the next few things she says sound romantic and unreal.*) Everything was so right. Bertha was beautiful; Kevin was sublime. Their life together would forever be a storybook romance. A flood of memories washed over me. I cried for our lost childhood,

B (*quietly, unfrozen, crying*): I cried for adulthood. I cried for the beauty, (*B freezes*)

N: and the ugliness inside me. I cried for Bertha, and I cried for myself. (*B unfreezes*) She looked at me again, witnessing the silent tears streaming down my face, and she smiled. She smiled at me. Her smile told me that

B (*to N*): Everything is going to be all right.

N: It told me that she still cared,

B: and she always would.

N: My tears turned to joy as I smiled in return, trying to tell her that I understood. After the ceremony, we were rushed into a receiving line. (*F1 pushes the bridal party into a line up left. The chorus members become guests, shaking B's hand, etc. Congratulations are heard. N and B are on opposite sides of the "line."*) People I had never met nor cared to meet (*she laughs*) shook my hand, and tried to make small talk about

F2 (*condescending*): How lovely the wedding was

M2 (*suggestive*): and how nice you look in your dress. (*F1, F2, M1, M2, go back to B and then to N, recycling the motions again and again.*)

N: Every moment I could, I stole a glance at Bertha, hoping to get an instant to talk to her, hug her, tell her I was proud of her. (*Chorus surrounds B, blocking her from the audience's and N's view.*) But she was swamped with people. I was sure I wouldn't have a chance to tell her anything. (*The chorus and B begin moving left.*) The hordes of people began shuffling into the hallway like cattle,

B: Bertha in the center of them all.

N: I decided to wait until it cleared out before I followed, just to avoid the crowd. (*They are all gone, N sighs and looks down.*) I took a moment to inspect my shoe. (*to audience*) Some of the beads had fallen off during the course of the day. (*B enters and touches N. N*

looks over when she feels B's hand on hers.) She leaned in very close and whispered,

B (*to N*): You're like a sister to me. (*B smiles again and leaves in a hurry. Chorus enters and B joins the others and freezes in a pose suggesting she is going to throw the bouquet.*)

N (*to self*): That touched me more than anything anyone has ever said to me. (*to audience*) She took time that she didn't have to tell me she cared. I loved her for that. (*to self*) I stood there, silent and still for a moment. Then I smiled. I knew that I had lost sight of the most important thing of all. Bertha. (*Looks over at B*) When she had entered high school and I was still in middle school, had we lost touch?

B (*unfreezing*): No.

N: When I moved, had she forgotten me?

B: No.

N (*to B, laughing*): We are blood brothers.

B (*to N, laughing*): Bosom buddies.

N (*softly out*): Friends

B (*softly out*): Forever. (*B holds out her hand to N who takes it and they hug. Smile. Then B freezes again in her bouquet-throwing pose.*)

N (*center stage, to audience*): And I knew that even though she was married, we would always be like sisters, and just because we were growing up, didn't mean we were growing apart. (*N looks at the others, and they unfreeze. B throws the bouquet and F2 catches it then looks at M2 who looks at N, who looks at the audience, shrugs, and laughs.*)

The End

Acknowledgments

(continued from page ii)

Chapter 2

36–38, excerpted/adapted with permission of Scribner, a division of Simon & Schuster, from *The Short Stories of Ernest Hemingway*. Copyright © 1927 Charles Scribner's Sons. Copyright renewed 1955 by Ernest Hemingway; **41–43,** from "the letting down of the hair," *The Book of Folly*. Copyright © 1972 by Anne Sexton. Reprinted by permission of Houghton Mifflin Co. All rights reserved. Performance rights to this selection must be obtained from Sterling Lord Literistic Inc., One Madison Ave., New York, NY 10021; **49,** reprinted by permission of Don Congdon Associates, Inc. Copyright © 1957, renewed 1985 by Ray Bradbury; **50,** "Jazz Fantasia" from *Smoke and Steel* by Carl Sandburg, copyright © 1920 by Harcourt Brace & Company and renewed 1948 by Carl Sandburg, reprinted by permission of the publisher; **58–59,** from *The Scarlet Letter* by Nathaniel Hawthorne, Riverside Edition, Harry Levin, ed. Copyright © 1960 by Houghton Mifflin Company; **59–60,** "For Witches" by Susan Sutheim in *Women: A Journal of Liberation*, Fall 1969.

Chapter 4

106, 107, excerpts from *If on a Winter's Night a Traveler* by Italo Calvino, copyright © 1981 by Harcourt Brace & Company, reprinted by permission of the publisher; **107,** Yukio Mishima, *Death in Midsummer*. Copyright © 1966 by New Directions, translated by Ivan Morris. Reprinted by permission of New Directions Publishing Corp.; **107,** "I Stand Here Ironing," copyright © 1956, 1957, 1960, 1961 by Tillie Olsen, from *Tell Me a Riddle* by Tillie Olsen, Introduction by John Leonard. Used by permission of Delacorte Press/Seymour Lawrence, a division of Bantam Doubleday Dell Publishing Group, Inc.; **107–108,** reprinted with permission of Scribner, an imprint of Simon & Schuster, Inc. from "Haircut" in *The Love Nest and Other Stories* by Ring Lardner. Copyright © 1925 and renewed 1953 by Ellis A. Lardner; **113,** from "The Gift of the Magi" by William Sydney Porter in *The Complete Works of O. Henry,* copyright © 1953 Bantam Doubleday Dell; **117,** from "The Worm in the Apple" by John Cheever in *The Short Stories of John Cheever.* Copyright © 1979 Alfred A. Knopf, a subsidiary of Random House, Inc. Used with permission; **117,** reprinted with permission of Scribner, an imprint of Simon & Schuster, Inc., from *The Short Stories of Ernest Hemingway* by Ernest Hemingway. Copyright © 1933 Charles Scribner's Sons. Copyright renewed © 1961 by Mary Hemingway; **117–118,** "The Horse-Dealer's Daughter," copyright © 1922 by Thomas B. Seltzer, Inc., renewed 1950 by Frieda Lawrence, from *Complete Short Stories of D. H. Lawrence* by D. H. Lawrence. Used by permission of Viking Penguin, a division of Penguin Books USA, Inc.; **122–124,** adapted from "The Third Prize" by A. E. Coppard in *The Collected Tales of A. E. Coppard.* Copyright © 1929, 1948 by A. E. Coppard, published by Robert Hale. Reprinted by permission of David Higham Associates; **125,** excerpt from "Rope" in *Flowering Judas and Other Stories,* copyright © 1930 and renewed 1958 by Katherine Anne Porter, reprinted by permission of Harcourt Brace & Company; **126,** from *Misery* by Stephen King. Copyright © 1987 by Stephen King, Tabitha King, and Arthur B. Greene, Trustee. Used by permission of Viking Penguin, a division of Penguin Books USA, Inc.; **126,** excerpt from "Good Country People" in *A Good Man Is Hard to Find and Other Stories,* copyright © 1955 by Flannery O'Connor and renewed 1983 by Regina O'Connor, reprinted by permission of Harcourt Brace & Company; **131, 137,** adapted from *The Great Gatsby* by F. Scott Fitzgerald. Reprinted by permission of Harold Ober Associates Incorporated. Copyright © 1925 by Charles Scribner's Sons. Copyright renewed 1953 by Frances Scott Fitzgerald Lanahan; **133,** from "The Open Window" by H. H. Munro in *The Complete Stories of Saki.* Copyright © 1930 and renewed 1958 by The Viking Press, Inc.; **140–142,** "Jack and the Beanstalk" by Mark Hillenbrand. Reprinted by permission of the author; **149–150,** "A Wife's Confession" by Guy de Maupassant. Adapted by Michael T. Downey. Used with permission.

Chapter 5
167, from "Yellow Wall Paper" by Charlotte Perkins Gilman in *The Charlotte Perkins Gilman Reader.* Copyright © 1980 by Pantheon Books; **179–181,** excerpt from *Lost in the Funhouse* by John Barth. Copyright © 1963, 1966, 1968, 1969 by John Barth. Used by permission of Doubleday, a division of Bantam Doubleday Dell Publishing Group, Inc.; **182–183,** "The Boarding House," from *Dubliners* by James Joyce. Copyright © 1916 by B. W. Heubsch. Definitive text copyright © 1967 by the Estate of James Joyce. Used by permission of Viking Penguin, a division of Penguin Books USA, Inc.

Chapter 7
227, 241, "The Tow" by Nick Foster. Used with permission; **228–230, 236–240,** "Now I Know" by Andy Catron. Used with permission; **234,** from "She Smiled at Me" by Carrie Schlatter. Used with permission; **235–236,** from "One Last Starry Night" by Cassandra Strandin. Used with permission.

Chapter 8

250–256, "The Last Rung on the Ladder" from *Night Shift* by Stephen King. Copyright © 1976, 1977, 1978 by Stephen King. Used by permission of Doubleday, a division of Bantam Doubleday Dell Publishing Group, Inc. Adapted by Joshua Coomer, used with permission; **257–260,** "One Last Starry Night" by Cassandra Strandin. Used with permission; **261–270,** "World War II from the Homefront: Those Fabulous 40s" compiled by Donald E. Heady and members of The Third Age Theatre. Used with permission; **271–276,** "Alcoholics Anonymous" by Ken Dingledine, Laura Jansen, Audrey Snyder, and Michelle Hensley. Used with permission; **277–296,** "Growing Pains" by Marjorie Duehmig. Used with permission; **297–303,** "the letting down of the hair," reprinted by permission of Sterling Lord Literistic, Inc. Copyright © 1972 by Anne Sexton. Adapted by Judy E. Yordon; **304–312,** script of naturally occurring conversation, transcribed by Laura Jansen and Melissa Jones. Used with permission; **313–317,** "The Open Window" by H. H. Munro in *The Complete Stories of Saki.* Copyright © 1930 and renewed 1958 by The Viking Press, Inc. Adapted by Judy E. Yordon; **318–322,** "We the People" by Melissa Van Meter. Used with permission; **323–327,** "She Smiled at Me" by Carrie Schlatter. Used with permission.

Bibliography

Sources on Readers Theatre and Chamber Theatre

Abel, Leslie Gillian, and Robert M. Post. "Towards a Poor Readers Theatre." *Quarterly Journal of Speech* 559 (December 1973): 437–42.

Allison, John M., Jr. "Narrative and Time: A Phenomenological Reconsideration." *Text and Performance Quarterly* 14 (April 1994): 108–25.

Bacon, Wallace A. *The Art of Interpretation*. 3rd ed., 457–72. New York: Holt, Rinehart & Winston, 1979.

_____. "Readers Theatre As Humanizing Process." *Readers Theatre* (Fall 1975): 3, 11.

Barchers, Suzanne I. *Readers Theatre for Beginning Readers*. Englewood, Colo.: Teacher Ideas Press, 1993.

Beck, Roy. *Group Reading: Readers Theatre for Interscholastic Speech Contestants*. Skokie, Ill.: National Textbook Co., 1969.

Bennett, Gordon C. *Readers Theatre Comes to Church*. Richmond, Va.: John Knox Press, 1972.

Bowen, Elbert R. "Adapting the Novel for the Production in Readers Chamber Theatre." In *Studies in Interpretation*, vol. 2, edited by Esther M. Doyle and Virginia Hastings Floyd. Amsterdam: Rodopi N.V., 1977.

Bowman, Michael S. "Novelizing the Stage: Chamber Theatre After Breen and Bakhtin." *Text and Performance Quarterly* 15 (January 1995): 1–23.

Brecht, Bertolt. "A Short Organum for the Theatre." In *Brecht on Theatre*, edited and translated by John Willet. New York: Hill and Wang, 1964.

_____. "The Modern Theatre Is the Epic Theatre." In *Brecht on Theatre*, edited and translated by John Willet. New York: Hill and Wang, 1964.

Breen, Robert S. *Chamber Theatre*. Evanston, Ill.: Wm. Caxton Ltd., 1978.

331

Brown, Joseph Epolito, and Nancy Palmer Stump. "Genre Theory and the Practice of Readers Theatre." *Speech Teacher* 23 (January 1974): 1–8.

Coger, Leslie Irene, and Melvin R. White. *Readers Theatre Handbook: A Dramatic Approach to Literature.* 3rd ed. Glenview, Ill.: Scott, Foresman and Company, 1982.

Doll, Howard D. *Oral Interpretation of Literature: An Annotated Bibliography With Multimedia Listings.* Metuchen, N.J.: Scarecrow Press, 1982.

Donovan, Jane. "Audience Roles in a Compiled Readers Theatre Script: 'Who Are You This Time.' " Paper presented at SCA Convention, Boston, November 1987.

Foley, John Miles, ed. *Oral Tradition in Literature: Interpretation in Context.* Columbia: University of Missouri Press, 1986.

Haas, Richard, et. al. *Theatres for Interpretation.* Ann Arbor, Mich.: Roberts Burton, 1976.

Heston, Lilla A. "A Note on Prose Fiction: The Performance of Dialogue Tags." *Speech Teacher* 22 (January 1973): 69–72.

Hirschfield-Medalia, Adeline. "Stylized Movement in Interpreters Theatre." *Communication Education* 25 (March 1976): 111–20.

Hopkins, Mary Frances, and Brent Bouldin. "Professional Group Performance of Non-Dramatic Literature in New York." In *Performance of Literature in Historical Perspectives,* edited by David W. Thompson. Lanham, Md.: University Press of America, Inc., 1983.

Johnson, Albert, and Bertha Johnson. *Plays for Readers' Theatre: A Collection of Six Popular Classics.* Boston: Baker's Plays, 1972.

King, Judy Yordon. "Chamber Theatre by Any Other Name . . .?" *Speech Teacher* 21 (September 1972): 193–96.

Kleinau, Marion L., and Janet Larsen McHughes. *Theatres for Literature.* Sherman Oaks, Calif.: Alfred Publishing, 1980.

Latrobe, Kathy Howard. *Readers Theatre for Young Adults: Scripts and Script Development.* Englewood, Colo.: Teacher Ideas Press, 1989.

_____. *Social Studies Readers Theatre for Young Adults: Scripts and Script Development.* Englewood, Colo.: Teacher Ideas Press, 1991.

Laughlin, Mildred. *Readers Theatre for Children: Scripts and Script Development.* Englewood, Colo.: Teacher Ideas Press, 1990.

_____. *Social Studies Readers Theatre for Children: Scripts and Script Development.* Englewood, Colo.: Teacher Ideas Press, 1991.

Lee, Charlotte I., and Timothy J. Gura. *Oral Interpretation.* 7th ed, 436–52. Boston: Houghton Mifflin, 1987.

Liggett, Clayton E. *Concert Theatre.* New York: R. Rosen Press, 1970.

Logan, Christie A. "Form and Rhythm in Compilation Productions: Progressing the Audience's Field of Experience." Paper presented at SCA Convention, Boston, November 1987.

Long, Beverly Whitaker, Lee Hudson, and Phillis Rienstra Jeffrey. *Group Performance of Literature.* Englewood Cliffs, N.J.: Prentice-Hall, 1977.

Ludwig, Dale. "Performing the Authorial Novel: A Chamber Theatre Production of *Joseph Andrews.*" *Literature in Performance* 6 (April 1986): 71–82.

Maclay, Joanna H. *Readers Theatre: Toward a Grammar of Practice.* New York: Random House, 1971.

Meyer, Janice Jones. " 'Bartleby the Scrivener': Performing the Narrator's Inner Conflict in Chamber Theatre." *Communication Education* 26 (November 1977): 348–51.

Miller, Cynthia A. "Concepts for Adapting and Directing a Readers Theatre Production: Symbolism, Synecdoche and Metonymy." *Communication Education* 33 (October 1984): 343–50.

Miller, Lynn Christine. "The Subjective Camera and Staging Psychological Fiction." *Literature in Performance* 2 (April 1982): 35–45.

Oliver, Douglas L. *Poetry and Narrative in Performance.* New York: St. Martin's Press, 1989.

Paden, Frances Freeman. "Narrative Dynamics in *Animal Farm.*" *Literature in Performance* 5 (April 1985): 49–55.

Parella, Gilda. "Through the 'I' of the Beholder: A Rationale for Physicalization in the Performance of Narratives." *Central States Speech Journal* 25 (Winter 1974): 296–302.

Park-Fuller, Linda. "Voices: Bakhtin's Heteoglossia and Polyphony, and the Performance of Narrative Literature." *Literature in Performance* 7 (November 1986): 1–12.

Pearse, James Allen. "Montage: A Paradigm for Readers Theatre." In *Studies in Interpretation*, vol. 2, edited by Esther M. Doyle and Virginia Hastings Floyd. Amsterdam: Rodopi, N.V., 1977.

Pelias, Ronald J. "The Use and Misuse of Multiple Casting." *Western Journal of Speech Communication* 43 (Summer 1979): 224–30.

Pickering, Jerry V. *Readers Theatre.* Encino, Calif.: Dickinson Publishing, 1975.

Scrivner, Louis M., and Dan Robinette. *A Guide to Oral Interpretation: Solo and Group Performance*, 2nd ed. Indianapolis: Bobbs-Merrill Co., 1980.

Sloyer, Shirlee. *Readers Theatre: Story Dramatization in the Classroom.* Urbana, Ill.: National Council of Teachers of English, 1982.

Taft-Kaufman, Jill. "Creative Collaboration: The Rehearsal Process in Chamber Theatre." *Communication Education* 32 (October 1983): 428–34.

Wade, Alan. "From Text to Television: A Chamber Theatre Approach." *Literature in Performance* 2 (April 1982): 23–34.

Yordon, Judy E. *Roles in Interpretation.* 3rd ed. Dubuque, Ia.: Wm. C. Brown, 1993, chapter ten.

Zachary, Samuel J. "A Language Rationale for Conventional Readers Theatre of the Deaf." *Literature in Performance* 5 (November 1984): 20–28.

Sources on Ethnography, Conversation Analysis, and Personal Narratives

Allison, John M., Jr. "Narrative and Time: A Phenomenological Reconsideration." *Text and Performance Quarterly* 14 (April 1994): 108–25.

Atkinson, J. Maxwell, and John Heritage, eds. *Structures of Social Action: Studies in Conversation Analysis.* New York: Cambridge University Press, 1984.

Bacon, Wallace. "A Sense of Being: Interpretation and the Humanities." *The Southern Speech Communication Journal* 41 (winter 1976), 135–41.

Bakhtin, Mikhail M. *The Dialogic Imagination.* Translated by Caryl Emerson and Michael Holquist. Austin: University of Texas Press, 1981.

Balder, C. E. *Performance in Family Narratives: An Ethnographic Study of Oral Interpretation Components.* Unpublished masters thesis. University of Iowa, 1984.

Baldwin, K. " 'Woof!' A Word on Women's Roles in Family Storytelling." In *Women's Folklore, Women's Culture*, edited by R. A. Jordan and S. J. Kalcik. Philadelphia: University of Pennsylvania, 1985.

Bateson, Gregory. "A Theory of Play and Fantasy." In *Steps to an Ecology of Mind*, 177–93. New York: Ballantine Books, 1972.

Bauman, Richard. "The Field Study of Folklore in Context." In *Handbook of American Folklore*, edited by Richard M. Dorson. Bloomington: Indiana University Press, 1983.

———. *Story, Performance, and Event.* Cambridge: Cambridge University Press, 1986.

———. *Verbal Art As Performance.* Reprint. Prospect Heights, Ill.: Waveland Press, 1977.

———. ed. *Folklore, Cultural Performances, and Popular Entertainments: A Communications-Centered Handbook.* New York: Oxford University Press, 1992.

Bauman, Richard, and Joel Sherzer, eds. *Explorations in the Ethnography of Speaking.* 2nd ed. Cambridge: Cambridge University Press, 1989.

Beach, Wayne A. "Everyday Interaction and Its Practical Accomplishments: Progressive Developments in Ethnomethodological Research." *Quarterly Journal of Speech* 68 (1982): 314–44.

Berleant, Arnold. *Art and Engagement.* Philadelphia: Temple University Press, 1991.

Boatright, Mody C. "The Family Saga As a Form of Folklore." In *The Family Saga and Other Phases of American Folklore.* Urbana: University of Illinois Press, 1958.

Brandes, Stanley. "Family Misfortune Stories in American Folklore." *Journal of the Folklore Institute* 12 (1975): 5–17.

Brunvand, Jan H. *The Study of American Folklore.* New York: W. W. Norton, 1968.

Carlson, Lauri. *Dialogue Games: An Approach to Discourse Analysis*. Dordrecht, Holland: D. Reidel Publishing Company, 1983.

Clements, William M. "Personal Narrative, the Interview Context, and the Question of Tradition." *Western Folklore* 39 (1980): 106–12.

Clifford, James, and George E. Marcus. *Writing Culture: The Poetics and Politics of Ethnography*. Berkeley: University of California Press, 1986.

Colson, Ted, ed. *Renewal and Revision: The Future of Interpretation*. Denton, Tex.: NB Omega Publications, 1986.

Conquergood, Dwight. "Communication As Performance: Dramaturgical Dimensions of Everyday Life." In *The Jensen Lectures: Contemporary Communication Studies*, edited by John Sisco, 24–43. Tampa: University of South Florida, 1983.

_____. " 'A Sense of the Other': Interpretation and Ethnographic Research." In *Proceedings of the Southwest Conference on Oral Traditions*, edited by Isabel Crouch, 148–55. Las Cruces: New Mexico State University, 1983.

_____. "Performing As a Moral Act: Ethical Dimensions of the Ethnography of Performance." *Literature in Performance* 5 (April 1985): 1–13.

Crow, Bryan K. "Conversational Performance and the Performance of Conversation." *The Drama Review* 119 (1988): 23–54.

Dundes, Alan. "From Etic to Emic Units in the Structural Study of Folktales." *Journal of American Folklore* 75 (1962): 95–105.

_____. "The Study of Folklore in Literature and Culture: Identification and Interpretation." *Journal of American Folklore* 78 (1965): 136–42.

_____. *Interpreting Folklore*. Bloomington: Indiana University Press, 1980.

Ellis, Donald G., and William A. Donahue, eds. *Contemporary Issues in Language and Discourse Processes*. Hillsdale, N.J.: Lawrence Erlbaum Associates, 1986.

Fine, Elizabeth C. *The Folklore Text: From Performance to Print*. Bloomington: Indiana University Press, 1984.

Fine, Elizabeth C., and Jean Haskell Speer. "A New Look at Performance." *Communication Monographs* 44 (November 1977): 374–89.

Fine, Elizabeth C., and Jean Haskell Speer, eds. *Performance, Culture, and Identity*. Westport, Conn.: Praeger, 1992.

Fisher, Walter. *Human Communication as Narration: Toward a Philosophy of Reason, Value, and Action*. Columbia: University of South Carolina Press, 1987.

Garfinkel, H. "Studies of the Routine Grounds of Everyday Activities." In *Studies in Ethnomethodology*, 35–75. Englewood Cliffs, N.J.: Prentice-Hall, 1967.

Geertz, Clifford. *The Interpretation of Cultures*. New York: Basic Books, 1973.

Georges, Robert A. "Toward a Resolution of the Text/Context Controversy." *Western Folklore* 39 (1980): 34–40.

_____. "Toward an Understanding of Storytelling Events." *Journal of American Folklore* 82 (1969): 313–29.

Georges, Robert A., and Michael Owen Jones. *People Studying People: The Human Element in Fieldwork*. Berkeley: University of California Press, 1980.

Glenn, Phillip J., and Ronald J. Pelias. "Talking about *Talking Relationships*: Reporting Textual Understanding." Paper presented at the Central States Communication Association Convention, Cleveland, Ohio, April 1992.

Goffman, Erving. *Frame Analysis*. New York: Harper Colophon, 1974.

_____. *Interaction Ritual*. Garden City, N.Y.: Doubleday, 1967.

_____. *The Presentation of Self in Everyday Life*. Garden City, N.Y.: Doubleday, 1959.

Goldstein, Kenneth L. *A Guide for Field Workers in Folklore*. Hatboro, Pa.: Folklore Associates, 1964.

Gumperz, John J. *Discourse Strategies*. Cambridge: Cambridge University Press, 1982.

Gumperz, John J., and Dell Hymes, eds. *Directions in Sociolinguistics: The Ethnography of Communication*. New York, 1972.

Gumperz, John J., ed. *Language and Social Identity*. Cambridge: Cambridge University Press, 1982.

Hayano, David M. "Auto-Ethnography: Paradigms, Problems, and Prospects." *Human Organization* 38 (1979): 99–104.

Jackson, Shannon. "Ethnography and the Audition: Performance As Ideological Critique." *Text and Performance Quarterly* 13 (January 1993): 21–43.

Jason, Heda. "A Model for Narrative Structure in Oral Literature." In *Patterns in Oral Literature*, edited by Heda Jason and Dimitri Sega. The Hague: Mouton, 1977.

Jefferson, Gail. "Sequential Aspects of Storytelling in Conversation." In *Studies in the Organization of Conversational Interaction*, edited by J. Schenkein, 219–47. New York: Academic, 1978.

_____. "A Technique for Inviting Laughter and its Subsequent Acceptance Declination." In *Everyday Language: Studies in Ethnomethodology*, edited by G. Psathas, 97–122. New York: Irvington, 1979.

Jennings, Gayle G. *Storytales: Performing Features of Conversational Storytelling Between Ministers*. Unpublished dissertation, Southern Illinois University, 1992.

Jones, Steven Swann. "Slouching toward Ethnography: The Text/Context Controversy Reconsidered." *Western Folklore* 38 (1979): 42–47.

Jordan, Rosan A., and Susan J. Kalcik, eds. *Women's Folklore, Women's Culture*. Philadelphia: University of Pennsylvania Press, 1985.

Kalcik, Susan. " ' . . . Like Ann's Gynecologist or the Time I Was Almost Raped': Personal Narratives in Women's Rap Groups." *Journal of American Folklore* 88: 3–11. Reprinted in *Women and Folklore*, edited by Claire R. Farrer. Austin: University of Texas Press, 1975.

Kirschner, Suzanne R. " 'Then What Have I to Do with Thee?': On Identity, Fieldwork, and Ethnographic Knowledge." *Cultural Anthropology* 2 (1987): 211–34.

Labov, William, and Joshua Waletzky. "Narrative Analysis: Oral Versions of Personal Experience." In *Essays in the Visual Arts*, edited by June Helm, 12–44. Seattle: University of Washington Press, 1967.

Langellier, Kristin. "Personal Narratives: Perspectives on Theory and Research." *Text and Performance Quarterly* 9 (October 1989): 243–76.

_____. "From Text to Social Context." *Literature in Performance* 6 (April 1986): 60–70.

Leeds-Hurwitz, Wendy. *Communication in Everyday Life: A Social Interpretation*. Norwood, N.J.: Ablex, 1989.

Littleton, C. Scott. "A Two-Dimensional Scheme for the Classification of Narratives." *Journal of American Folklore* 78 (1965): 21–27.

Lord, Albert B. *The Singer of Tales*. New York: Atheneum, 1970. Reprinted from Harvard University Press, 1960.

Madison, D. Soyini. " 'That Was My Occupation': Oral Narrative, Performance, and Black Feminist Thought." *Text and Performance Quarterly* 13 (July 1993): 213–32.

Maranhao, Tullio, ed. *The Interpretation of Dialogue*. Chicago: The University of Chicago Press, 1990.

Moerman, Michael. *Talking Culture: Ethnography and Conversation Analysis*. Philadelphia: University of Pennsylvania Press, 1988.

Moore, Sally F., and Barbara Myerhoff, eds. *Secular Ritual*. Amsterdam: Van Gorcum, 1977.

Myerhoff, Barbara. "Life History Among the Elderly: Performance, Visibility, and Remembering." In *Studies of the Human Life Course*, edited by Kurt Beck. American Association for the Advancement of Science, 1980.

Narula, Uma, and W. Barnette Pearce, eds. *Cultures, Politics, and Research Programs: An International Assessment of Practical Problems in Field Research*. Hinsdale, N.J.: Lawrence Erlbaum Associates, 1990.

Nofsinger, R. *Everyday Conversation*. Newbury Park, Calif.: Sage Publications, 1991.

Pellowski, Anne. *The World of Storytelling: A Practical Guide to the Origins, Development and Applications of Storytelling*. Expanded and revised ed. New York: H.W. Wilson Company, 1990.

Pollock, Della. "Telling the Told: Performing *Like a Family*." *Oral History Review* (1990): 1–36.

Psathas, G., ed. *Everyday Language: Studies in Ethnomethodology*. New York: Irvington, 1979.

Robinson, John A. "Personal Narratives Reconsidered." *Journal of American Folklore* 94 (1981): 58–85.

Sacks, Harvey. "An Analysis of the Course of a Joke's Telling in Conversation." In *Explorations in the Ethnography of Speaking*, edited by Richard Bauman and Joel Sherzer. Cambridge: Cambridge University Press, 1974.

Sacks, Harvey, E. A. Schegloff, and Gail Jefferson. "A Simplest Systematics for the Organization of Turn-Taking for Conversation." In *Studies in the Organi-*

zation of Conversational Interaction, edited by J. Schenkein, 7–55. New York: Academic Press, 1978.

Stahl, Sandra Dolby. *Literary Folkloristics and the Personal Narrative*. Bloomington: Indiana University Press, 1989.

_____. "The Oral Personal Narrative in Its Generic Context." *Fabula* 18 (1977): 18–39.

_____. "Personal Experience Stories." In *Handbook of American Folklore*, edited by Richard M. Dorson. Bloomington: Indiana University Press, 1983.

_____. "The Personal Narrative As Folklore." *Journal of the Folklore Institute* 14 (1977): 9–30.

Stanley, David H. "The Personal Narrative and the Personal Novel: Folklore As Frame and Structure for Literature." *Southern Folklore Quarterly* 43 (1979): 107–20.

Stern, Carol Simpson, and Bruce Henderson. *Performance: Texts and Contexts*. New York: Longman, 1993.

Stucky, Nathan. "Unnatural Acts: Performing Natural Conversation." *Literature in Performance* 8 (1988): 28–39.

Tannen, Deborah. " 'Oh Talking Voice That Is So Sweet': Constructing Dialogue in Conversation." In *Talking Voices: Repetition, Dialogue, and Imagery in Conversational Discourse*, edited by Deborah Tannen. Studies in Interactional Sociolinguistics 6. Cambridge: Cambridge University Press, 1989.

_____. *You Just Don't Understand: Women and Men in Conversation*. New York: William Morrow, 1990.

Tedlock, Dennis. *The Spoken Word and the Work of Interpretation*. Philadelphia: University of Pennsylvania Press, 1983.

Thompkins, Jane P., ed. *Reader-Response Criticism*. Baltimore: Johns Hopkins University Press, 1980.

Titon, Jeff Todd. "The Life Story." *Journal of American Folklore* 93 (1980): 276–92.

Turner, Victor. *The Anthropology of Performance*. New York: PAJ Publications, 1986.

Turner, Victor, and Edward Bruner, eds. *Anthropology As Experience*. Urbana: University of Illinois Press, 1986.

Turner, Victor, and Edith Turner. "Performing Ethnography." *The Drama Review* 26.2 (Summer 1982): 33–35.

_____. "Performing Ethnography." In *The Anthropology of Performance*. New York: PAJ, 1986.

Werth, Paul, ed. *Conversation and Discourse: Structure and Interpretation*. New York: St. Martin's Press, 1981.

West, C., and D. Zimmerman. "Conversation Analysis." In *Handbook of Methods in Nonverbal Behavior Research*, edited by Klaus R. Scherer and Paul Ekman, 506–35. Cambridge: Cambridge University Press, 1982.

Wolfson, N. "A Feature of Performed Narrative: The Conversational Historical Present." *Language in Society* 7 (1978): 215–37.

Yordon, Judy E. *Roles in Interpretation.* 3rd ed. Dubuque, Ia.: Wm. C. Brown, 1993. Especially chapter 9.

Zan, Yigal. "The Text/Context Controversy: An Explanatory Perspective." *Western Folklore* 41 (1982): 1–27.

Author/Title Index

Subject Index